The Complete Shakespearience

Peter Thomas

I hope you and
your students
get as much
joy out of
this as I
did putting it
together!

Peter Thomas

NATE

The Complete Shakespearience is published by the National Association for the Teaching of English (NATE), the UK subject association for all aspects of the teaching of English from pre-school to university.

NATE
50 Broadfield Road
Sheffield
S8 OXJ

T: 0114 2555419
F: 0114 2555296
E: info@nate.org.uk
www.nate.org.uk

ISBN 9781904709275

British Library Cataloguing in Publication Data
A catalogue record for this book is available from the British Library.

Printed by Henry Ling Limited, at the Dorset Press, Dorchester, DT1 1HD

Foreword

This book has developed from my previous (1999) NATE publication called *Shakespeariences*. It includes material first published as articles in *Inkpellet* magazine and in various NATE publications. Its classroom practicality comes from my own practice as a teacher, teacher-trainer and Inset provider. The principles and practices behind the book are neither unique nor original: they are common to many others who have sought to make Shakespeare accessible, appealing and relevant to youngsters. The most notable of these was Rex Gibson, whose Cambridge Shakespeare and Schools project did more to enthuse teachers and students than could be dreamed by politicians or functionaries of government agencies.

The Complete Shakespearience is dedicated to the students of Wheatley Park School in Oxfordshire and the PGCE trainees at the University of Hull who shared in the growth of my own happy and satisfying Shakespearience.

My heartfelt thanks to Anne Fairhall for all the sensitivity, practicality, enthusiasm and patience she unfailingly maintained through her editing of this book.

Acknowledgements

We are grateful to the following copyright holders for permission to reproduce extracts from the following texts:

Shakespeare Made Easy – Hamlet by Alan Durband, reproduced with the permission of Nelson Thornes Ltd, ISBN 9780748703463, first published 1987

Crowther, John, ed. *No Fear Hamlet*. SparkNotes.com. SparkNotes LLC. 2005. Web. 3 Dec. 2009

The Marowitz Shakespeare – Hamlet, from *The Marowitz Shakespeare* – Adaptations and collages of *Hamlet, Macbeth, The Taming of the Shrew, Measure for Measure*, and *The Merchant of Venice* by Charles Marowitz (published by Marion Boyars London & New York 1978, 1990)

'To be or not to be in Lakewood, Marowitz is there' by Tony Mastroianni, originally published by Cleveland Press July 28 1972, now at www.clevelandmemory.org

'Oor Hamlet' by Adam McNaughtan, published in *The Best of Scottish Poetry* by Chambers 1989

Comic Book Shakespeare (*Twelfth Night*) ISBN 978054432546, edited and illustrated by Simon Greaves, published by Timber Frame Publications Ltd, www.shakespearecomics.com

Much Ado about Nothing – The Graphic Shakespeare series, retold by Hilary Burningham and published by Evans Brothers Ltd (illustrations by Tracy Fennell). Reprinted here by kind permission of Evans Brother Limited. Copyright © in the text Hilary Burningham 2005. Copyright © in the illustrations Evans Brothers Ltd 2005. All rights reserved

Macbeth © Classsical Comics Ltd. Original artwork Jon Haward; Inking Assistant Gary Erskine; Colourist and letterer Nigel Dobbyn

Romeo and Juliet screenplay by Baz Luhrmann ISBN 9780340698181, reproduced by permission of Hodder Children's Books

Contents

Throughout the book, this CD icon is used to indicate that there is electronic copy available on the CD which contains files of resources separated by chapters 1–8 as listed below. Click on 'How to use this CD' to find a full list of contents.

Introduction

Getting Shakespeare into them and them into Shakespeare

If ever there was a title to make an author, never mind a reader, wince, this must be it. *The Complete Shakespearience*? Complete? The Lot? Everything? All? The Complete Works on the Complete Works? In 170 pages?

Well, no. This book makes no claim to be a comprehensive survey, a complete compendium or a triumph of new scholarship. It's much simpler, and all the better for that. And anyway, the more truthful title 'The Incomplete Shakespearience' doesn't have the same ring. The point is that it's Shakespear*ience* – not Shakespeare the cultural heritage icon, national totem or quarry of PhD theses – that the book is about completely. It's a book that aims to give English teachers all they need to give their students a satisfying, memorable, enjoyable, worthwhile active experience of Shakespeare, in the classroom and without facilities of stage or studio. Not only that, but it's a book that aims to make the English teacher more confident in subject specialist expertise, justifying practical strategies by reference to Shakespeare's mind and art beyond the usual narrow repertoire of plays that may be studied in schools. The bottom line is that it will make up for that undergraduate mix'n'match, option-choice omission or evasion of canonical texts that may, for some teachers, be seeming not so smart now that untouched texts have to be confidently delivered to groups of thirty or more. The top line is that it will make Shakespearean scholars and enthusiasts build the necessary bridges to do what matters more than academic study: to get Shakespeare into youngsters and youngsters into Shakespeare.

Now that's enough to make the first paragraph seem easy by comparison.

The book comes from a lifetime's work in and out of schools, with students, teachers and trainee teachers. It draws on previous publications, on broadcasting and writing for ETV, and on 25 years of assessment for examination purposes. More importantly, all of these draw on what I have done in timetabled lessons in normal school days and in a normal classroom. What I call Shakespearience started with the belief that what gave me pleasure and inspiration should also give others pleasure and inspiration, but finding that this simple aim was thwarted by obstacles more numerous than I care to list. All English teachers will recognise them: student mistrust, apathy, incomprehension and distaste; texts which were large, annotated, falling apart and full of language you'd never hear on MTV; groups of 30 plus, mixed in ability and aptitude in a classroom full of desks; an examination regime which turned the experience into traps, pitfalls and memory tests; and also, a personal history as a confident silent reader, enjoying texts as a private pleasure – a bookworm, unfamiliar with actors, acting or the professional trade and craft of the theatre.

Given all this, I am pleased to record that some of the best experiences I have ever shared with students from 6 to 66 were moments of Shakespeare in the classroom. These best experiences include the buzz of directing youngsters to bring out what I thought implicit in a scene and the bigger buzz of seeing youngsters take on ownership of scenes as they found their own interpretations of words, events, relationships and meanings. The biggest buzz of all was the discovery that academic ability was not the key to success: many of the less able were advantaged by their lack of academic ambition and programming, nearly always requiring writing; and some of the most academically able were advantaged by venturing into more vulgar, physical, emotional and communal territories. I relish the memory of the two very unacademic and anti-school year 9 lads who made the rivalry between Dogberry and Verges larger than Life and Literature and who, seeing the scene done by Ben Elton and others in the Brananagh version, declared, 'Rubbish! Not half as good as ours' – and they were right. I also relish the memory of the very academic A level group who decided to make a deal of the Ceres masque in *The Tempest*, which I'd tended to see as a naff interlude obstructing the play's progress, and with costume, music, dance and the realism of several imported bales and sheaves, created something beautiful, inspiring and totally central to the play's concerns with Nature, Nurture, Magic and Love.

This book is my attempt to share the buzz, to make those classroom experiences happen for many more than those I have personally taught. Welcome. And thank you to all who have, in more ways than one, played a part in my own Shakespearience.

Shakespeare, youngsters, culture and literary heritage

For many youngsters, the Shakespeare experience is a duty, an imposition or a test of reading. The plays are long, complicated, about people called Leontes, Malvolio and Benedick and in grammatically and lexically unfamiliar language. It's not surprising if the experience seems alien or irrelevant. For 15 years, it was not helpful that their early secondary Shakespeare experience was confined to practice for tariffed questions to test reading under the discredited and thankfully dismantled SATs regime.

Shakespeare has become an institution rather than a person, processed into a cultural totem; badged, stamped and shelved as heritage literature. He has become 'monumentalised' as James Stredder calls it, and scaling a monument requires stamina and skill, hence the title of his book, *The North Face of Shakespeare*. Yet Shakespeare was not literature, or heritage, in his time. If he had been, he could never have bought the smartest house in Stratford. He was a successful popular entertainer who, as a former actor, knew what the public wanted and knew what actors needed to strut their stuff. His plays were appreciated in his day by the educated and by those who would not have met a government target of level 4 in literacy. His scripts democratised theatre-going by being unashamedly popular in appeal and variety. As a democratic entertainer he presented on stage the fears, woes and dreams of all, irrespective of rank or wealth or education, and he presented them *for* all, irrespective of rank or wealth or education.

Shakespeare and education in general

If Shakespeare is to be accessible and appealing today, students need to see him as a scripter for popular and public performance rather than a loan tome from the Literary Heritage vault. He needs to be seen as an entertaining dramatist. If the focus is on Shakespeare as a dramatist, internally assessed work can be made more than essays (or 'S.A.s' !) on books.

My concern most directly is with the teaching of Shakespeare within English, but there is a great potential gain from this across a wider educational territory. The approach to Shakespeare presented in this book is active, collaborative and creative. It is an approach with a long history but is well matched to some of the principles underpinning education in the twenty-first century. These include equal opportunities for all children and young people, irrespective of gender, ability or culture, the traditional democratic instinct of educators now given novelty acronymic status as ECM (Every Child Matters). This is closely related to another re-badging of ancient wisdom, that of varying the stimulus and mode to appeal to different kinds of learner and learning. This is now given novelty acronymic status as VAK (a reduction of a wide range of receptivities to visual, auditory and kinaesthetic.) These two notions combine in the glibness of a politician's mind to produce the novelty called personalised learning. Broader educational thinking accepts that education is not a matter of exclusively cognitive exercise and development, but of emotional, social and spiritual growth. The subject matter of the Shakespeare texts is itself a rich foundation for understanding oneself, others and society, but the method of presenting this subject matter to youngsters is also a means of developing insight into self, others and society. I think we can have our cake, eat it, keep it and bring it out again: education for whole-personal growth and for active, responsible and productive citizenship can be the longer-term outcome of Shakespearience. In the shorter term, teacher and student enjoyment and satisfaction will be more than enough to be getting on with. Enjoyment is a human energy which can fuel many other human attributes within the English teacher's shorter-term agenda, or the longer term agenda which goes beyond crude governmental measurements and targets.

Shakespeare and 'English'

The place of Shakespeare in the English curriculum is assured by statute. The national curriculum requires that all students read two Shakespeare plays over Key Stages 3 and 4. What statutes cannot do is ensure that Shakespeare is well taught or regarded with pleasure by students. Indeed, some of the inevitable results of statutory curricular existence have worked against good teaching and pleasure; the Key Stage 3 SATs for example. This book is not intended to have any bearing on these. The main concern of the book is to make the teaching of Shakespeare productive and enjoyable in its own right, across the age and ability range of the whole secondary school. The approaches are equally applicable to year 7 and to year 13, and would be an advantage to future generations if also applied to undergraduate Shakespeare modules. Whilst there is immense pleasure to be gained from treating Shakespeare as Literature, for reading the texts, this book works on the assumption that he is not a writer of Literature but a writer of dramascripts for performance, for entertainment. It is also true that much of what we call education rests upon turning reading into writing but the approach here is not necessarily concerned with writing about Shakespeare. Writing may result from active approaches but it is not the reason for them. Breaking the link of Shakespeare with 'Writing about Shakespeare' is perhaps the best way of presenting him to a wider constituency than the confidently and readily literate. This is not to say that the approach is tailored to the needs of the unacademic. Rather, it is tailored to embrace the non-academic as well as the academic, especially in the case of those who, successfully academic already, need other faculties and abilities exercised. There will always be a particular value in the academic distinctions that are individual, private, cerebral and expressed in writing. However, the broader agenda of living and being needs distinctions in the communal, public and emotional, expressed in physical and practical 'doing'. The 'Doing Shakespeare' approach is for the 'Gifted and Talented' as well as the disaffected and less able. It is about expanding the repertoire of gifts and talents in all youngsters. It is also about making this a basis for a more personal and insightful appreciation of Shakespeare for purposes traditionally enshrined in our curriculum and assessment arrangements. What matters for teachers and students alike is that one can be academically successful in fulfilling traditional goals without enjoying the experience but that enjoying the experience is worthwhile in itself and can also fulfil traditional goals. In the process, the mingling of faculties, abilities, personalities and preferences brings students together in ways that the rest of the curriculum does not.

Shakespeare and dramatic tradition

Drama before Shakespeare and his contemporaries amounted to learned re-creations of Latin and Greek plays and stories, or simple moralistic tales in the Everyman tradition, or masques and shows by Mummers and travelling troupes of singing, dancing artistes. Shakespeare was more than these. He took what he wanted from earlier traditions, and added things that others had not dreamed of. And he was not bothered by academic notions about Aristotelian Classical Unities, or the integrity of genres of tragedy, comedy or history. 'Mix, match and lay on whatever keeps the punters coming' seems to have been his working motto.

The blending of genres in the plays – history, comedy, tragedy, romance – and of styles – dialogue, monologue, chorus, song, dance and spectacle – appealed to a wider audience than the scholarly, the cultured and the privileged. Studying examples of script shaped by the needs of his stage, his audience and his actors gives a more practical approach to Shakespeare's craft.

Perhaps the most distinctive way in which Shakespeare departed from the dramatic tradition was in his realistic presentation of characters. He avoided the simple moral stereotypes of Good Characters and Bad Characters in order to show something fundamentally human in all characters: the mixture of elements that makes the powerful fallible and the oppressed strong; the hero with faults and the villain with virtues. Audiences can feel fleeting pity and admiration for characters like Macbeth and Richard III when they know them to be morally beyond the pale, and they can wince and sigh at the faults of Hamlet and Prospero just as they may, more than sometimes in real life, feel irritated by those they love and in awe of those they despise.

Shakespeare the impresario

It's no good expecting youngsters to embrace Shakespeare because he's Good For Them, or An Important Part of the English National Heritage. The only way I've found for giving them some real rather than artificial acquired respect, if any, for his achievement, is to present him as a great popular entertainer, despite the limitations of his theatre. The stage he wrote for lacked most of what we take for granted in the age of electric spectacle: he had to work in an open, unroofed, daytime space with

- no sound amplification
- no spot-lights, floodlights, footlights, houselights
- no curtains to signify act and scene changes
- no set changes, scenery, flies, revolves or back-projections.

This means that Shakespeare's scripts needed to help audibility in an acoustically poor environment. Changes of setting and passages of time had to be signalled by embedded cues in the dialogue. Some events too difficult to stage needed to be described rather than shown.

The audience he wrote for (other than private audiences) also shaped the way he constructed his plays. He was writing for a mixed audience of:

- literate, educated and familiar with history and modern politics
- illiterate, uneducated and paying for entertainment
- men and women.

Most of what he wrote was for a public playhouse and a paying public.

The appeal of any single play for this audience had to be wide, and the structure of a three-hour performance needed pace and variety. Appealing to the varied tastes of this wide audience meant putting together plays with something for everybody – comedy, violence, romance, suspense and references to current and past events in English life and history. Those best pleased by verbal abuse, drunkenness and foolery could enjoy Falstaff, Sir Toby Belch, Petruchio – others best pleased by witty puns, parodies and conceits could enjoy the subtler parts of *Much Ado About Nothing, Twelfth Night* and *Hamlet*. I'm not suggesting that the uneducated liked bawdy farce and the educated liked elaborate conceits and classical allusion; then, as now, both appreciated amusing representations of human excess and fallibility, both appreciated the drive to doom provoked by human excess and fallibility, and both appreciated recreated pageantry of great events and heroes of the English past. Twentieth century television demonstrated a similar way of finding the common ground appealing to both sophisticated and rough-hewn in the writing of Croft and Perry (*Dad's Army*), Simpson and Galton (*Steptoe, The Likely Lads*), John Cleese (*Fawlty Towers*) and John Sullivan (*Only Fools and Horses*). What these writers developed as a popular entertainment was, with Shakespeare, a mingling of strands within each dramatic performance. The strands were not united by an explicit or implicit moral or commercial view but by the realistic, ironic and non-moralistic display of unchanging human behaviour, driven by selfish or idealistic motives, thwarted by circumstance, human error or Fate, resulting in absurd or pitiful consequences which make the audience feel that the world is not such a bad place after all, and if it is, it's worse for others than for oneself. What else makes a man writing a play about the clash between two of the best-known figures in Roman history, and the love between one of them and the fabled 'Beauty of the Nile', write a scene (Act 1 Scene 2) in which two of Cleopatra's servants, in her palace in Alexandria, 1600 years before, discuss what is most desirable in a man like this (to paraphrase):

> 'And where would you choose to have an extra inch in a man?'
> 'Not in his nose, forsooth.'

In his time, Shakespeare offered the equivalent of a modern multi-channel, multi-modal entertainment: sitcom, *News at Ten*, History Channel, conjuring tricks and a bit of a dance-show thrown in.

Other aspects of contemporary life had an impact on his craft:

- no copyright law to protect his plays from rival companies
- uncertain employment dependent on a successful repertoire
- a hostile, Puritan control of London entertainment.

Parts needed to be written to make the most of the talents of individuals in the company. Popular characters may need to be re-written into other plays. Actors could not be given scripts in case they got into the hands of rival companies, so had to learn lines by heart. Hence the rhythms of blank verse helped memory.

The prevailing hostility to popular entertainment meant that all theatres had to ply their trade outside the city limits, on the south bank of the Thames, along with other entertainments subject to the disapproval of the authorities.

What made him popular then was what has made television the popular medium it is today: a provider of entertainment for all, depending on the time of day or channel selected. Shakespeare was all channels in any one play: he could please the groundlings with scenes of verbal abuse, drunkenness and outrageous behaviour (Falstaff, Sir Toby Belch, Petruchio) and he could please the educated with puns, parodies, conceits and references to classical literature (*Much Ado*, *Twelfth Night*, *Hamlet*).

These conditions he worked in shaped the way he wrote; youngsters need to know that he did not write for art and posterity but for profit, in which audibility, visible stunts and appealing plots were his means to the biggest house back in Stratford. He sold entertainment and, whilst I would rather extol virtues other than the mercenary, the truth can be of service to teachers in this case. His own disarming honesty about the limits he worked under is evident in the prologue to Henry V:

> Piece out our imperfections with your thoughts:
> Think, when we talk of horses, that you see them
> Printing their proud hoofs i' the' receiving earth…
> …eke out our performance with your mind…
> …behold, in the quick forge and working house of thought…

The practicality of his writing for such a stage and such an audience is evident in the way he starts his plays. The function of the opening is to still an audience which lacked the procedural prompts of dimming house-lights, usherettes and an educated acceptance that one has to shut up for one's consumption of Culture.

A manifesto

Ideally, the building of a relationship between students and Shakespeare needs to start early and be frequently reinforced. Active and interactive encounters with scenes and selective texts establish that Shakespeare is something you *do*, not something you study. *Shakespearience* is more than reading and is open to all levels of ability. Although it aims to give youngsters pleasure and excitement, it is also a sound basis for the more formal appreciation of Shakespeare which tends to be the assessment focus at 16+ and 18+. *The Complete Shakespearience* aims to be just what it says – a handbook for all that is needed in the secondary school classroom from year 7 onwards. As a handbook, it is based on the principles embodied in my Teachers' Manifesto, first published in *NATE Classroom* magazine (Autumn 2007).

This manifesto has many sources. Personally, it comes from my own pleasure in Shakespeare and my experience as a teacher trying to get youngsters of all abilities to get pleasure out of Shakespeare. Academically, it comes from my interest in Shakespeare scholarship and Shakespeare in performance over the last four hundred years. Professionally, it comes from my experience as an examiner and moderator, reading many scripts in which Shakespeare is written about as a psychological novelist with a penchant for dialogue, and little sense of him as a craftsman working in a particular theatre and for a particular audience. All three threads have woven into my experience as a teacher trainer, both in ITT and Inset, helping others to see how Shakespeare can be at least one good reason for going to school on Monday. I've spent a lot of my working life noticing what is wrong in teaching and learning Shakespeare. This is my attempt to take the high ground and declare what we should all be doing.

A manifesto for classroom Shakespearience

1) Shakespeare's texts are playscripts – prompts for performance.

2) Students need to be physically active – performing lines and scenes.

3) Playscript needs to be vocalised not merely verbalised.

4) Performances need to be shared with others – in performing groups and in audiences.

5) Students need to be confident at editing, extending, re-working and improvising from text.

6) Writing does not need to be the outcome of work with playscript.

7) Improvisation and performance are for all, regardless of academic or acting ability.

8) Critical appreciation of professional performance on stage and screen should be built into the experience of playtext.

9) Students should see Shakespeare as a writer who exposed the darker, unworthy sides of human nature and society, as well as one who eloquently expressed the sublime, the spiritual and the beautiful.

10) 'Shakespeare' is more important than any individual play. Students should experience the range of Shakespeare's ideas and dramatic skills rather than be committed to one play only; selections which allow comparison and variety will engage them with his craft.

2. The Close Shakespearience: teaching Shakespeare in the classroom

Developing confidence

Preparing the ground

As preparation for getting close up and personal with Shakespeare's playtext and dramatic craft, students need to develop confidence in their relationship with Shakespeare. They need to feel that they have something to say to Shakespeare, not just that Shakespeare has something to say to them. This is best done by giving them some status as authors working alongside Shakespeare, re-treading some of his territory, dealing with some of the issues he dealt with, perhaps facing some of the same problems and arriving at similar or different solutions. The teacher's aim is to promote empathy with Shakespeare as a maker of meaning and shaper of texts.

One quick and easy way to do this is to set students the task of producing a modern version of 'The Seven Ages of Man', Jaques' speech from *As You Like it*. They don't need to read the text to start this task. They need only know that Shakespeare's text charts a life-scale of seven stages. Their task is to represent either their own life so far or (perhaps more ambitiously) human life at large in seven stages. I have sometimes started this with a reading of Jaques' speech and found it a useful model for some. I have also held back Shakespeare's original until students have completed their own, and found that this gives them more interest in his version, appraising it as equal practitioners in the art of representing life symbolically.

If the task is representing their own life so far, they can begin without writing. Sketching objects significant to them as signposts of their growing up can be done by prompting them to illustrate their seven ages by any of these:

- seven favourite foods
- seven favourite TV programmes
- seven favourite toys
- seven important moments
- seven best friends and why
- seven biggest disappointments
- seven best memories

If the task is representing human life in general, it's made easier by deciding on some key ages – e.g. 4, 11, 16, 21, 30, 50, 70 – or any other way of marking key life stages, e.g. childhood, school, work, social life, marriage, children, retirement. Here's the text, in case it's needed.

> All the world's a stage,
> And all the men and women merely players:
> They have their exits and their entrances;
> And one man in his time plays many parts,
> His acts being seven ages.

At first the infant,
Mewling and puking in the nurse's arms.

Then the whining school-boy, with his satchel
And shining morning face, creeping like snail
Unwillingly to school.

And then the lover,
Sighing like furnace, with a woeful ballad
Made to his mistress' eyebrow.

Then a soldier,
Full of strange oaths and bearded like the pard,
Jealous in honour, sudden and quick in quarrel,
Seeking the bubble reputation
Even in the cannon's mouth.

And then the justice,
In fair round belly with good capon lined,
With eyes severe and beard of formal cut,
Full of wise saws and modern instances;
And so he plays his part.

The sixth age shifts
Into the lean and slipper'd pantaloon,
With spectacles on nose and pouch on side,
His youthful hose, well saved, a world too wide
For his shrunk shank; and his big manly voice,
Turning again toward childish treble, pipes
And whistles in his sound.

Last scene of all,
That ends this strange eventful history,
Is second childishness and mere oblivion,
Sans teeth, sans eyes, sans taste, sans everything.

                                     (*As You Like It* Act 2, Scene 7)

Here is an example of a year 7 student's up-dating and personalizing of the seven ages, using a favourite pastime – computer gaming – as his theme:

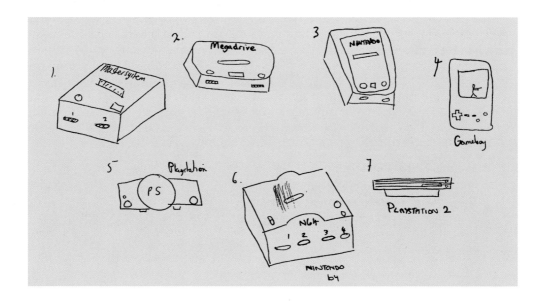

Here is an example of another year 7 student's re-working of the theme, taking Life in general for her approach:

> # Human Life
>
> Birth, screaming, tears and muckiness.
>
> Child, adventurous will to explore anything possible.
>
> Teenager, moody, love struck person afraid of many things.
>
> Young adult, fun loving, wild child like, stuck with responsibilities.
>
> Middle age, regrets the past, longing to be young again.
>
> Old age, babies, not able to do things for themselves.
>
> Death, leaving others sad and depressed.
>
> Lauren

Approaching the play – some guidelines

The top-whack measure of an English teacher's success for me is that your class is still talking about its Shakespeare session during the Maths lesson that follows. But, as every English teacher knows, it takes some getting to that point. And what may have got *us* to that point when we were at school may not work for our students: we were the odd ones who probably wanted to be teachers when the rest were more concerned with getting a set of wheels with a bad-ass rear spoiler, or making it as the next Madonna.

The most unproductive approach to Shakespeare in the classroom is to begin with a class reading of the play, however skilfully, sensitively or selfishly the teacher assigns the parts. Students struggling to get the plot into their heads have to be stopped and re-started at mis-readings or for vocabulary glosses. It's a recipe for failure. It's a bit more productive to start with a story outline and some character detail. Most teachers will prepare the ground by showing clips from a recorded performance, or use the *Animated Tales* as a starter. Anything that gets the students over the obstacle of decoding unfamiliar language is a help. This section provides some more elaborate (though simple) ways of making Shakespeare's language less alien and obstructive. This is not to say that Shakespeare's language is alien and obstructive, but that those of us who find it familiar and appealing tend to have English degrees. The students we teach do not – and will not have – this possible advantage. What they can appreciate, though, is the way he wrote as a jobbing pro for conditions that were unlike those of today – specifically, for an audience that was not like a modern theatre audience, and for a theatre that was unlike a modern theatre.

Starting with beginnings – understanding scriptcraft

Here's the scene: it's a Wednesday in London and the sun is shining. Some people are legitimately off work; others are taking a sickie; others are not in regular work. Where best to go for a day out? Over the Thames, where taverns, sideshows, theatres and places of ill repute compete for trade. What to choose? Everyone says the new Shakespeare's got to be seen – ghosts, murders, clowns and some conjuring tricks. Maybe follow with a few drinks and some freak shows. Or do them first…

The play is due to start at two o'clock but the manager thinks waiting another quarter of an hour will boost the sales if his criers roll some more in. It's chat, slurp and crunch time, as well as watch the posh gits in the boxes with their clothes and fancy women.

There are no house lights to go down. No tannoy reminder that the performance begins in two minutes. No comfortable seats to sink back in and enjoy being cultured and refined in a visit to the theatres. The public space is all a-buzz after lunch on the early afternoon.

Now that's a challenge. How to settle the audience into concentration on the scene before them? Drawing the curtain helps but it's daylight and something more is needed. With all this in mind, there is something beautifully and simply appropriate about the openings of Shakespeare's plays. They have a job to do.

A common device is to begin with a sudden loud call and an answer, from one or two, possibly invisible, characters. The effect needed is to signal the start of something and get the audience to concentrate its attention:

1

BARNARDO: Who's there?

FRANCISCO: Nay, answer me. Stand and unfold yourself.

BARNARDO: Long live the King!

FRANCISCO: Barnardo?

BARNARDO: He.

FRANCISCO: You come most carefully upon your hour.

BARNARDO: Tis now struck twelve. Get thee to bed Francisco.

FRANCISCO: For this relief, much thanks. Tis bitter cold and I am sick at heart.

(***Hamlet***)

Shutting an audience up is part of the function of these lines, but there's more. *Hamlet* is a play about doubt, challenge, danger and intrigue – all of which are signalled in the opening seconds by dialogue between the sentries on the battlements at night. This is not just play-starting, but tone setting and theme-foreshadowing. Impressive stuff, in few small words. The device can also be used to gain attention by curiosity, beginning a play in apparent mid-conversation, so that the audience thinks they may have missed something:

2

PHILO: Nay, but this dotage of our general's doth o'erflow the measure.

(***Antony and Cleopatra***)

Lacking back-projections, dry ice and electrically-operated scene drops, Shakespeare had to get what visual stimulus from his actors. Rags and, perhaps, disfigurements were cheap enough when supported by a general willingness to believe in witchy stuff to make the Macbeth opening an arresting one. The three hags and their chant are visually and verbally enough to stop the punters' chat:

3

MASTER: Boatswain!

BOATSWAIN: Here master. What cheer?

MASTER: Good: speak to the mariners; fall to't, yarely, or we run ourselves aground: bestir, bestir.

(***The Tempest***)

More than that, the scene established a context of the supernatural that gives the mortal drama a wider and more sinister context. It's tone-setting and theme-foreshadowing again. In some ways, things have not moved on that much today. Violent action and danger may start a film today, assisted by computer graphics or digital whizzery. Smart though these may be, they do little more than the shouted alarm and sense of danger rendered by two sailors in a wreck at the start of *The Tempest*:

4

FIRST WITCH: When shall we three meet again?
                    In thunder, lightning or in rain?

(*Macbeth*)

Sometimes, it's vision alone that can still the theatre. Before a word is spoken at the start of *All's Well*, some respect is cued by the appearance on stage of a cortege party, silent and slow, and sombrely dressed:

5

(Enter young Bertram, Count of Rousillon, his mother, the Countess, Helena and Lord Lafeu, all in black.)
COUNTESS: In delivering my son from me I bury a second husband.

(*All's Well That Ends Well*)

That's more than audience-hushing: it's setting an agenda of emotions and relationships that will eventually be resolved in the fulfilment of the title of the play – all's well that ends well, however it begins.

Students can check the ways that Shakespeare's openings settle an audience in the first few lines. A group should speak the lines against the buzz and chat of the rest of the class (grouped mutters of *'rhubarb, rhubarb'… 'slice of nice'… 'chops and chips'* if they can't spontaneously generate some pre-play talk). This context is usually enough to give the rendering more than a mechanical barking at the print. If they get the point that the audience needs to be shut up and its eyes drawn to something on stage, they're there.

Check this out further. Flick to the opening scene of five randomly-chosen plays by Shakespeare and assess their effectiveness in settling and engaging an audience. It's a good activity for English teachers and for students needing a grasp of writing for the theatre.

It's not just the openings that show the influence of Shakespeare's working conditions. The plays are put together to deal with attention span and varied interests. The structure of the plays shows more than a logical and sequential unfolding of a plot-line. There's a craft of varying tone and pace and topic – of juggling different kinds of appeal – to keep all sections of the audience engaged. Look at any of the plays from the point of view of theatrical competition for bums on seats and it becomes apparent that Shakespeare offered not only variety of story and character, but a whole range of audience-pleasing tricks and delights. Most of the plays are a rich mix of ingredients designed to please the rich mix of audience tastes. Apply this brief list of ingredients to any play to see how the recipe works:

*   Satire – sardonic and ironic comment on past or current events
*   Farce – improbably chaotic and comic exploitation of a situation
*   Documentary – recording events before the lives of those watching
*   Feature – examining two or more ways of valuing an event or a character
*   Soap – extending the sentiment or comedy of a sub-plot involving ordinary mortals with recognisably ordinary motives and manners
*   Showbiz spectacle: masques, illusions, tableaux, dance and song

Pick one of the following plays and test the recipe: *Antony and Cleopatra, Much Ado About Nothing, Romeo and Juliet, The Winter's Tale, As You Like It, King Lear, Twelfth Night, The Tempest, Macbeth*.

The development and progression that will take youngsters through suspicion or insecurity to active appreciation needs careful planning and resourcing. There needs to be some controlled phasing of their encounter with the text as readers. The sequence of practical activities proposed is:

1. **Voice practice: speaking Shakespeare**
2. **Action practice: doing Shakespeare**
3. **Group practice: sharing Shakespeare**
4. **Reading practice: appreciating Shakespeare**

Voice practice: speaking Shakespeare

There's no getting away from the fact that the students have to read Shakespeare. This is not to say that they have to read long stretches, or read to get it right first time, or read to 'get through' the play in class. What they need is to understand that reading Shakespeare is about reading playscript – reading aloud, and reading for tone and feeling. Comprehension matters, but there are ways to comprehending that are not limited to the absorption of print for cerebral processing. They need to sound Shakespeare. As a starting point, they need to get their tongues and mouths round some unfamiliar phonic clusters, some unfamiliar morphology and some unfamiliar syntax. Take some examples of expressions they will be encountering in the activities which follow: 'shrugst thou?', 'durst', 'avouch' and 'In the poisoned entrails throw'. This is without the added confusion of the verbal 'false friends' – those words which appear familiar but which mean something very different in Elizabethan English – e.g. 'happy', 'humour', 'naughty', 'fell' and 'sack'. If the unfamiliarities are encountered at the same time as reading the whole text, the process becomes constantly interrupted by glossing. The result is that students may think that Shakespeare is something requiring translation, like a foreign language. What they need to experience is what is familiar in Shakespeare before encountering the less appealing unfamiliarity. And the familiarities are there in attitude, feeling and manner. They need to enjoy some language which conveys these things without glossing.

The usual way of getting youngsters to relish sounds and vocalize meaning is to let them loose with a Shakespeare insult kit. This one has been compiled from various versions easily accessible on the Internet.

Shakespearian insult kit

Here is a useful activity to get students' mouths around some unfamiliar sounds, and their heads around some very familiar aspects of abuse, contempt and insult.

If individuals are lacking verve in their renderings, split the class into two (or four) and get some mass abuse of opposite groups. Volume matters! Emphatic enunciation of plosives, fricatives and sibilants is a good basis for understanding Shakespeare's writing in activities which follow.

Combine one word from each column below, prefaced with 'Thou':

artless	base-court	baggage
bawdy	bat-fowling	barnacle
beslubbering	beef-witted	basket-cockle
bootless	beetle-headed	bladder
burly-boned	boil-brained	blind-worm
caluminous	apple-john	boar-pig
churlish	brazen-faced	bugbear
clouted	bunch-back'd	bum-bailey
cockered	clapper-clawed	canker-blossom
craven	clay-brained	clack-dish
cullionly	common-kissing	clotpole

currish	crook-pated	codpiece
dankish	death-token	coxcomb
dissembling	dismal-dreaming	devil-monk
droning	dizzy-eyed	dewberry
errant	doghearted	flap-dragon
fawning	dread-bolted	flax-wench
fishified	earth-vexing	flirt-gill
fobbing	elf-skinned	foot-licker
frothy	fat-kidneyed	fustilarian
froward	fen-sucked	giglet
fusty	flap-mouthed	gudgeon
gleeking	fly-bitten	haggard
goatish	folly-fallen	harpy
gorbellied	fool-born	hedge-pig
impertinent	full-gorged	horn-beast
infectious	guts-griping	hugger-mugger
jarring	half-faced	joithead
loggerheaded	hasty-witted	jolt-head
lumpish	hedge-born	knave
mammering	hell-hated	lewdster
mangled	idle-headed	lout
mewling	ill-breeding	maggot-pie
misbegotten	ill-nurtured	malcontent
odiferous	knotty-pated	malt-worm
paunchy	leaden-footed	mammet
poisonous	lily-livered	measle
pribbling	malmsey-nosed	minnow
puking	milk-livered	miscreant
puny	motley-minded	moldwarp
qualling	muddy-mettled	mumble-news
rank	onion-eyed	nut-hook
reeky	pigeon-liver'd	pigeon-egg
roguish	plume-plucked	pignut
ruttish	pottle-deep	popinjay
saucy	pox-marked	pumpion
spleeny	reeling-ripe	puttock
spongy	rough-hewn	rampallian
surly	rude-growing	rascal
tottering	rump-fed	ratsbane
unmuzzled	shard-borne	scullian
vain	sheep-biting	scut
venomed	spur-galled	skainsmate
villainous	swag-bellied	strumpet
warped	tardy-gaited	toad
wart-necked	tickle-brained	varlot
wayward	toad-spotted	vassal
weedy	unchin-snouted	wagtail
wimpled	unwash'd	whey-face
yeasty	weather-bitten	whoreson

The more that these insults encourage speakers in lip-smacking, spitting and plosive contempt, the better they will be able to embrace the principle of dramatic writing: that audibility and meaning are evident to even those at the back of the 'wooden O'.

Taking this a stage further, they need to be edged towards speaking words that seem alien or unfamiliar, and whose meaning is at odds with current idiom. Becoming familiar with the words will make them familiar with some of the grammatical forms no longer current today.

Elizabethan and modern: a glossary of common 17th-century words

arrant – out-and-out, downright

art – are

avaunt – go away!

avouch – testify, prove

begat – gave birth to

betimes – soon; early

betwixt – between

caitiff – cowardly wretch

canst – can

capon – chicken

charms – spells

choler – irritable temper

con – study

conceit – idea

cozen – cheat

divers – various

doth/dost – does

doublet – a man's close-fitting jacket

drab – an immoral woman

durst – dare to

entreat – beg, plead

ere – before

enow – enough

fain – inclined to

fardel – burden

fealty – loyalty

fell – terrible

forsooth – truly, honestly

gainst – against

groat – a small coin

hath/hast – has

hose – stockings

humour – mood

husbandry – maintenance

ifaith – honestly

ist – is it

jade – worn out horse

jakes – lavatory

lest – unless

lief (I had as lief) – prefer

methinks – I think

naught – nothing

noisome – harmful

o'er – over

orisons – prayers

parley – talk

pate – head

post – haste

prithee – I beg you

quoth – says

quaff – drink

railst thou – do you complain?

rend – split or break

repair – make your way to

riggish – playful

rude – rough

sack – wine

sirrah – young man

sith – since (because)

taper – candle

thee – you (to a friend)

thou, thine – you, yours

'tis – it is

twain – two/both

varlet – low-class person

visage – face

wanton – reckless

welkin – sky

wench – young woman

wilt – will

ye – you

yore – time gone/ago

yon, yonder – there, over there

zounds! – God's wounds!

Working from word level to sentence level, as the orthodoxy has it, students are ready to practise some extended examples of Elizabethan language.

Practise your Elizabethan

Give these sentences just a touch of the seventeenth century by using the list above

1. Honestly, I think your face has the look of a worn-out horse.
2. Go away! I've had enough of this quarrelling between you two.
3. Honestly, I cannot drink this unpleasant wine.
4. Let's make our way to the pub and have a talk about this terrible business immediately.
5. I suspect you've got some terrible burden on your mind.
6. That wretched coward has cheated you. I would be inclined to testify how he has treated you in a harmful manner.

What do the following mean in modern English?

1. Prithee, let us repair post-haste to yonder tavern for a pot of sack and some capon.
2. Yon wench seems in a choler. Her humour hath been thus sith days of yore.
3. Ifaith, the caitiff hath been justly punished for cozening divers townsfolk.
4. Yon jade hath not the worth of a groat.
5. Con this page for divers conceits concerning husbandry.

Now try these lines from plays by Shakespeare – how might they translate into modern English?

1. I had as lief the town crier spoke my lines. (*Hamlet*)
2. To go to bed after midnight is to go to bed betimes. (*Twelfth Night*)
3. Who would fardels bear, to grunt and sweat under a weary life? (*Hamlet*)
4. Sir John, there's one Master Brook below would fain speak with you, and be acquainted with you; and hath sent your worship a morning's draught of sack. (*The Merry Wives of Windsor*)
5. Lorenzo, I commit into your hands
   The husbandry and manage of my house. (*The Merchant of Venice*)

Action practice: doing Shakespeare

The next stage is to get some sort of performance criteria established. Acting, this isn't – at least, not the sort of acting that gets an Equity card. Let's call it animating story. And let's accept that what Hamlet complained of in coarse acting is just what we need here: sawing the air with arms and all the rest of grimacing and gesturing in ways that out-Herod Herod. Subtle, we don't need: this is English, not RADA.

First, they need to be confident with story detail, sequence and characters. This in itself is a useful way of emphasising the power of ear rather than eye. They need to be made to listen carefully, to reproduce what they have heard – no reading or writing allowed or necessary.

Getting a grip on story structure and detail

This exercise encourages learning by hearing, rather than by reading. The teacher reads the story of e.g. *The Tempest*, using the summary below, emphasising the words in bold type.

A long time ago in a country called **Milan** there was a Duke called **Prospero** who was more interested in **studying** than in ruling his country. Apart from his books, he enjoyed talking to his little daughter and practising **magic**.

His brother **Antonio** was a very **jealous** man who thought he would be better at running the country and plotted with his close friend **Alonso** how he could become Duke.

One day, when Prospero was deep in one of his books, his cousin and his friends seized him and bundled him and his daughter, **Miranda**, into a boat which they sent off to sea. **Gonzalo** kindly gave the pair some small items of food and Antonio took over as Duke.

After days on the **storm tossed** ocean wave through thunder and lightning, through suffering **despair** and **anger** and **fear** and care for his little girl, Prospero and Miranda landed on an island. It was a beautiful island, full of **enchanting** noises. The two were glad to find fruit and shelter, and a place to rest.

1. Re-tell the story, leaving gaps (bold words) for the class to complete.

2. Choose individuals to re-tell the story. Others to correct error or omission.

3. Challenge one student to repeat the story in double-quick time.

4. Challenge a group to mime the story so far, without narration.

5. Challenge another group to present the story in a sequence of five freeze-frames.

This sequence secures the necessary knowledge and introduces the necessary discipline for the practical activities which can now be developed.

Responding to textual cues: miming *The Tempest*

Again, the teacher reads the text, with pauses for a group to respond with physical gesture and or facial expression. Students need to become familiar and confident with some disciplines of performance. Again, using an animated story technique, they can be allowed wild excesses of thespian flurry in taking the prompts as the story is read.

A long time ago in a country called Milan there was a Duke who was more interested in studying than in ruling his country *(mime reading and ignoring flunkeys or Gonzalo as a Minister bringing in letters etc)*. Apart from his books, he enjoyed talking to his little daughter and practising magic *(cue tricks)*.

His brother was a very jealous man who thought he would be better at running the country *(cue trying on the crown/regalia)* and plotted with his close friend *(cue whispers of schemes and graphic gesture)* how he could become Duke.

One day, when Prospero was deep in one of his books, his brother and his friends seized him and bundled him and his daughter into a boat which they sent off to sea *(cue melodrama)*. Gonzalo kindly gave the pair some small items of food *(cue pathos)* and the brother took over as Duke *(cue swagger, strut and orders)*.

After days on the storm tossed ocean wave *(cue action)* through thunder and lightning *(cue FX)*, through suffering despair and anger and fear and care for his little girl *(cue emotions and sea noises)*. Prospero and Miranda landed on an island. It was a beautiful island, full of enchanting noises *(cue music and birdsong)*. The two were glad to find fruit and shelter, and a place to rest *(cue gathering and settling)*.

The next morning, Prospero was walking in the woods when he came across an odd tree that was making strange noises *(cue FX)*. He stopped and listened. It sounded like 'Help me'. He looked, listened and suddenly realised there was something in the tree. Remembering one of his magic spells *(cue gibberish)* he released from the tree a spirit. The spirit was a beautiful winged creature called Ariel... *(cue graceful flight and hover)*. The spirit was very impressed and pleased to serve this new master.

Prospero found another spirit on the island. This one was a lumbering, ungraceful *(cue movement)* creature called Caliban. Caliban was very grateful to be given attention and began to fetch fruit and precious objects for Prospero. He tried to make the two spirits friends but they obviously didn't like each other *(cue gesture and facial expression)*.

Years passed by. Miranda grew up. She looked after her Dad. One day, when she was sitting on her own and Prospero was reading, Caliban sneaked up on her and started to stroke her hair *(cue sneaky movement)*. She was frightened. Prospero heard her scream and thrashed Caliban with his stick *(cue howl and roll and squeal and abuse from Prospero)* and said he would never trust him again and he would now be a slave. After this, Caliban hated Prospero and Miranda. Ariel thought he'd best keep on the good side of Prospero.

Then, one day, there was a storm. There was a shipwreck on the island *(cue FX)*. Amazingly, hardly believably, astonishingly, some people survived and were cast on the beach. Amazingly, hardly believably, astonishingly it was the Duke's wicked brother and his wicked friend and the good Gonzalo and the wicked friend's son. All were suddenly in Prospero's power. All those years of suffering loneliness and anger and hatred had resulted in the chance to get his own back on these evil people who had spoiled his life. He had all the power and the advantages now.

Next, groups present a mimed version of the story without narration and with five freeze-frame or tableau pause-points. To make the most of these tableaux, other students need to advise the performing group about posture and expression, sculpting the group to present key features of the scene.

When the class has story and presentation methods firmly in its grasp, it is time to move on to another story, with a more ambitious outcome.

Story through tableau and mime to performance

An introduction: to be read slowly, as before:

Once upon a time, a long time ago, in Scotland, there was a King called Duncan. He was a **very old** King and needed someone to fight against the **Norwegians**. One of his bravest supporters was the **Thane of Glamis** whose name was **Macbeth**.

Macbeth and his friend **Banquo** were proud to go serve the King, so with their army they went to fight the Norwegians. They got on their horses and rode for days **over hills** and **down dales, across rivers** and **marshes** and **bogs** and **rocky places** until they met the Norwegians. Then there was a fierce battle. Macbeth **lunged** and **stabbed** and **hacked** and **chopped** until the Norwegians were **vanquished**. A sergeant who saw Macbeth fighting reported how he **unseamed one foe from the nave to the chaps** with one stroke of his sword.

Then Macbeth and Banquo and their army rode back to see King Duncan. They rode for days over **rocky places, bogs, marshes** and **rivers, down dales** and **up hills** until they came to a **murky place** that was **evil** and **sinister** and weird, where, suddenly, out of nowhere, there emerged **three witches**. They were **evil** and **sinister** and **weird** and they cackled. One said, '**Hail Macbeth, Thane of Glamis**', which surprised him because he was. Another said '**Hail Macbeth, Thane of Cawdor**', which surprised him because he wasn't. The third then said, '**Hail Macbeth, that shall be King hereafter**', which surprised him even more because he wasn't a member of the royal family. Banquo asked, '**What about me?**' and one of the witches said, 'You won't be King, but your children's children will be.' Then suddenly, just like that, they disappeared into thin air.

Macbeth and Banquo rode on, deep in thought. Then they reached Duncan's palace and they knelt before to tell him about defeating the Norwegians. The King was pleased, and made Macbeth **Thane of Cawdor**. Macbeth thought, '**That's what the witch seemed to know already. I wonder if…. But no!**'

So he wrote a letter to his wife, **Lady Macbeth**, telling her all about these strange events. When she read the letter, she started to think. And what she started to think was, '**Hmmm. Aha. What if…**' and '**So…**'

1.   Knowing the facts

Challenge anyone in the class to tell the story as accurately as possible. Any omission of detail means that the story passes to the person who gets it right. (Alternatively, the teacher can prompt the story-teller, allowing three, four or five faults before choosing someone else to tell the story from the start.) The story can be split into parts for different groups to work on.

2.   Speed trial

The teacher can read this narrative very fast to make it more difficult. If pupils can repeat the story accurately at normal speed, challenge them to repeat it at superfast speed.

3.   Approaching performance: auditions for mime parts.

Choose four pupils to be Macbeth, Banquo, Duncan and Lady Macbeth. Choose three to be witches. Volunteers to play the part must first undergo the audition challenge. This can be a lengthy business, with a panel awarding marks for performance, or the teacher commenting and asking for repeats and freezes.

The audition tests for playing the roles are in no way rigorous, challenging and wholly based upon authentic evocation of character, mood and situation:

Macbeth:	lunging and hacking and stabbing and chopping and ripping foes open from navel to chaps
Banquo:	riding up hills and down dales and across rivers and bogs and marshes and rocky places, through thickets and thorns, and at night
Duncan:	being a wise and kind and weary and worried and (of course) old King
Lady Macbeth:	thinking and plotting and scheming and saying 'Hmmmmm' and 'Ahhh...'
Three witches:	a) cackling b) stirring c) cackling and stirring d) cackling and stirring and filling a cauldron with nasty stuff, e.g. eye of bat and tongue of frog.

4. **Miming the story**

   As with **The Tempest**, the Narrator reads slowly, emphasising the underlined parts, repeating if necessary until performers give suitable exaggerated gestures and movements (silently).

   Volunteers who didn't get the main parts can be the Norwegian army – scope for dramatic mass dying here.

5. **Speed trial miming**

   Narrator reads story very rapidly, forcing performers to mime at double speed, silent movie-style.

6. **Modern English improvisation**

   Narrator disappears. Performers accompany mime routine with improvised dialogue.

7. **Learning aloud: an adaptation of the witches' chants.**

   In this activity, the class as a whole learns 12 lines of Shakespearian text by heart. In reality, one pair of students learns one line, although all students learn the first two lines to get the rhythm established. The rhythm is the guide to sense and action. The teacher speaks the line and the student pair repeats it. It's worth doing this twice, asking for likely rhyme-words for the next line after the first reading. Gradually, add the second line to the first line, then the third and so on until the whole speech is rendered by the class. This takes about 10–15 minutes and demonstrates how students can learn by hearing. Learning aloud! No reading or writing allowed!

   Double, double, toil and trouble;
   Fire burn and cauldron bubble.

   Round about the cauldron go;
   In the poisoned entrails throw,
   Sweltered venom sleeping got,
   Boil thou first in the smelly pot
   Fillet of a fenny snake
   In the cauldron boil and bake;
   Eye of newt and toe of frog,
   Wool of bat and tongue of dog,
   Adder's fork and blindworm's sting,
   Lizard's leg and barn owl's wing.
   For a charm of powerful trouble,
   Like a hell-broth boil and bubble.

   Double double toil and trouble
   Fire burn and cauldron bubble.

Adapted from (*Macbeth* Act 4, Scene 1)

8.   Creating a text for performance

Add the (almost) authentic Shakespeare text for the witches to the improvised text. A performance now has confident story knowledge, rehearsed action sequences, modern English script and some original learned lines from Shakespeare. Impressive! Perform at suitable volume for disrupting maths class in next block. Seek funding for lavish UK/USA/World TV co-production in line for more Oscars than Titanic hits Matrix in Dumbledore.

9.   One more story version for the same practical activities.

Once upon a time, a long time ago, there was a young man called **Hamlet** who was the **Prince of Denmark**. He was a student at **Wittenburg University**, where he sometimes studied very hard *(cue pose)* and sometimes didn't *(cue action)*. One day he received a letter from his mother, **Queen Gertrude**, with some very bad news *(cue action)*. It said that his father, the King of Denmark, had died and that he, Prince Hamlet, was needed at home.

Hamlet received the news with **confusion** and **distress**. Did this mean that he was now to become King? *(Cue action.)* He wanted to carry on being a student, not be responsible for the country. He had always loved his Dad and felt miserable that he was now dead. There was no mention of how he had died, and Hamlet did not know of any illness his father had.

Hamlet returned at once to **Elsinore Castle** in Denmark, with his friend **Horatio**. *(Cue energetic journeying as per Macbeth if wished...)* When he got there, he comforted his mother and she comforted him *(cue action)*. Then he got a shock *(cue pose)*. His mother told him that she had already, within days of her husband's death, married her husband's brother, Hamlet's **Uncle Claudius**. Gertrude begged her son to accept his uncle as the new King and as his new father. Hamlet left her and spent many hours in confusion, turmoil, anguish, anger and sadness. *(Cue all these.)*

Hamlet could not get to sleep. He paced about for hours, wondering what to do with himself. Then his friend Horatio knocked on his door and said he had something to tell him. Two soldiers had reported seeing a ghost for **three nights** running, in the **hours before dawn**, upon the **battlements**. They said the ghost was a dead ringer for Hamlet's Dad. Hamlet was astonished *(cue pose)*. He thought it was not true. Students at Wittenburg University didn't believe in ghosts. Horatio said he didn't either, but he had been with the soldiers last night and he had seen the ghost, and it was just like King Hamlet.

Hamlet said he would go to the battlements that night. As he stood in the cold and the dark *(cue both)* nothing happened. Then, suddenly, there appeared before him a grisly, horrifying sight. It was the ghost! *(Cue action.)* And it was his father! It beckoned him. Horatio grabbed him and told him to be careful, because you couldn't trust ghosts but Hamlet broke free and said he would do what this ghost said.

Then it happened. When Hamlet and the ghost were alone, the ghost of his father spoke to him. It said that he had been murdered, poisoned by his brother, Claudius, so that he could become King and marry Gertrude. He wanted Hamlet to take revenge and kill Claudius, but be kind to Gertrude.

Hamlet was in a terrible state. He..........................

Activities based on this sketch can be adapted from the sequence following the Macbeth sketch.

Group practice: sharing Shakespeare

Getting it together: performance of a Shakespeare text

1. **Working towards a performance of a scene from** *A Midsummer Night's Dream*

   Read a version of the story as before:

   Once upon a time there were two young people who lived next door to each other, a boy and a girl *(cue entrance)*. The boy was handsome and brave and in love with the girl *(cue stance)*. The girl was beautiful and intelligent and in love with the boy *(cue stance)*. But their parents did not approve, and told them not to see each other *(cue scene)*. The boy's name was ..... and the girl's name was ...... (most classes will guess *Romeo and Juliet*) Pyramus and Thisby.

   The only way they could see each other was to talk through a chink in the wall at the bottom of their gardens *(cue action)*. There, they would whisper sweet words of love, in fear of being found out by their parents. One night Pyramus had an idea. He was so fed up that he suggested, through the chink in the wall, that they should run away together. Thisby agreed *(cue plans for elopement obscured by a wall...)*. They planned to meet that night, at midnight, in the churchyard, near Ninny's tomb etc.

2. **Test knowledge of the story** – get individuals to recount it, gonging them out if they omit two key features.

3. **Call for mime volunteers** to perform as the story is read again, with suitable pause and emphasis.

3. **Do double-quick silent movie mime** to a rapid story reading.

4. **Normal speed mime** without the story.

5. **Tableau snapshots** (also known as **film stills**) with promotional captions written on A3 paper as a luxury addition.

6. **Modern English improvisation**

   Students make up whatever dialogue that fits the purpose. Any flourishes of language indicating extremity of passion to be approved. Modern idiom welcomed. 'O' and 'Oh!' and 'Ah!' and 'Aaagh!' worth practical attention as components of performance.

7. **The Shakespeare performance**

   This activity is very well suited to a group of five or six. The two main spoken parts will need some confident performers able to learn some lines, but there is also scope for others to be engaged in planning and performing without the lines. **Wall** and **Moonshine** offer scope for paired unscripted performance and every class in the country has someone willing to give the **Lion** role some roaring and pouncing verve.

   Auditions: volunteers are called for a stage test as follows, with a brief to demonstrate suitable gesture and movement.

   Pyramus test: being Romantic and Love-sick; discovering a bloody mantle with a) curiosity, b) recognition, c) disbelief, and d) shock and horror; dying by own sword.

   Thisby test: being Romantic and Lovesick; being Frightened and Cold in the Dark; dying by Pyramus' sword.

   Wall test: standing still when people do things around you (and no cracking up).

Moonshine test: shimmering gently in a dark sky.

Lion test: a) roaring, b) pouncing, c) roaring and pouncing together, d) roaring, pouncing and savaging a mantle.

8. **Whole class**

   Successful Pyramus and Thisby asked to read. If, as likely, expression lacks melodramatic and hyperbolic quality, whole class instructed to accompany each 'O' with dramatic and elongated choral effect. Success criteria: Senior Management Team crisis concerning tragic wailing coming from the English block.

9. **Group work**: groups of 5/6 to play Pyramus and Thisby, Wall, Lion, Moonshine. Larger groups or doubling-up if needed to include Narrator and Ninny's tomb.

Time scale: three lessons. Add non-lesson time to make costumes, Moon effect, Wall (cardboard box painted, blanket festooned) etc. A sword! A Lion costume! (I have always under-estimated the extent to which students can get carried away with costume and prop-construction, sometimes drawing parents into elaborate transformation of curtains, bed-linen and resurrected cardboard TV packaging. I have also learned that some students shy of spoken performance have a natural gift or talent for backstage work. I think this is sometimes described as kinaesthetic learning.)

The following script is generally authentic but is edited and adapted for classroom purposes. Any liberties taken with the original are respectfully offered as being in the spirit that Shakespeare would approve, including some of the worst rhymes.

The tragic love and death of Pyramus and Thisby

Scene 1: the secret meeting place, a wall which divides the gardens of the two families. It is night.

PYRAMUS: O! Grim-looked night! O night with hue so black!
            O! Night, O night! Alack! Alack! Alack!
            I fear my Thisby's promise is forgot!
            And thou, O wall, O sweet, O lovely wall,
            Behind whose stones my Thisby's garden lies,
            Show me thy chink, to blink through with my eyes.
            But what see I? No Thisby do I see.
            O wicked wall, through whom I see no bliss!
            Cursed be thy stones for thus deceiving me!

(Enter Thisby.)

            O wall, full often hast thou heard my moans
            For parting my fair Pyramus and me!
            My cherry lips have often kissed thy stones;
            The stones I kiss because I can't kiss he.

PYRAMUS: I see a voice! Now will I to the chink
            To see if I can hear my Thisby's face.
            Thisby! Thisby!

THISBY: My love thou art, my love I think.

PYRAMUS: O kiss me through the hole of this rough wall!

THISBY: I kiss the stone and not your lips at all.

PYRAMUS: Wilt thou at Ninny's tomb meet me straightway?

THISBY: O Pyramus, O Pyramus, I'll come without delay.

(They go off.)

Scene 2: later that night in the churchyard near Ninny's tomb.

(Enter Thisby, nervously.)

THISBY: O night! O dark! O cold! Be still, my heart!
            No more shall cruel father keep us two apart.
            I've left with mantle but no scarf or glove –
            Here is the tomb, now where's my love?

(Enter a ferocious lion which pounces on her. She escapes, leaving her mantle which the lion tears before going off.)

(Enter Pyramus.)

PYRAMUS: Sweet moon, I thank thee for thy sunny beams;
            I thank thee, Moon, for shining now so bright.
            For by thy gracious, golden, glittering beams
            I trust to take of truest Thisby sight.
            But stay! O spite!
            O Woe! O night!
            What dreadful deed is here?
            Eyes, do you see?
            O how can it be?
            The mantle I know you wear
            With rip and blood and tear!
            To live without my love I cannot bear!

(He draws his sword.)

            Thus die I, thus and thus and thus.
            Now I am dead.
            Now I am fled.
            My soul goes to the sky –
            I die! I die! Die... die...die..die..die...die...

(Enter Thisby, frightened.)

THISBY: Asleep, my love?
            What, dead my dove?
            O Pyramus, arise!
            Speak, Speak. Quite dumb!
            Dead! Dead! A tomb
            Must cover thy sweet eyes.
            These lily lips,
            This cherry nose,
            These yellow cowslip cheeks
            Are gone, are gone!
            Tongue, not a word!
            Come, trusty sword!
            And farewell friends,
            Thus Thisby ends...
            Adieu, adieu, adieu....

(Adapted from *A Midsummer Night's Dream* Act 5, Scene 1)

A more ambitious classroom performance – or an alternative one if time does not allow both – is to work with the following rehearsal scene for Pyramus and Thisby. This is a useful way of getting students to enjoy some 'Very Exaggerated Bad Acting' and Bottom's comic faith in his own thespian excellence.

The Mechanicals' first rehearsal

Casting the parts

(Enter QUINCE, SNUG, BOTTOM, FLUTE, SNOUT, and STARVELING.)

QUINCE: Is all our company here?

BOTTOM: You were best to call them man by man, according to the scrip.

QUINCE: Here is the scroll of every man's name thought fit to play in our interlude before the duke and the duchess on his wedding-day.

BOTTOM: First, good Peter Quince, say what the play treats on, then read the names of the actors, and then get to the point.

QUINCE: Well then, our play is, 'The most lamentable comedy, and most cruel death of Pyramus and Thisby'.

BOTTOM: A very good piece of work, I assure you. Now, good Peter Quince, call forth your actors by the scroll. Masters, spread yourselves.

QUINCE: Answer as I call you. Nick Bottom, the weaver?

BOTTOM: Ready. Name what part I am for, and proceed.

QUINCE: You, Nick Bottom, are set down for Pyramus.

BOTTOM: What is Pyramus? A lover, or a tyrant?

QUINCE: A lover, that kills himself for love

BOTTOM: That will ask some tears in the true performing of it: if I do it, let the audience watch out; I will move storms, I will suffer miserably in good measure. Yet my best talent is for a tyrant: I could play a tyrant or a hero full of passion.
                The raging rocks
                And shivering shocks
                Shall break the locks
                Of prison gates.
Now name the rest of the players.

QUINCE: Francis Flute, the bellows-mender.

FLUTE: Here, Peter Quince.

QUINCE: Flute, you must take Thisby on you.

FLUTE: What is Thisby? a wandering knight?

QUINCE: It is the lady that Pyramus must love.

FLUTE: Nay, faith, let me not play a woman; I have a beard coming.

QUINCE: You shall play it in a mask, and you may speak as small as you will.

BOTTOM: Let me play Thisby too, I'll speak in a monstrous little voice. 'T'hisne, Thisne;' 'Ah, Pyramus, lover dear! Thy Thisby's here, thy love most dear!' 'Ah, Thisby, love. Tis me, thy love. Tis Pyramus my dove.'

QUINCE: No, no; you must play Pyramus; and, Flute, you Thisby.

BOTTOM: Well, proceed.

QUINCE: Snug, the joiner; you, the lion's part; and, I hope, here is a play fitted.

SNUG: Have you the lion's part written? If it be, give it me, for I am slow of study.

QUINCE: You may do it extempore, for it is nothing but roaring.

BOTTOM: Let me play the lion too! I will roar so every man can hear me; I will roar so the Duke will say 'Let him roar again, let him roar again.'

QUINCE: If you should do it too terribly, you would fright the duchess and the ladies.

BOTTOM: Then I will roar as gently as a dove; I will roar like a nightingale.

QUINCE: You can play no part but Pyramus; for he is as sweet-faced man as one shall see; a most lovely gentleman-like man: therefore you must play Pyramus.

BOTTOM: Well, I will undertake it. What beard were I best to play it in? I will discharge it in either your straw-colour beard, your orange-tawny beard, your purple beard, or your French beard, your perfect yellow.

QUINCE: I will draw a bill of properties, such as our play wants. There is two hard things: that is, to bring the moonlight into a chamber; for, you know, Pyramus and Thisby meet by moonlight. One must come in with a lanthorn, and say he comes to disfigure, or to present, the person of Moonshine. Then, we must have a wall; for Pyramus and Thisby says the story, did talk through the chink of a wall.

BOTTOM: Some man or other must present Wall; and let him have some plaster, or some rough-cast about him, to signify wall; and let him hold his fingers thus, and through that cranny shall Pyramus and Thisby whisper.

QUINCE: Then all is well. Here are your parts: know them by to-morrow night; and meet me in the palace wood by moonlight; there will we rehearse.

BOTTOM: We will meet; and there we may rehearse most obscenely and courageously. Take pains; be perfect: adieu.

* *

First read-through

QUINCE: Pyramus, you begin; and every one according to his cue. Thisby, stand forth.

BOTTOM: Thisby, the flowers of odious savours sweet –

QUINCE: 'Odours'! 'Odours'! Not 'odious'!

BOTTOM: …odours savours sweet:
           So hath thy breath, my dearest Thisby dear.
           But hark, a voice! Stay thou but here awhile,
           And by and by I will to thee appear.

(Exit)

(Adapted from *A Midsummer Night's Dream* Act 1, Scene 2 and Act 3, Scene 1)

The same play, and same sub-plot, provides material for another practical activity which focuses students on words, delivery and meaning. Two different performers can speak the lines, one with the mis-punctuation that Shakespeare has used to create a comic mis-rendering of meaning, and one with appropriate punctuation.

PROLOGUE   If we offend, it is with our good will.
            That you should think, we come not to offend,
            But with good will. To show our simple skill,
            That is the true beginning of our end.
            Consider then we come but in despite.
            We do not come as minding to contest you,
            Our true intent is. All for your delight
            We are not here. That you should here repent you,
            The actors are at hand and by their show
            You shall know all that you are like to know.

(*A Midsummer Night's Dream* Act 5, Scene 1)

Reading practice: appreciating Shakespeare

With some rousing performances behind them, students are ready to get some insight into the artistry of Shakespeare – particularly how he makes it easy for actors to know what to do with his script. This stage of Shakespearience is still preparing for any substantial encounter with a study text.

Working with sound cues – Shakespeare's implicit stage directions

In the following passages, various sounds are being worked on to give more expression. Actors are being cued to express emotion in sound effects.

It's a commonplace that Shakespeare (unlike, for example, Shaw, or Ibsen) wrote no stage directions to guide the performance of his text. True, there is that well-known exception, 'exit pursued by a bear' and various alarums, flourishes and fanfares, but nothing consistently explicit; no vocalisation prompts like 'whispers nervously' or 'speaks menacingly'. One reason for this is Shakespeare's understandable protectiveness of his property. Plays were business, and before a law of copyright protected authors' rights, a theatrical money-spinner had to be kept out of the hands of rivals. Complete text copies were, literally, a giveaway. It made sense to give actors only their own parts and cues. It also made sense to keep directions for performance to yourself. Thus, hand-in-hand go economics and aesthetics.

There is another reason, though. Audibility and expression needed help in the large public space of an open-air theatre. His words had to be heard by everyone – even at the back – and the mood of the character had to be clear from meaning and sound. Actors could not always be relied upon to get lines right. (See Shakespeare's scathing comments on 'sawing the air' and 'mouthing' lines in *Hamlet*, and his portrayal of duff thespians in *A Midsummer Night's Dream*.) As an actor himself by trade, Shakespeare understood what an actor needed, and how to direct an actor by embedding prompts within the script.

Consonantal cueing

Some consonants are particularly distinct and help audibility. They also help convey a sense of mood and purpose. Take sibilants, for example. 'S' sounds can express the hissing of urgent or vengeful intent, or of secretive whispers, or both. In this passage, Leontes is watching his wife and best friend, suspecting that they are sexually attracted to each other. As he looks on, his adviser tries to assure him that there is nothing suspicious going on. Leontes speaks to him so that his wife and best friend cannot hear, emphasising that what he sees with his own eyes cannot mean anything but the worst:

LEONTES: Is whispering nothing?
          Is leaning cheek to cheek? Is meeting noses?
          Kissing with inside lip? Stopping the career
          Of laughter with a sigh (a note infallible
          of breaking honesty)? Horsing foot on foot?
          Skulking in corners? Wishing clocks more swift?
          Hours, minutes? Noon, midnight? And all eyes
          Blind with the pin and web, but theirs, theirs only.
          That would, unseen, be wicked? Is this nothing?

(The Winter's Tale **Act 1, Scene 2)**

There is more than poetically alliterative sound-patterning here. This is direction of utterance, making it easy for an actor to find the feeling and the voice within the text. Shakespeare wants the actor to speak in a whisper so that others on stage apparently don't hear what he says, but the audience does. It's important that his mood of bitter anger is expressed. Adding stage directions would be superfluous when the lines are so stuffed with hissing sibilants an actor could hardly fail to render fierce seethings. Students can count the sibilants and practise saying the lines with as fierce a hiss as possible.

The same use of sibilance helps the actor playing Hamlet to express the passionate revulsion and disgust of thinking about his mother and Claudius: '... in the rank sweat of an enseamed bed.'

Something similar is going on in the scene where Macbeth, anxiously considering awful deeds and the need to act quickly and secretively, mutters audibly:

MACBETH: If 'twere done, when 'tis done, then 'twere well
          It were done quickly: if the assassination
          Could trammel up the consequence, and catch
          With his surcease, success.....

(Macbeth **Act 1, Scene 7)**

It's enough for the audience to hear the sounds of Macbeth's voice, with individual words indistinct, for mood and meaning to be conveyed. Shakespeare makes the speech sound whispered and nervous, with lots of T sounds. Students can count the T and S sounds, colour-code the script for sound-patterning and practise saying the lines.

Likewise, Shakespeare's directional alliteration can work to prompt an actor to violent physical anger and repugnance. In this passage from *The Tempest*, Prospero is angry with Caliban, the island monster he has tried to help and who has repaid his help by trying to rape his daughter, Miranda.

PROSPERO: Hag-seed, hence!
          Fetch us in fuel; and be quick, thou'rt best,
          To answer other business. Shrug'st thou, malice?
          If thou neglect'st, or dost unwillingly
          What I command, I'll rack thee with old cramps,
          Fill all thy bones with aches, make thee roar,
          That beasts shall tremble at thy din.

(The Tempest **Act 1, Scene 2)**

Shakespeare wants the actor to be angry and threatening. He makes the actor draw in lots of air to thrust out again by stacking the opening lines with a number of aspirates at the start. The violence of his mood and threats of rough physical punishment are conveyed in lines brutally jammed with forced aspirates and harsh consonants linked by short vowels. The consonantal cueing exploits the K – G – R sounds produced by forceful use of the back of the throat.

Students can count the harsh consonants and score the passage by colour-coding the sound pattern for its sound effects.

Then they can test it. This needs some vigorous exercise of lungs and voices! Vocalise the cues. Read aloud, with emphatic stress on all the short vowels.

Start by vocalising the vowels only:

> **a – ee – e !**
> **e – u – i – ue – a – ee – i – oua – e,**
> **oo – a – e – u – e – i – e . u – ou – a – i?**
> **i– ou – e – e –o – u – u – i – i – ee**
> **o – I – o – a – I – a – ee – i – o – a,**
> **i – o – I – ow – i – aa – aa – ee – oa,**
> **a – ee – a – e – a – I – i.**

Now vocalise the consonants. Start with the harsh, back-of throat, guttural ones.

> Ha**g**-seed, hence!
> Fetch us in fuel; and be **q**ui**ck**, thou'rt best,
> To answer other business. Shru**g**'st thou, malice?
> If thou ne**g**le**c**t'st, or dost unwillingly
> What I **c**ommand, I'll ra**ck** thee with old **c**ramps,
> Fill all thy bones with a**ch**es, ma**k**e thee roar,
> That beasts shall tremble at thy din.

Now vocalise emphasis upon the rolling 'r' in:

> 'answe**R** other business', 'sh**R**ugst', '**R**ack', 'c**R**amps', '**R**oar' and 't**R**emble'.

Now put the whole speech together and vocalise all the cues, including any 'F' and 'B' sounds that help to produce an utterance of anger and loathing. That 'shrug'st' on its own is enough to squeeze full vocal value from an actor with its demand for five consonants and a vowel in the space of a syllable. Try it: SH-R-U-G-S-T…! Even the most SE (Standard English? South East? Stylistically Emotionless?) speaker will be moved to rolled 'r' elocution with lines like these.

There is similar patterning in the lines written for Coriolanus when he angrily turns on the Roman people who have dared to banish him after he has saved them and the city. The recurring C and R sounds prompt the actor to expressive contempt and fury.

CORIOLANUS: You common cry of curs! whose breath I hate
             As reek o'th'rotten fens, whose loves I prize
             As the dead carcasses of unburied men
             That do corrupt my air: I banish you!

                                    (*Coriolanus* Act 3, Scene 3)

Students can count the C and R sounds and colour-code the passage, then practise saying the lines.

In a theatre lacking effective acoustics, electronic sound amplification and a reverential audience in a darkened auditorium, it's the embedded amplification which helps an actor reach the rear rows. Matching audibility to expressive utterance and emphasis is alliteration put to public use rather than private silent-reading delight. If the subject is violent, the words need to be chosen for violent sound as well as for visual suggestion.

HENRY   The **b**lind and **b**loody soldier with **f**oul hand
          Defile the locks of your **sh**rill-**sh**rieking **d**aughters;
          Your **f**athers taken by their **s**ilver **b**eards,
          And their most reverend hea**ds d**ash'd to the walls;
          Your naked infants **sp**i**tt**ed up**o**n **p**ikes...

                                    (*Henry V* Act 3, Scene 3)

The 'b', 'f', 'd', 's' and 'p' consonants emerge like crags from the valley-bottom of English vowels. Combinations of 's' and 'p', combining sibilant and plosive, are particularly effective in forcing an actor's use of breath and lip muscles. It's not just in colloquial abuse and contemptuous name-calling that the plosive is so satisfyingly gestural. When Shakespeare, in *Henry IV Part One*, wanted his Hotspur to convey outraged contempt for the effete King's messenger who arrived on the battlefield fresh-barbered, trimly dressed and waving a perfume box against the unwholesome smell of corpses (Act 1, Scene 3), he could have written that Hotspur was 'annoyed by this parroter'. That would be enough to communicate an image of impatience with a gaudy, vain repeater of words. What he wrote, however, shows care for an actor's vocalisation as well as for communicating meaning. 'Annoyed' is vocally weak. 'Parrot' is OK, vocally and for sense, but the more plosive-packed, short-vowelled

> **To be** so **pestered** of **t**his **pop**injay

makes the line an unavoidable prompt to lip-curling expulsion of feeling.

Vowel cues

It is not only consonants that can help an actor find the right mood and attitude, and reach the back of the theatre. Vowels can also be used for the same purpose. Shakespeare understood that in real speech we sometimes deliberately or unintentionally choose certain sounds to express our feelings. Short a, e, i, o, u create a sense of rapid action; long a, e, i, o, u a sense of drawn out feeling. Compare 'Get off that rug you git!' with 'O don't leave me alone in these dark ruined mines!'

Here is King Lear's anguished plea to his daughters who have refused to let him have as many comforts and servants as he wants:

LEAR: O, reason not the need...

(*King Lear* Act 2, Scene 4)

If Shakespeare wants to cue his actors to passionate, romantic utterance, he tends to rely on long open vowels to get the desired effect, as in his sending-up of melodramatic love-drama in Pyramus and Thisby:

PYRAMUS   O kiss me through the hole of this rough wall.

THISBY   I kiss the stone, and not your lips at all.

(*A Midsummer Night's Dream* Act 5, Scene 1)

Long open vowels can suggest sorrow and passion. Shakespeare sometimes presents this as genuine emotion. He also has a crafty insight into how some people – politicians, for example – may use the device in a less than sincere way. King Claudius, having killed his brother, is making a public speech in which he wants the audience to think him sad and sincere for his brother's death.

CLAUDIUS: Though yet of Hamlet our dear brother's death
           The memory be green and that it us befitted
           To bear our hearts in grief, and our whole kingdom
           To be contracted in one brow of woe...

Shakespeare has packed the speech with long vowels. Students can colour code the long vowels to see how much the expression is cued by them, and contrast it with what follows as he shifts from the grieving role to the role of statesman with business to do. As Claudius moves from the posture of the man of feeling into the posture of the man of action, his lines become by contrast stacked with the short vowels of the role of the new ruler – brisk, efficient, prompt and expedient.

CLAUDIUS: Thus much the business is: we have here writ
            To Norway, uncle of young Fortinbras
            Who, impotent and bed-rid, scarcely hears
            Of this his nephew's purpose, to suppress his further gait herein…

(*Hamlet* Act 1, Scene 2)

Students can contrast the colour-coded long vowels of the first extract with the short vowels of the second.

It's not surprising that a writer who started as an actor understands what an actor needs, writing script that assists breath and pause and emphasis. Many who study Shakespeare don't appreciate the practicality of his stagecraft because they read him with the eye, not the ear and see his work as literature. His gift is for uniting poetry and drama. Open-space performance calls for open-mouthed expression from an actor. His scriptcraft is poetry put to work for public purpose. Let's hear it for the back row of the wooden O. Let's hear it in the next block, in the Maths suite…

Imagery

Shakespeare is famous for the choice of words to evoke mental images and this technique matches the use of sound cues to make an impact on the audience. In the following passage, it is important that the audience gets the message that these two Roman soldiers take a very dim view of the way their former great leader has now thrown away his life and reputation by cavorting with Cleopatra. The sounds of the words are important but the words themselves are rich in imagery of military life and values, and of their view of sexual indulgence.

(Enter Demetrius and Philo.)

PHILO: Nay, but this dotage of our general's
         O'erflows the measure: those his goodly eyes
         That o'er the files and musters of the war
         Have glowed like plated Mars, now bend, now turn
         The office and devotion of their view
         Upon a tawny front. His captain's heart,
         Which in the scuffles of great fights hath burst
         The buckles on his breast, reneges all temper,
         And is become the bellows and the fan
         To cool a gypsy's lust.

(Flourish. Enter Antony, Cleopatra, her ladies, the Train, with Eunuchs fanning her.)

(*Antony and Cleopatra* Act 1, Scene 1)

Students can pick out the words which suggest that it is a soldier speaking: technical terms drawn from the military life. They can then pick out words intended to show behaviour far from military life: terms of comfortable homely activity. Contrasting the images helps to show how these two Roman soldiers feel about the man they used to admire.

For further reading on Shakespeare's imagery as something designed to reflect the lives of the speakers, and to draw on experiences familiar to audiences, see page 146.

Syntactical patterning

It's not just sound cues and imagery that help and actor and reach the back rows. Although rather inconsistent and neglectful of punctuation, Shakespeare does use grammatical features of phrases and clauses to cue actor.

In the next extract, Prince Hamlet is in an emotional turmoil. He cannot believe – does not believe – that his mother can have re-married so soon after her husband's death. Hamlet feels disgusted that she could have seemed so much in love with her first husband, his father, but then so quickly marry his brother, a far less worthy man in Hamlet's view. The speech needs to show the audience how fond memory, anger, disbelief, disgust and contempt mingle in Hamlet. The confusion makes him temporarily incapable of controlling his thoughts and feelings.

HAMLET: Heaven and earth,
                Must I remember? Why, she would hang on him
                As if increase of appetite had grown
                By what it fed on; and yet within a month –
                Let me not think on't – Frailty, thy name is woman –
                A little month, or ere those shoes were old
                With which she follow'd my poor father's body,
                Like Niobe, all tears, why she –
                O God, a beast that wants discourse of reason
                Would have mourned longer – married with my uncle,
                My father's brother, but no more like my father
                Than I to Hercules.

                                                        (*Hamlet* Act 1, Scene 2)

Modern editors punctuate the passage so that the cues are more obvious, but they are pretty obvious without any added signs. Shakespeare has constructed the speech so that thoughts seem to interrupt each other, though there is a logical order throughout. Perhaps it's more accurate to say that he shows Hamlet trying to keep to a logical order of meaning ('My mother, who seemed so fond of my father, has married his brother only days after his death') but that feelings disrupt the order throughout. This is a form of naturalistic writing. It reproduces the way people speak in distress in real life.

Students can track the thought-and-feeling nature of the speech by commenting on what is happening inside Hamlet's head at each point of the speech.

Mark the speech with notes on Hamlet's thoughts and feelings.

Heaven and earth, /Must I remember?

Why, she would hang on him /As if increase of appetite had grown
By what it fed on;

and yet within a month –

Let me not think on't –

Frailty, thy name is woman –

A little month, or ere those shoes were old/With which she follow'd my poor father's body,/Like Niobe, all tears

– why she –

God, a beast that wants discourse of reason/Would have mourned longer

– married with my uncle,

My father's brother

but no more like my father/Than I to Hercules.

Put all these together and you have script that doesn't need much in the margin to explain how to perform it – as long as the cues are seen for what they are.

Embedded stage directions

In the following speech, Macbeth is, like Hamlet, in a state of confusion and conflict. He has begun to face the fact that he is losing all that he has worked for. His wife has died, his followers are deserting him and the enemy army is approaching to punish him for what he has done. He remains a brave, powerful man, but he is so tormented by fear and anger that he cannot be decisive. Shakespeare writes lines that help the actor to show this rapid change in mood, the lurching swings between one decision and another. What is especially skilful about the scene is that it also helps the four or five other people on stage, who have no lines to speak, to know what to do to make the scene active and convincing. There is no marginal stage direction for Seyton to go off-stage or to return. There is no marginal stage direction for the servant – or two servants – trying to put Macbeth's armour on to be finding the job difficult because of his movements and moods. There is no marginal stage direction to the Macbeth actor to alternate between pitiful self-doubt and angry assertiveness and back to doubt. It's all in the script.

MACBETH: Throw physic to the dogs; I'll none of it. –
              Come, put mine armour on; give me my staff. –
              Seyton, send out. – Doctor, the Thanes fly from me. –
              Come sir, despatch. – If thou couldst, Doctor, cast
              The water of my land, find her disease,
              And purge it to a sound and pristine health,
              I would applaud thee to the very echo,
              That should applaud again. – Pull't off, I say! –
              What rhubarb, cyme or what purgative drug
              Would scour these English hence? Hearst thou of them?

(*Macbeth* Act 5, Scene 3)

Students can track the thoughts and feelings and mark the clash-points which the actor needs to display on stage.

**Mark the speech with notes on mood and action
to help an actor:**

Throw physic to the dogs; I'll none of it.

Come, put mine armour on; give me my staff. –

Seyton, send out. –

Doctor, the Thanes fly from me. –

Come sir, despatch. –

If thou couldst, Doctor, cast/The water of my land, find her disease,
And purge it to a sound and pristine health,/I would applaud thee to
the very echo,/That should applaud again. –

Pull't off, I say! –

What rhubarb, cyme or what purgative drug/Would scour these English
hence? Hearst thou of them?

Advanced embedded stage directions for performance

What we've done so far has involved studying Shakespeare's technique as a writer of playscript, a maker of drama. We have seen how he makes conflicts within a person come to life, and how he makes conflicts between people come to life. Personalities clashing, moods changing and situations developing all make good drama. The next example is of Shakespeare's writing a speech for an actor to be credibly himself, but also to impersonate another character. The lines cue an actor to act as a character acting as another character...

In *Henry IV*, young Hotspur is called to face the King for apparently refusing to carry out his orders to send prisoners to the king so that he could ransom them for lots of money. He knows the king is angry and has to find a reason for having caused offence. If he can make the king laugh and blame someone else (i.e. the messenger), he can get himself off the hook. So the actor on stage has to act as Hotspur acting as the messenger.

HOTSPUR:		My liege, I did deny no prisoners,
		But I remember, when the fight was done,
		When I was dry with rage and extreme toil,
		Breathless and faint, leaning upon my sword,
		Came there a certain lord, neat and trimly dressed,
		Fresh as a bridegroom, and his chin new reaped
		Showed like a stubble land at harvest home.
		He was perfumed like a milliner,
a)		And twixt his finger and his thumb he held
		A pouncet-box, which ever and anon
b)		He gave his nose, and took't away again –
		Who, therewith angry, when it next came there,
		Took it in snuff, and still he smiled and talked:
		And as the soldiers bore dead bodies by,
c)		He called them untaught knaves, unmannerly,
		To bring a slovenly unhandsome corpse
		Betwixt the wind and his nobility.
		With many holiday and lady terms
		He questioned me, amongst the rest demanded
		My prisoners in your majesty's behalf.
		I then, all smarting with my wounds being cold,
		To be so pestered with a popinjay,
		Out of my grief and my impatience,
		Answered neglectingly, I know not what...

(Henry IV Part One Act 1, Scene 3)

Students can probe the speech for the cues which help to make this a clever, amusing and cunning performance on stage.

1. What actions do you think Hotspur will be using to mime the messenger at a), b) and c)?

2. Which words does he deliberately choose to make the messenger seem like a woman?

3. Which actions does he think will make the King feel critical of the Messenger?

4. How does Hotspur remind the King of his own efforts in his cause?

5. Where does he hope to make his listeners and the King laugh?

Relating Shakespeare to our world

Students (and others) need to feel some linkage between Shakespeare's text and the world they are familiar with. Generations of zealous English teachers have worked on defustifying language and drawing common threads of motive, passion and relationship to make the links with varying degrees of success or dismay. Too much explanation is itself a turn-off. Any amount of patient explaining that Elsinore is in Denmark and that Polonius is a high-level courtier can still result in students' sense that these people with funny names in a place they've never heard of are not in any way meshed with the lives we lead today. They need to have visual and physical links to real life before they find the more subtle links.

Creating a context (1): a press conference

Take *Hamlet*, for example, and we already have. The ingredients of murder, ghost, dodgy marriage and revenge are strong features of a teacher's sales pitch. They can produce a willingness to follow the plot when the lines get tough, but they can also result in disappointment that the trailer is better than the show that follows. They need to feel that the words are sometimes secondary to the action. Much of what I have recommended before is based on finding the action in the words. The tack here is slightly different. The activity is based on Claudius' speech in Act 1 Scene 2 – a scene previously used to illustrate Shakespeare's scriptcraft.

CLAUDIUS: Though yet of Hamlet our dear brother's death
            The memory be green and that it us befitted
            To bear our hearts in grief, and our whole kingdom
            To be contracted in one brow of woe...

Whatever other interest there is in this scene (and other interests include character study, plot development and dramatic craft in cueing an actor through systematic vowel-patterning) it is a scene fascinating in its grasp of the skill of political leadership. It is not cynical to observe that 21st century politics is as much about presentation as it is about policy. Sound-bites, spinning, manipulating the media and winning public confidence. On both sides of the Atlantic, mature democracies resolve issues of national leadership not by inviting judgements of relative intelligence, experience or morality, but by news management and personality appeal. Image is all. If a man sounds serious, he must be a serious man. If he sounds confident that he has the answers, he must have the answers. If he sounds as if his dreams are the same as ours, he must be one of us. Politics may once have been the art of getting things done. It now seems more like the art of seeming to get things done. It may once have been about leading people to what they may not understand to be a better way, but now it seems about telling people what they want to hear, while despising people and having contempt for what it is they think they want. Two of the scripts for study and performance in 'The Collaborative Shakespearience' (see page 47), show how Shakespeare understood these things 400 years ago. Mark Antony is the ultimate exemplar of the art of turning round a hostile crowd by cunning presentation of sentiment and appeal to economic gain and nationalistic pride. Coriolanus is the ultimate exemplar of the art of saying what people want to hear while despising their stupidity. At the point where English becomes Citizenship Studies without a government-controlled curriculum and ring-binder guidance, these two sections from the Roman plays are as powerful an insight into how we may be manipulated today as any we could lay hands on in Literature.

This activity is worth a lesson on its own, as an example of how to give some text a social relevance and how to enhance text with some directorial embellishment. It is also a good introduction to the longer selections in the next section, from *Coriolanus* (page 86) and *Julius Caesar* (page 93). It has the double practical merit of involving the whole class and giving some a role that requires no speaking.

THE PRESS CONFERENCE

1   Casting

Seven individuals need to be cast as Claudius, Gertrude, Polonius, Hamlet and three Heavies. No audition necessary and only Claudius has to speak – or read – from a script. Claudius needs some distinguishing garment to betoken kingly status. (For years I have used the same purple corduroy – cord du Roi…! – jacket that has also been Malvolio's modern equivalent of yellow cross-garters.) The Heavies need big coats with collars up, padded armpits and cuff-mikes. Sun-glasses finish the image. The rest of the class are reporters and photographers .

2   A model

Show the class a newsclip of the President of the US getting off a plane and/or making his way to the podium at the White House for a press conference, top flunkey beside him and security service at all corners of the presidential square.

3   Briefing the class

Teacher as Director explains to class (court players sent outside) that they have been called to the palace for an important announcement following the recently-broken news of the death of the King. Rumours have been flying around. Nobody knows what to believe. It's a 'Bad Business' and some insiders have said that it may turn out even worse. Not only that, but other news just in concerns a Norwegian army led by Fortinbras approaching the Danish frontier. Teacher explains that this is very solemn occasion and respects need to be paid.

4   Briefing the court players. Scenario 1

Polonius is briefed to be a fussy, forgetful and feeble assistant to the king, occupying himself with tidying the podium, adjusting the King's chair etc.

The King is briefed to be purposeful, authoritative and annoyed with Polonius' fussiness. He has written his own speech, is totally confident and is reassuring to Gertrude.

Hamlet is briefed to be sullen, detached and uncomfortable.

The Heavies are briefed to enter closely before and behind Claudius, staying behind Claudius throughout. Claudius bids the audience sit, and reads his prepared speech. (Lines may be learned, but this is a case where evident reading is both naturalistic and gives scope for choices.)

5   Play the scene

This first version is about putting a layer of recogniseable modernity upon the situation. Discussion with the class should involve aspects of direction such as:

    a) the best moment for Claudius to offer the photo-opportunity

    b) a good moment for the audience to call out 'Long live the King'

    c) how best to conclude the scene

    d) any relevant audience response to the first part of the speech and to the second part of the speech

    e) what Gertrude can do at various points.

6   Briefing for Scenario 2

Polonius is briefed to be the genius who has arranged the coup and is stage-managing the succession and the press conference. He steers the King to the chair, adjusts the microphone and produces the speech from his pocket and gives it to the King, who reads it.

Claudius is briefed to be hesitant, fearful and ill at ease. Gertrude may have to help him. He may need a stick and glasses.

This time the class as audience plays reporters, photographers and two members of the King's entourage selectively placed. Polonius enters, with two Heavies, to announce the imminent arrival of the King and Queen and a photo-opportunity, but that will be at a time to be announced. In the meantime, cameras are to be put away apart from one court official who photographs the photographers.

The Heavies are briefed to enter the room first, prepare the audience ('Stand when His Majesty arrives'), and maintain watchful guard over all, possibly checking identity cards and confiscating a voice-recorder. At a sign from Polonius, someone may be removed.

7   **Play the scene**

Discussion with the class should involve aspects of direction such as: a), b), c), d) and e) as before, and f) how best to make it clear that Claudius has been manipulated, as well as the situation, g) how Hamlet and Gertrude should respond to Polonius and to Claudius

Clearly, Scenario 2 is not easy to justify by reference to the play as a whole and the text at this point, but the importance of the exercise is in demonstrating how much can be done with a scene in the interests of making it relevant and credible. The text has gaps in it which a director can turn into a plausible story.

Creating a context (2): chairing a meeting

Putting together students' experience of embedded cues and the need to make something dramatic occupy the stage, they need to see how far actors and directors are entitled to improvise action from the cues provided. Here is a scene which I have seen many teenagers exploit ingeniously to show what happens when rivalry, jealousy and cunning are the main things an audience needs to see in the sparse lines written for the two great figures, Octavius Caesar and Mark Antony.

The two great Roman leaders are to meet in the house of Lepidus, the third member of the leadership. He is nervous because he knows that the two leaders are jealous of each other and may fall out. Antony is much older than Caesar, and resents the way he behaves as an equal. Caesar thinks Antony is old and past it, wasting his time on wild living in Egypt. It is a potentially explosive situation, and Lepidus does all he can to make it peaceable, appealing to Antony's friend, Enobarbus, to keep things calm.

LEPIDUS: It shall become you well to entreat your captain
              To soft and gentle speech.

ENOBARBUS: I shall entreat him
              To answer like himself.

LEPIDUS: 'Tis not a time for private stomaching.
              But small to greater matters must give way.

ENOBARBUS: Not if the small come first.

LEPIDUS: I pray you, stir no embers up. Here comes
              the noble Antony.

(Enter Antony and Ventidius busily talking to each other right.)

ENOBARBUS: And yonder, Caesar.

(Enter Caesar and Maecenas and Agrippa, busily talking left.)

ANTONY: If we compose well here, to Parthia.
              Hark, Ventidius.

CAESAR: I do not know, Maecenas. Ask Agrippa.

LEPIDUS: Noble friends
             That which combined us was most great, so let not
             a leaner action rend us. What's amiss,
             May it be gently heard. Touch you the sourest
             points with sweetest terms, I beg, my Lords.

ANTONY: Tis spoken well.

(Flourish of trumpets.)

CAESAR: Welcome to Rome

ANTONY: Thank you.

CAESAR: Sit.

ANTONY: Sit, sir.

CAESAR: Nay, then.

(He sits, followed by Antony.)

                                              (*Anthony and Cleopatra* Act 2, Scene 2)

With the last ten words of this piece of script, Shakespeare creates a very tense and hostile atmosphere. What is each character thinking at each stage of this exchange? What must they do on stage to make this an exciting scene about power and rivalry?

Students can add the thoughts that each character has before and after each bit of speech, showing what is the motive and the response to the other in this exchange.

Annotate the following piece of script with characters' thoughts:

(Flourish of trumpets.)
CAESAR: Welcome to Rome

ANTONY: Thank you.

CAESAR: Sit.

ANTONY: Sit, sir.

CAESAR: Nay, then.

(He sits, followed by Antony.)

Here are some practical things to do with the scene. This can be done by one group in front of the class then other groups can practise on their own before returning to show how they would treat the script and use chairs as props.

1.   **The anxious host** (one performer)

     As host, Lepidus needs to make the arrangements for the meeting. Choose a pupil to play Lepidus arranging the chairs for the meeting, thinking out loud what will happen if Caesar or Antony thinks he has the second best chair, or an inferior position, or if either of them thinks that Lepidus is making himself more important.

2. **Status and position**

   Practise ways in which one person sitting and the other standing can convey different messages about status. Try:

   a) called in to talk to the headteacher about work. Headteacher sits, pupil stands.

   b) sitting in a police cell, answering questions. Suspect sits, detective stands.

   c) called into an interview in front of a panel of four people. All sit.

3. **Body language** (five performers)

   Make players try various ways of expressing a state of mind or a status by sitting in a chair. Try:

   • casual, bored and indifferent

   • impatient, ready to start business

   • angry, not wanting to start talking

   • confident, relaxed, poised (my chair, my place)

   • waiting to be called for an interview (inspect soles of shoe, cuffs, watch)

4. **Status and chairs** (one performer)

   Give Lepidus a problem by not making all the chairs similar. One could be much better than the other two or there could be three chairs of different status.

5. **How will Antony sit?** (try five performers)

6. **How will Caesar sit?** (try five performers)

7. **How does Caesar sit – and in which chair?** (one performer)

8. **How does Antony take the remaining available chair?** (reversed? moved?)

9. **What part is played by their respective supporters?** (four performers for Maecenas, Agrippa and Ventidius and Enobarbus)

10. **What does Lepidus do?**

For discussion and perhaps writing: 'Is this scene serious and menacing or comical?'

Shakespeare's stagecraft and dramatic devices

Much of Shakespeare's skill as a dramatist was in exploiting a range of devices to keep an audience engaged, amused or in suspense. This meant serving up plots involving comic mistakes, romantic tangles and devious doings by nasty bits of work. With, of course, some highflown bits about life, society, conscience and the nature of evil thrown in. It was a mixed ability audience, after all.

Props for revealing and for concealing

Revealing: the letter

Take one common device: the letter. A letter brought on stage can fill the audience in on what's happened before or elsewhere especially if what's happened was too tricky to do with limited resources. Did Shakespeare really want to write a scene in which Hamlet, embarked on a cross-channel vessel is involved in a sea-fight with pirates, switches vessel and is returned to Denmark by the public-spirited swashbucklers? No way. Write it in a letter to Horatio and it's done, sorted, pictured economically in the audience's head.

On the other hand, a letter can be used to move the plot on, set sub-plots in motion and illuminate character. In the same play, Hamlet sends another letter to the King. Claudius, receiving this letter, shows frustration at the failure of his plan and swiftly improvises an alternative plan, manipulating Laertes into the assassin role.

Another letter used for more than narration of past or off-stage events is the one Macbeth writes to Lady Macbeth. The audience doesn't need its news as it's seen the witchy business. Shakespeare uses this letter to show Lady Macbeth's astute reading of her husband and spontaneous planning to shape events.

Another interesting use of a letter is in *Twelfth Night*, where the bogus declaration of his mistress's love is placed before the box tree where Malvolio will find it. This letter is used to create comic irony, mockery and farcical humour as those behind the tree observe the way the self-loving steward falls for the ruse.

Elsewhere, Shakespeare uses the device of a letter for tragic effect – think of the one that doesn't arrive in *Romeo and Juliet*.

Concealing: the arras and the cloak

The variety of the plays was and is their winning ingredient. Hence his winning repertoire of stories with comic moments in tragedies, tragic moments in comedies and lyrical moments in both. Mistaken identity, love's passion and blindness, revenge, jealousy, vanity and ambition are equally elements of human folly and tragedy. And both were made visual on a stage lacking lighting, sound amplification, rolling sets or back projections.

If we revere Shakespeare most for the music of his verse, the dense allusion of his imagery or the riches of his word-hoard, it says more about us than about him. We're more *literate* these days. We *read* his plays more than watch them. Which is why we forget his stagecraft, his niftiness in scripting for performance.

Look at the way he uses concealment devices to pull off comedy, suspense or tragedy.

Hamlet's 'To be or not to be' soliloquy is clever psychological realism, richly evocative in sound, syntax and imagery – poetry, you might say. Yet it's a soliloquy with an on-stage audience, delivered to Ophelia, twitchily aware her father and the King are listening behind the arras. The presence of these earwiggers – if only evident by their boots poking through the bottom of the drape – changes the speech. We should *see* it as it seems to a fearful King, looking for signs of a step-son's murderous intent. We forget what Hamlet was on about as we are aware of Claudius and Polonius listening for clues that the lad was bad. Or mad. To be parcelled off to England. ('Why England?' 'Faith, all the men there are as mad as he. His madness will not show there.' The English do like a joke at the expense of their own eccentricity…)

Shakespeare's stagecraft consisted of making much of simple props. Other uses of concealment for serious purposes occur in *Measure for Measure*, where The Duke learns much from speaking to those who don't recognise him wrapped in a cloak. And in *Henry V* the King, the night before the battle, incognito in a borrowed cloak, debates the lot of humble subjects with… some humble subjects.

Then there's the parallel gulling in *Much Ado About Nothing*, where an arras or a hedge is used as Benedick believes what people say about him on the other side, then Beatrice is similarly tricked. We laugh at the way both visibly struggle with insult, pride and prejudice and show themselves more alike than any quarrelling twosome would care to admit.

In *The Merry Wives of Windsor*, Falstaff hides himself in a laundry basket in a lady's boudoir when her enraged husband arrives, unaware of her previous instruction to her servants to take the basket and tip it in the Thames. Dramatic irony is often a simple matter of the simplest props: cheap, practical and worth repeating in another play.

The repertoire of devices

As previously considered, Shakespeare was highly skilled in cueing actors to performance and in making the most of the resources he had. It's not surprising if, in the course of writing 38 plays, he used many tricks and devices a number of times. We can get a grasp of his repertoire by thinking of the ways he caught and kept an audience's interest.

Students need to see how he uses a particular device for a range of purposes and effects if they are to have a practical understanding of him as a dramatist. This is best done by using extracts from various plays rather than a lengthy flog through character description and action summaries that treat the plays as if they were dialogue-heavy novels.

In the following lists, asterisks mark the extracts edited for classroom use in the next section, 'The Collaborative Shakespearience'. The other references are to plays which provide other examples of the device. The examples are a sample only and not intended to be comprehensive. They are intended to give evidence of well-exploited stage business and to suggest further possibilities for teachers' use.

1   Visual devices

unknown or mistaken identity: *Hamlet** (graveyard scene), *Measure for Measure*, *Henry V*

deliberately disguised identity: *Henry IV** (Falstaff and the Robbery), *The Merry Wives of Windsor*, *Henry V*, *The Merchant of Venice*, *A Midsummer Night's Dream*

gender swap/twins: *Twelfth Night*, *A Comedy of Errors*

mistaken situation: *Much Ado About Nothing**, *Twelfth Night*

other dramatic irony: *Much Ado About Nothing**, *The Merchant of Venice** (the rings), *Troilus & Cressida**

props and costumes: *Merry Wives of Windsor** (Falstaff the Great Lover), *The Tempest* (Caliban and Trinculo); *Henry V* (the leek and the gloves); *Hamlet* (Yorick's skull), *Othello* (the handkerchief (see 'Shakespearience for teachers: the wider picture', page 132)

2   Aural devices

over-hearing: *Hamlet*

aside: *Measure for Measure*; *Richard III*, *Macbeth*

soliloquy: *Much Ado About Nothing**, *Hamlet*, *Richard III*

mispronunciation/malapropism: *Much Ado About Nothing** (Dogberry), *Henry IV* (Mistress Quickly), *Henry V* (Fluellen)

national stereotype and accent: *Henry V* (Scots, Welsh, Irish)

parody/mimicry: *Henry IV** (Hotspur), *A Midsummer Night's Dream** (the Mechanicals), *Hamlet* (Priam and Troy)

3   Narrative devices

chorus: *Henry V*, *Romeo and Juliet*

dialogue exposition of non-staged events: *Hamlet* (Hamlet's letter to Horatio)

dialogue introduction to unseen character: *Macbeth* (captain's description before entry of Macbeth)

letters and reports: *Macbeth* (letter to Lady Macbeth); see also 'Shakespearience for teachers: the wider picture' (page 132)

4   Directorial devices

Sound: expressive cues to an actor such as sibilants, plosives, fricatives, vowels (see page 26) action cues to other actors: *Macbeth* (MACBETH: 'Doctor, the thanes fly from me…')

cues to audience: *Macbeth* (DUNCAN: 'This castle hath a pleasant seat. See where the temple-haunting martlets…')

5   Structural devices

act structure: e.g. setting; arrivals; dilemma; effects; resolution

scene structure: e.g. varying mood, plot, setting, character *Henry IV*

scene parallel: *Much Ado About Nothing**

scene contrast: *Macbeth* (the porter)

plots & sub-plots: *King Lear*, *A Midsummer Night's Dream*

6   Stylistic devices

characterisation in speech: e.g. idiom, rhythm

verse/prose: e.g. status, sentiment

imagery: e.g. cue audience

7   Audio-visual devices spectacular

pleasing the groundlings: verbal abuse and hurling props in *The Taming of the Shrew**; verbal abuse, drunkenness in *Henry IV* (Hal and Falstaff)

pleasing the educated: e.g. puns, parodies, conceits

dance: *Antony and Cleopatra*

song: *As You Like it*, *Twelfth Night*, *The Winter's Tale*

spectacle: *The Tempest*, *The Winter's Tale*, *Macbeth*

ghosts: *Hamlet*, *Macbeth*

The ultimate in theatrical craftsmanship: *Troilus and Cressida* Act 5, Scene 2

Here is an example of Shakespeare doing his best to make his bare stage flexible and dynamic in order to sustain interest and appeal. It's a complex piece of theatre and it needs some grappling with the complexity of the situation Shakespeare was representing on stage.

Where a lesser scriptwriter would have the scene dominated by a single level of interest, he manages to bring off a coup using the device available to a modern film director of a split screen. Cressida has a secret meeting with her passionate suitor, Diomedes, who wants her to give him the love-token scarf given her by her lover, Troilus. Romantic interest assured? Will-she/Won't she suspense guaranteed? Women's fickleness or constancy of interest to a largely male audience?

The following study is intended as an example of Shakespeare's dramatic craft at its highest for more able and more experienced students. The scene is re-presented in three versions to show the levels of complexity of Shakespeare's stagecraft and diversity of appeal to audience.

Version 1

(Enter Diomedes)

DIOMEDES: What, are you up here, ho? speak.

CALCHAS: *(Within)* Who calls?

DIOMEDES: Calchas, I think. Where's your daughter?

CALCHAS: *(Within)* She comes to you.

(Enter Cressida)

DIOMEDES: How now, my charge!

CRESSIDA: Now, my sweet guardian! Hark, a word with you. *(Whispers)*

DIOMEDES: Will you remember?

CRESSIDA: Remember! Yes.

DIOMEDES: Nay, but do, then. And let your mind be coupled with your words.

CRESSIDA: Sweet honey Greek, tempt me no more to folly.

DIOMEDES: Nay, then, –

CRESSIDA: I'll tell you what, –

DIOMEDES: Foh, foh! come, tell a pin: you are forsworn.

CRESSIDA: In faith, I cannot: what would you have me do?

DIOMEDES: What did you swear you would bestow on me?

CRESSIDA: I prithee, do not hold me to mine oath;
               Bid me do anything but that, sweet Greek.

DIOMEDES: Good night.

CRESSIDA: Diomed, –

DIOMEDES: No, no, good night: I'll be your fool no more.

CRESSIDA: Hark, one word in your ear.

This is dramatically interesting in its own right, as it presents the audience with a whispered discussion between two lovers, making us feel we are eavesdropping on something secret, sexually intriguing and dangerous. Shakespeare deliberately gives little explicit guidance as to what is going on to maintain curiosity but it is clear that the young man is asking Cressida to prove her affection for him by giving him the scarf which her previous lover, Troilus, gave to her. There are hints related to some previous cause of friction and distress. The young man threatens to leave if Cressida can't make up her mind: she is under pressure and torn between being loyal to Troilus and placing her affections in a new quarter. This is gripping as an example of love's tensions and lovers' wiles and blackmails – Cressida's plight is a touching one, and the scene a rich display of passionate and romantic feelings tinged with uncertainty and dilemma. It would be strong enough in character, situation and anticipation as it stands.

Version 2

(Enter Diomedes)

Diomedes: What, are you up here, ho? speak.

Calchas: *(Within)* Who calls?

Diomedes: Calchas, I think. Where's your daughter?

Calchas: *(Within)* She comes to you.

(Enter Troilus and Ulysses, at a distance)

ULYSSES: Stand where the torch may not discover us.

(Enter Cressida)

TROILUS: **Cressid comes forth to him.**

DIOMEDES: How now, my charge!

CRESSIDA: Now, my sweet guardian! Hark, a word with you. *(Whispers)*

TROILUS: **Yea, so familiar!**

ULYSSES: **She will sing any man at first sight.**

DIOMEDES: Will you remember?

CRESSIDA: Remember! Yes.

DIOMEDES: Nay, but do, then. And let your mind be coupled with your words.

TROILUS: **What should she remember?**

ULYSSES: **List.**

CRESSIDA: Sweet honey Greek, tempt me no more to folly.

DIOMEDES: Nay, then, –

CRESSIDA: I'll tell you what, –

DIOMEDES: Foh, foh! come, tell a pin: you are forsworn.

CRESSIDA: In faith, I cannot: what would you have me do?

DIOMEDES: What did you swear you would bestow on me?

CRESSIDA: I prithee, do not hold me to mine oath;
Bid me do anything but that, sweet Greek.

DIOMEDES: Good night.

TROILUS: **Hold, patience!**

ULYSSES: **How now, Trojan!**

CRESSIDA: Diomed, –

DIOMEDES: No, no, good night: I'll be your fool no more.

TROILUS: **Thy better must.**

CRESSIDA: Hark, one word in your ear.

TROILUS: **O plague and madness!**

Shakespeare does not let it stand as a conversation overheard by the audience. The scene becomes more suspenseful and ironic because Shakespeare adds to the whispered lovers' scene the extra dimension of being seen and heard by Troilus, Cressida's previous lover. He now watches as Cressida, struggles not to give in to the new suitor, and watches as his love token becomes the emblem of her besieged affections. This is doubly gripping as it exploits audience feelings for Cressida and for Troilus: it creates a rich ambivalence in that the audience sympathises both with Cressida's dilemma, and with Troilus' feelings of betrayal. It also sharpens expectation of some consequence – Troilus' feelings of hurt and rejection must lead him to further, possibly violent actions. The scene is now overlaid with menace and fear for what will happen. The romantic and passionate scene now has all the ingredients for tragedy. This is certainly enough to move an audience in respect of character, situation and anticipation

Version 3

(Enter Diomedes)

DIOMEDES: What, are you up here, ho? speak.

CALCHAS: *(Within)* Who calls?

DIOMEDES: Calchas, I think. Where's your daughter?

CALCHAS: *(Within)* She comes to you.

(Enter Troilus and Ulysses, at a distance; after them, Thersites)

ULYSSES: Stand where the torch may not discover us.

(Enter Cressida)

TROILUS: Cressid comes forth to him.

DIOMEDES: How now, my charge!

CRESSIDA: Now, my sweet guardian! Hark, a word with you. *(Whispers)*

TROILUS: Yea, so familiar!

ULYSSES: She will sing any man at first sight.

THERSITES: And any man may sing her, if he can take her cliff; she's noted.

DIOMEDES: Will you remember?

CRESSIDA: Remember! Yes.

DIOMEDES: Nay, but do, then. And let your mind be coupled with your words.

TROILUS: What should she remember?

ULYSSES: List.

CRESSIDA: Sweet honey Greek, tempt me no more to folly.

THERSITES: Roguery!

DIOMEDES: Nay, then, –

CRESSIDA: I'll tell you what, –

DIOMEDES: Foh, foh! come, tell a pin: you are forsworn.

CRESSIDA: In faith, I cannot: what would you have me do?

THERSITES: A juggling trick, to be secretly open.

DIOMEDES: What did you swear you would bestow on me?

CRESSIDA: I prithee, do not hold me to mine oath;
           Bid me do anything but that, sweet Greek.

DIOMEDES: Good night.

TROILUS: Hold, patience!

ULYSSES: **How now, Trojan!**

CRESSIDA: Diomed, –

DIOMEDES: No, no, good night: I'll be your fool no more.

TROILUS: **Thy better must.**

CRESSIDA: Hark, one word in your ear.

TROILUS: **O plague and madness!**

As if this isn't enough, Shakespeare adds yet another dimension. Not only do we have the two lovers on stage, and Troilus observing them, but Shakespeare adds a third party, Thersites, observing both the lovers and the observers of the lovers. As a lower class, mouthy upstart who thinks all his so-called superiors are corrupt and despicable, he delights in seeing this apparently noble lady tempted into sexual indiscretion, and delights in seeing his superior mortified by her disloyalty. His coarse comments on sexuality provide a comic overlay on the romantic and tragic elements already developed.

Hence we have a scene richly romantic, tragic and comic, represented by a complex stage setting which gives the audience three sources of interest and three different perspectives and calls upon their sympathies. In a primitive open theatre and a relatively bare stage, Shakespeare has contrived to position his audience visually and emotionally: he makes us eavesdrop on Thersites eavesdropping on Troilus eavesdropping on Cressida. The ambivalence exploited in this three-dimensional setting is extraordinary: we can despise or feel sorry for Cressida; we can disapprove of or feel sorry for Troilus; and we can despise or laugh with Thersites all whilst remaining in suspense regarding the outcome of what is happening.

Now that's what I call stagecraft. As a scene, this takes some beating for complexity of theme and action on a simple stage. Try it in class!

3. The collaborative Shakespearience: working with scenes

Ten scripts for classroom study and performance

These ten scripts have been edited – some quite heavily – for practical use in the classroom. With a brief introduction to situation and character, they can be treated as stand-alone texts. The scripts should be presented as the starting point for performance, with *the first decisions focused on how much of the text is to be used.* Where cuts are judged necessary, and additions and amendments are judged appropriate, students should feel free to do what directors do in editing and adapting a text for performance. That is the basis for owning what results from the collaboration with each other and with Shakespeare.

All the scripts are available as Word documents, on the CD included with this book.

The following practical sequence for classroom activity with all the scripts establishes a working method that can be applied to other texts:

Getting involved:

- **edit** text – cutting words, lines or speeches

- **rework** text – re-sequencing or re-allocating lines to different characters or a narrator

- **elaborate** text – inserting words, phrases or lines and/or adding stage directions

- **translate** text – substituting more familiar words, phrases or references to modern contexts

- **improvise** text – perform what may be implied or omitted (use freezeframe, tableau and sculpting as in 'The Close Shakespearience', pages 15–20)

- **perform** text – present to an audience or camera

- **compare** texts – evaluate each others' final results or evaluate professional versions on stage or screen.

Some starting points for applying this sequence to the scripts are provided in examples of questions related to each script.

Not all of the scripts will require the same measure of attention to parts of the sequence: some of the scripts are already heavily edited and have been tested in many classrooms for performability. For example, '**Getting his garters in a twist**' will need very little or no editing and adapting as it is already a re-worked script. **'Roman public relations'** has not been edited but is so tight a script that it is hard to decide what may go or need amendment. The ten scripts are arranged under four thematic headings to emphasise Shakespeare's characteristic patterns of thought and interest, and his methods of presenting them, across a number of plays. This helps to focus on Shakespeare as an artist and craftsman, and minimise any tendency to turn Shakespeare study into plot recall or character description.

Each of these scripts gives scope for putting into practice 'The Close Shakespearience' methods in the second chapter of this book. Equally, there is much to be gained from comparing scripts within and across the four groupings here.

NB: To emphasise the point made in the first paragraph, *the scripts – even where already edited from the originals – should not be seen as ready for class use.* The first task with these, as with any other scripts, is to edit them: teachers and students need to decide how much they need to be faithful to the spirit of the text in a classroom setting.

Men and Women (1)
How do you get a man/woman to change their mind? From *Much Ado About Nothing*

Some background

Benedick is a young man who enjoys the freedom of being single. Marriage, to him, is a trap, and the key to staying free is not getting caught up with a woman, and certainly having nothing to do with Love. He pities his friend, Claudio, for giving up his friends and his bachelor habits now that he's in a relationship with Hero. Benedick thinks it's especially pitiful because Claudio used to boast that he was the last person likely to give up freedom for a woman.

And if Benedick was to get into a close relationship with a woman, the last woman on the planet he would choose is Beatrice, because she mocks him, outwits him and always seems to manage to get the last word. Benedick's friends, however, think they'd make a well-matched pair…

Beatrice is intelligent, independent and a witty speaker in argument. She is too proud to have strong feelings for a mere man, and enjoys making fun of Benedick in public and in private. Her pride may have something to do with the fact that she once cared for him and he hurt her by not returning her care.

Shakespeare writes parallel scenes in which each of them is gulled, or tricked, into dropping their defence and doing what others know to be right for them.

Parts and the whole

Plot

These scenes develop the relationship between the two main characters: we have seen them mocking and vocally indifferent to each other. We now see them moved to express affection – and then see the relationship tested by Beatrice's command to 'Kill Claudio', Benedick's best friend, for the hurt he has caused Hero, her best friend.

Audience appeal

The light-hearted and satirical humour contrasts with the clownish Watch sub-plot and the serious sub-plot of Don John's devious scheme and the cruel effects it has on the relationship between Hero and Claudio.

What's so good about these scenes:

- humour based on observation of feelings and behaviour particular to men and to women
- insight into feelings and behaviour common to men and to women
- dramatic irony of seeing characters tricked into changing their minds by friends who know them well.

Getting involved:

- **edit** text – how much needs to be cut to make the essential comedy performable? For example, does Claudio's first speech need anything more than 'How still the evening is'?
- **rework** text – what are the modern equivalents of references to 'tabour' and 'fife', 'doublet' and 'armour'?
- **elaborate** text – does the text need stage directions such as voice and movement cues?
- **translate** text – should words like 'hath' be substituted by 'has'?

- **improvise** text – any props? (e.g. photos or a mirror)
- **perform** text – how should Benedick be concealed but able to hear; be seen by the audience but not, apparently, by others on stage?
- **compare** texts – either the gulling of Benedick with the gulling of Beatrice or of different performances of others in the class, or different screen versions.

How do you change a man's mind?

Scene 1 LEONATO'S orchard

BENEDICK: I do much wonder that one man, seeing how much another man is a fool when he dedicates himself to love, will, after laughing at such shallow folly in another, fall in love himself. And such a man is Claudio. I have known when there was no music with him but the drum and the fife; and now he would rather hear the tabour and the pipe. I have known when he would walk ten miles to see some good armour; and now will he lie awake ten nights, thinking of himself in a new fashion of doublet. He used to speak plain and to the purpose, like an honest man and a soldier; and now his words are like a fantastic feast, full of strange dishes. May this happen to me? I think not! Ha! The prince and Monsieur Love! I will hide behind the hedge.

(Enter Don Pedro, Claudio and Leonato.)

CLAUDIO: How still the evening is, as hush'd on purpose to grace harmony!

DON PEDRO: *See you where Benedick hath hid himself?*

CLAUDIO: *O, very well, my lord.*

DON PEDRO: Come hither, Leonato. What was it you told me of to-day, that your niece Beatrice was in love with Signior Benedick?

CLAUDIO: *O, ay: stalk on. The fowl sits.* I did never think that lady would love any man.

LEONATO: No, nor I neither; but most amazing that she should so dote on Benedick, who, in all outward behaviours, she has seemed to loathe.

BENEDICK: Is't possible? Sits the wind in that corner?

LEONATO: By my troth, I cannot tell what to think of it but she does seem to love him with astonishing affection: it doth not bear thinking on.

DON PEDRO: Maybe she doth counterfeit affection.

LEONATO: Counterfeit! False feeling could not come near the passion she shows for him.

DON PEDRO: What effects of passion shows she?

LEONATO: What effects, my lord? Hear what my daughter told me. (*Whispers.*)

CLAUDIO: *Bait the hook well; this fish will bite.*

DON PEDRO: You amaze me! I would have I thought her spirit too strong to surrender to such feelings of affection, especially for Benedick.

BENEDICK: I should think this a trick but that the white-bearded fellow speaks it.

CLAUDIO: *He hath ta'en the infection: hold it up.*

DON PEDRO: Hath she made her affection known to Benedick?

LEONATO: No; and swears she never will: that's her torment.

CLAUDIO: 'Tis true, indeed; so your daughter says: 'Shall I,' says she, 'that have so oft encountered him with scorn, write to him that I love him?'

LEONATO: She'll be up twenty times a night, and there will she sit till she have writ a sheet of paper: my daughter tells us all.

CLAUDIO: Now you talk of a sheet of paper, I remember a witty jest your daughter told us of.

LEONATO: O, when she had writ it and was reading it over, she found Benedick and Beatrice between the sheets?

LEONATO: O, she tore the letter into a thousand pieces; railed at herself, that she should be so immodest to write to one that she knew would reject her.

CLAUDIO: Then down upon her knees she falls, weeps, sobs, beats her heart, tears her hair, prays, curses; 'O sweet Benedick! God give me patience!'

LEONATO: She doth indeed; my daughter says so, and she is sometime afeared she will do something desperate.

DON PEDRO: Benedick should know of her passion if she will not reveal it.

CLAUDIO: To what end? He would make sport of it and torment the poor lady.

DON PEDRO: Shame if he did. She's an excellent sweet lady; and very virtuous.

CLAUDIO: And very wise.

DON PEDRO: In everything but in loving Benedick.

LEONATO: I am sorry for her, as her uncle and guardian.

DON PEDRO: If she had bestowed this feeling on me: I would have thought myself a lucky man. I pray you, tell Benedick, and hear what he will say.

LEONATO: Were it good, think you?

CLAUDIO: Hero thinks surely she will die; for she says she will die, if he love her not, and she will die, ere she make her love known.

DON PEDRO: She hath reason: if she should make her love known, he'll scorn it; for the man, as you know all, hath a contemptible spirit.

CLAUDIO: He is a very proper man with a good outward happiness and sometimes wise.

DON PEDRO: He doth indeed show some sparks that are like wit.

DON PEDRO: Well I pity her. Shall we seek Benedick, and tell him of her love?

CLAUDIO: Never tell him, my lord: let her wear it out with good counsel.

LEONATO: Nay, that's impossible: she may wear her heart out first.

DON PEDRO: Well, we will hear further of it by your daughter. I wish Benedick could examine himself, to see how he is unworthy so good a lady.

LEONATO: My lord, will you walk? Dinner is ready.

CLAUDIO: *If he do not dote on her upon this, I will never trust my expectation.*

DON PEDRO: *Let there be the same net spread for her; and that must your daughter and her gentlewomen carry. The sport will be, when they hold an opinion of each other's dotage: that's the scene that I would see. Let us send her to call him in to dinner.*

(Exeunt Don Pedro, Claudio, and Leonato.)

BENEDICK: This can be no trick: the conference was sadly borne. They have the truth of this from Hero. They seem to pity the lady: it seems her affections are strong. Love me! I hear how I am censured: they say I will bear myself proudly; they say she will rather die than give any sign of affection. I did never think to marry: I must not seem proud: happy are they that hear their detractions and can put them to mending. They say the lady is fair; 'tis a truth; and virtuous; 'tis so; and wise, but for loving me. I will be horribly in love with her. I may have some quirks and remnants of wit broken on me, because I have railed so long against marriage: but doth not the appetite alter? A man loves the meat in his youth that he cannot endure in his age. Shall quips and sentences awe a man from what he wills? No, the world must be peopled. When I said I would die a bachelor, I did not think I should live till I were married. Here comes Beatrice. By this day she's a fair lady: I do spy some marks of love in her.

(Enter Beatrice.)

BEATRICE: Against my will I am sent to bid you come in to dinner.

BENEDICK: Fair Beatrice, I thank you for your pains.

BEATRICE: I took no more pains for those thanks than you take pains to thank me: if it had been painful, I would not have come.

BENEDICK: You take pleasure then in the message?

BEATRICE: Yea, just so much as you may take upon a fingertip and choke a canary with. If you have no stomach, signior: fare you well. *(Exit.)*

BENEDICK: Ha! 'Against my will I am sent to bid you come in to dinner;' there's a double meaning in that 'I took no more pains for those thanks than you took pains to thank me.' That's as much as to say, 'Any pains that I take for you is as easy as thanks.' If I do not take pity of her, if I do not love her, I am a villain. I will go get her picture.

(Exit.)

(Much Ado About Nothing Act 2, Scene 3)

And now, the difference between men and women…

Scene 2 LEONATO'S orchard

(Enter Hero, Margaret, and Ursula.)

HERO: Good Margaret, find my cousin BEATRICE
               Whisper her ear and tell her, I and Ursula
               Walk in the orchard and our whole discourse
               Is all of her; say that thou overheard'st us;
               And bid her steal into the pleached bower
               To listen our purpose.

MARGARET: I'll make her come, I warrant you, presently. *(Exit.)*

HERO: Now, Ursula, when Beatrice doth come,
Our talk must only be of Benedick.
When I do name him, let it be thy part
To praise him more than ever man did merit:
My talk to thee must be how Benedick
Is sick in love with Beatrice.

(Enter Beatrice.)

                    Now begin;
For look where Beatrice, like a lapwing, runs
Close by the ground, to hear our conference.

URSULA: *Fear you not my part of the dialogue.*
The pleasant'st angling is to see the fish
Cut with her golden oars the silver stream,
And greedily devour the treacherous bait:
So angle we for Beatrice.

HERO: *Then go we near her, that her ear lose nothing*
Of the false sweet bait that we lay for it.
(Approaching the bower.)
No, truly, Ursula, she is too disdainful;
Affection cannot live in one so self-endeared.

URSULA: But are you sure
That Benedick loves Beatrice so entirely?

HERO: So says the prince and my new-trothed lord.

URSULA: And did they bid you tell her of it, madam?

HERO: They did entreat me to acquaint her of it;
But I persuaded them, if they loved Benedick,
To never to let Beatrice know of it.

URSULA: Why did you so? Doth not the gentleman
Deserve as full as fortunate a bed
As ever Beatrice shall couch upon?

HERO: O god of love! I know he doth deserve
As much as may be yielded to a man:
But Nature never framed a woman's heart
Of prouder stuff than that of Beatrice;
Disdain and scorn ride sparkling in her eyes,
Misprising what they look on, and her wit
Values itself so highly that to her
All matter else seems weak.

URSULA: Sure, I think so; and sure it were not good
She knew his love, lest she make sport at it.

HERO: Why, you speak truth. I never yet saw man,
How wise, how noble, young, how rarely featured,
But she would find him lacking: if fair-faced,
She would swear the gentleman should be her sister;
If speaking, why, a vane blown with all winds;
If silent, why, a block moved with none.
She never gives to truth and virtue that
Which sense and merit would judge true worth.

URSULA: Sure, sure, such carping is not commendable.

HERO: No, to be so odd and from all fashions
As Beatrice is, cannot be commendable:
But who dare tell her so? If I should speak,
She would but mock me; silence me with wit.
Therefore let Benedick, like cover'd fire,
Consume away in sighs, waste inwardly:
It were a better death than die with mocks,

URSULA: Yet tell her of it: hear what she will say.

HERO: No; rather I will go to Benedick
And counsel him to fight against his passion.

URSULA: O, do not do your cousin such a wrong.
She cannot be so much without true judgment—
Having so swift and excellent a mind
As she is prized to have, as to refuse
So rare a gentleman as Signior Benedick.

HERO: He is the only man of Italy. Always excepted my dear Claudio.

URSULA: I pray you, be not angry with me, madam,
Speaking my fancy: Signior Benedick,
For shape, for bearing, argument and valour,
Goes foremost in report through Italy.

HERO: Indeed, he hath an excellent good name.

URSULA: His excellence did earn it, ere he had it.

HERO: Come, let's in: I'll show thee some attires, and have thy counsel
Which to wear to-morrow.

URSULA: *She's limed, I warrant you: we have caught her, madam.*

HERO: *If it proves so, then loving goes by haps:*
Some Cupid kills with arrows, some with traps.

(Exeunt Hero and Ursula.)

BEATRICE: *(Coming forward)*
What fire is in mine ears? Can this be true?
Stand I condemn'd for pride and scorn so much?
Contempt, farewell! and maiden pride, adieu!
And, Benedick, love on; I will requite thee,
Taming my wild heart to thy loving hand:
For others say thou dost deserve, and I
Believe it better than reportingly.

(Exit.)

(*Much Ado About Nothing* Act 3, Scene 1)

Men and Women (2)
A tricky business of rings ... from
The Merchant of Venice

Some background

Portia is Bassanio's wife. Bassanio has got into financial trouble because he can't repay the loan he took out to help his friend Antonio. Shylock, the moneylender, loaned him money on condition he could cut a pound of his flesh if he failed to pay. Serious!

Portia disguises herself as a lawyer to defend him in court. She wins the case by claiming that the pound must be an exact pound as agreed, not an ounce more or less, or Shylock will be charged with murder. Result! Unaware that the 'lawyer' who has saved him is his own wife, Bassanio is full of gratitude. Portia, keeping up the disguise, decides to test Bassanio's loyalty by asking for the ring that she gave him, and which he swore never to give to anyone else... (To make the plot thicker her servant, Nerissa, is disguised as a lawyer's clerk and tests her husband, Gratiano, in the same way.)

Parts and the whole

Plot

Portia's wit and intelligence in disguising herself as a lawyer has a serious purpose in defeating Shylock's scheme and saving her future husband's life. The role she is adopting here is central to the play's resolution.

Audience appeal

Dramatic irony as we know who the 'lawyers' are, and a lighter contrast to the darker side of the play.

What's so good about this scene:

- comic situation where young men have to wriggle out of seeming to care nothing about precious love tokens given to them by their partners
- comic situation where women, knowing the truth, relish their power over their men, knowing that they are wriggling and enjoying their discomfort
- dramatic irony – the audience knows that the two 'men' who Antonio and Bassanio take to be lawyers are, in fact, Portia and Nerissa.

Getting involved:

- **edit** text – how much needs to be cut without losing suspense, irony and comedy? Is it best to keep the Nerissa/Gratiano parallel scenes?
- **rework** text – do all actors need all of their lines?
- **elaborate** text – render some of the plot by adding lines for a narrator?
- **translate** text – should terms like 'ducats' stay or be rendered into familiar currency?
- **improvise** text – what do characters do with the ring and the gloves? Which moments to select for a still shot or a tableau?
- **perform** text – should the performance be made amusing because the female characters seem cleverer than the male characters or because the male characters try hard to wriggle out of the tricky situation?
- **compare** texts – different groups in the class and/or show different film clips e.g. Al Pacino and David Bamber versions.

Scene 1 Outside the court

BASSANIO: Most worthy gentleman, I and my friend
Have by your wisdom been this day acquitted
Of grievous penalties; in thanks whereof,
Three thousand ducats, we do freely cope
Your courteous pains and all.

ANTONIO: And stand indebted, over and above,
In love and service to you evermore.

PORTIA: He is well paid that is well satisfied;
And I, delivering you, am satisfied
And therein do account myself well paid:
I wish you well, and so I take my leave.

BASSANIO: Dear sir, of force I must attempt you further:
Take some remembrance of us, as a tribute,
Not as a fee: grant me two things, I pray you,
Not to deny me, and to pardon me.

PORTIA: You press me far, and therefore I will yield.
(To Antonio.)
Give me your gloves, I'll wear them for your sake;
(To Bassiano.)
And, for your love, I'll take this ring from you:
Do not draw back your hand; I'll take no more;
And you in love shall not deny me this.

BASSANIO: This ring, good sir, alas, it is a trifle!
I will not shame myself to give you this.

PORTIA: I will have nothing else but only this.

BASSANIO: There's more depends on this than on the value.
The dearest ring in Venice will I give you,
Only for this, I pray you, pardon me.

PORTIA: I see, sir, you are liberal in offers
You taught me first to beg; and now methinks
You teach me how a beggar should be answer'd.

BASSANIO: Good sir, this ring was given me by my wife;
And when she put it on, she made me vow
That I should neither sell nor give nor lose it.

PORTIA: That 'scuse serves many men to save their gifts.
If your good wife be not a mad-woman,
And know how well I have deserved the ring,
She would not hold out enemy for ever,
For giving it to me. Well, peace be with you!

(Exeunt Portia and Nerissa.)

ANTONIO: My Lord Bassanio, let him have the ring:
Let his deservings be valued against
Your wife's commandment.

BASSANIO: Go, Gratiano, run and overtake him;
                  Give him the ring, and bring him, if thou canst,
                  Unto Antonio's house: away! make haste.

(Exeunt.)

Scene 2 at Belmont (Portia has arrived back before them, and has taken off her disguise)

(Enter Bassianio, Antonio, Gratiano.)

PORTIA: You are welcome home, my lord.

BASSANIO: I thank you, madam. Give welcome to my friend.
                  This is the man, this is Antonio,
                  To whom I am so infinitely bound.

PORTIA: You should in all sense be much bound to him.
                  For, as I hear, he was much bound for you.

ANTONIO: No more than I am well acquitted of.

PORTIA: Sir, you are very welcome to our house:

GRATIANO: *(To Nerissa.)* By yonder moon I swear you do me wrong;
                  In faith, I gave it to the judge's clerk:
                  Would he were gelt that had it, for my part,
                  Since you do take it, love, so much at heart.

PORTIA: A quarrel, ho, already! What's the matter?

GRATIANO: About a hoop of gold, a paltry ring
                  That she did give me, and thereon engraved
                  'Love me, and leave me not.'

NERISSA: You swore to me, when I did give it you,
                  That you would wear it till your hour of death
                  And that it should lie with you in your grave:
                  You should have been respective and have kept it.
                  Gave it a judge's clerk! No, God's my judge,
                  The clerk will ne'er wear hair on's face that had it.

GRATIANO: Now, by this hand, I gave it to a youth,
                  A kind of boy, a little scrubbed boy,
                  No higher than thyself; the judge's clerk,
                  A prating boy, that begg'd it as a fee:
                  I could not for my heart deny it him.

PORTIA: You were to blame, I must be plain with you,
                  To part so slightly with your wife's first gift.
                  I gave my love a ring and made him swear
                  Never to part with it; and here he stands;
                  I dare be sworn for him he would not leave it
                  Nor pluck it from his finger, for the wealth
                  That the world promise. Now, in faith, Gratiano,
                  You give your wife too unkind a cause of grief:
                  If it were me, I should be mad at it.

BASSANIO: *(Aside.)* Why, I were best to cut my left hand off
                  And swear I lost the ring defending it.

GRATIANO: My Lord Bassanio gave his ring away
            Unto the judge that begg'd it, then the clerk
            Begg'd mine; and neither man nor master would
            Take aught but our two rings.

PORTIA: What ring gave you my lord?
            Not that, I hope, which you received of me.

BASSANIO: If I could add a lie unto a fault,
            I would deny it; but you see my finger
            Hath not the ring upon it; it is gone.

PORTIA: Even so void is your false heart of truth.
            By heaven, I will ne'er come in your bed
            Until I see the ring.

NERISSA: Nor I in yours till I again see mine.

BASSANIO: Sweet Portia,
            If you did know to whom I gave the ring,
            If you did know for whom I gave the ring
            And would conceive for what I gave the ring
            And how unwillingly I left the ring,
            When nought would be accepted but the ring,
            You would abate the strength of your displeasure.

PORTIA: If you had known the virtue of the ring,
            Or half her worthiness that gave the ring,
            Or your own honour to contain the ring,
            You would not then have parted with the ring.
            Nerissa teaches me what to believe:
            I must assume some woman had the ring.

BASSANIO: No, by my honour, madam, by my soul,
            No woman had it, but a civil lawyer,
            Who did refuse three thousand ducats of me
            And begg'd the ring; the which I did deny him.
            What should I say, sweet lady?
            I was enforced to send it after him;
            I was beset with shame and courtesy;
            My honour would not let ingratitude
            So much besmear it. Pardon me, good lady;
            Had you been there, I think you would have begg'd
            The ring of me to give the worthy lawyer.

PORTIA: Let not that lawyer e'er come near my house:
            Since he hath got the jewel that I loved,
            And that which you did swear to keep for me,
            I will become as liberal as you;
            I'll not deny him any thing I have,
            No, not my body nor my husband's bed:
            Know him I shall, I am well sure of it:
            Lie not a night from home; if I be left alone,
            I'll have that lawyer for my bedfellow.

NERISSA: And I his clerk; therefore be well advised
            How you do leave me to my own desiring.

ANTONIO: I am the unhappy subject of these quarrels.

PORTIA: Sir, grieve not you; you are welcome notwithstanding.

BASSANIO: Portia, forgive me this enforced wrong;
            Pardon this fault, and by my soul I swear
            I never more will break an oath with thee.

ANTONIO: I dare be bound again, and promise you,
            My soul to be the forfeit, that your lord
            Will never more break faith, assuredly.

PORTIA: Then you shall be his surety. Give him this
            And bid him keep it better than the other.

ANTONIO: Here, Lord Bassanio; swear to keep this ring.

BASSANIO: By heaven, it is the same I gave the doctor!

PORTIA: I had it of him: pardon me, Bassanio;
            For, by this ring, the lawyer lay with me.

NERISSA: And pardon me, my gentle Gratiano;
            For that same 'scrubbed boy', the lawyer's clerk,
            Last night did lie with me, and gave this ring.

PORTIA: You are all amazed: here is a letter;
            Read it at your leisure; it proves our tale.
            There you shall find that Portia was the lawyer,
            Her clerk, Nerissa. And if you are not
            Satisfied of these events at full, we will
            Give answer, render all things faithfully.

BASSANIO: Were you the lawyer and I knew you not?

GRATIANO: Were you the clerk that is to make me cheated?

NERISSA: Ay, but the clerk that never means to do it,
            Unless he live until he be a man.

PORTIA: It is almost morning, let's all go in.

BASSANIO: Sweet lawyer, you shall be my bed-fellow:
            When I am absent, then lie with my wife.

GRATIANO: Well, while I live I'll fear no other thing
            So sore as keeping safe Nerissa's ring.

(Exeunt.)

(*The Merchant of Venice* Act 4, Scenes 1-2; Act 5, Scene 1)

Men and Women (3)
The best way to train a woman... from
The Taming of the Shrew

Some background

Katharina is a strong-minded, independent young woman who does not see why she should put up with foolish men in order to win a husband. Her father thinks he will never be able to find a husband for her, because she is so 'shrewish'. He is grateful when Petruchio offers to marry her and, as he says, teach her how to accept a woman's lot as grateful obedience to a man. He says he will use his experience in training hawks and horses and dogs...

This stage of his 'taming' her follows a long journey in the rain over rough country which has made her hungry and desperate for warmth and something to eat. They arrive at his house in the country.

Parts and the whole

Plot

This is a new stage in the relationship between the two – Petruchio's promise to tame the shrewish Katherina appears to be successful – leading to anticipation of further developments.

Audience appeal

This is a contrast in Katherina from the sharp-witted, sharp-tongued individual we've seen before. Will she be tamed? Will she fight back? If she does, how?

What's so good about this scene?

- outrageously extreme behaviour from Petruchio designed to make Katherina grateful when it stops
- coarse humour of physical action on stage as servants work hard to please and are abused
- display of worst male attitudes concerning marriage and how to treat a wife.

Getting involved:

- **edit** text – how much of the scene setting with Grumio and the servants is needed?
- **rework** text – is it necessary to keep separate parts for Curtis, Philip and Nathaniel?
- **elaborate** text – what stage directions would help to set the scene?
- **translate** text – what may be the modern equivalents of not touching a hair of the master's horse-tail and 'whoreson malt-horse drudge'?
- **improvise** text – what activity would show the preparations for Petruchio's visit and how could his treatment of servants and food be made dramatic?
- **perform** text – to groups or to camera
- **compare** texts – different groups or different screened performances e.g. BBC (John Cleese/Joan Hickson) and Richard Burton/Elizabeth Taylor.

Scene at Petruchio's country house

GRUMIO: Fie, fie on all tired jades, on all mad masters, and all foul ways! Was ever man so beaten? Was ever man so weary? I am sent before to make a fire, and they are coming after to warm them.

(Enter CURTIS.)

CURTIS: I prithee, good Grumio, tell me, how goes the world? Is my master and his wife coming, Grumio?

GRUMIO: O, ay, Curtis, ay: and therefore fire, fire. My master and mistress are almost frozen to death. Where's the cook? Is supper ready, the house trimmed, rushes strewed, cobwebs swept? The serving-men in their new fustian, their white stockings, and their wedding-garment on? Call forth Nathaniel, Gregory, Nicholas, Philip: let their heads be sleekly combed, their blue coats brushed and let them curtsy with their left legs and not presume to touch a hair of my master's horse-tail till they wash their hands. Call them forth.

(Enter Serving-men.)

NATHANIEL: Welcome home, Grumio!

PHILIP: How now, Grumiio.

GRUMIO: Now, my spruce companions, is all ready, and all things neat?

NATHANIEL: All things is ready. How near is our master?

GRUMIO: E'en at hand, alighted by this...

(Enter Petruchio and Katharina.)

PETRUCHIO: Where be these knaves? What, no man at door
To hold my stirrup nor to take my horse!
Where is Nathaniel, Gregory, Philip?

SERVING-MEN: Here, here, sir; here, sir.

PETRUCHIO: Here, sir! Here, sir! Here, sir! Here, sir!
You logger-headed and unpolish'd grooms!
What, no attendance? No regard? No duty?
Where is the foolish knave I sent before?

GRUMIO: Here, sir; as foolish as I was before.

PETRUCHIO: You peasant! You whoreson malt-horse drudge!
Did I not bid thee meet me in the park,
And bring along these rascal knaves with thee?

GRUMIO: There was not time to ready all, my lord,
And so much to be done to please you, sir.
Yet, as best they can, here come they to serve.

PETRUCHIO: Go, rascals, go, and fetch my supper in.
(Singing.)

'Where is the life that late I led? Where are those...'
Sit down, Kate, and welcome.
'It was the friar of orders grey, As he forth walked on his way'
Off with my boots, you rogues!
Nay, good sweet Kate, be merry!
Out, you rogue! you pluck my foot awry:

Take that, and mend the plucking off the other. (Strikes him.)
Be merry, Kate. Some water, here; what, ho!
Where's my spaniel Troilus? Sirrah, get you hence,
And bid my cousin Ferdinand come hither:
One, Kate, that you must kiss, and be acquainted with.
Where are my slippers? Shall I have some water?

(Enter one with water.)

Come, Kate, and wash, and welcome heartily.
You whoreson villain! Will you let it fall? *(Strikes him.)*

KATHARINA: Patience, I pray you; 'twas a fault unwilling.

PETRUCHIO: A whoreson beetle-headed, flap-ear'd knave!
Come, Kate, sit down; I know you have a stomach.
Will you give thanks, sweet Kate; or else shall I?
What's this? Mutton?

FIRST SERVANT: Ay.

PETRUCHIO: Who brought it?

PETER: I.

PETRUCHIO: 'Tis burnt; and so is all the meat.
What dogs are these! Where is the rascal cook?
How durst you, villains, serve it thus to me?
There – take it to you, trenchers, cups, and all;

(Throws the meat, etc. about the stage.)

You heedless joltheads and unmanner'd slaves!

KATHARINA: I pray you, husband, be not so disquiet:
The meat was well, if you were so contented.

PETRUCHIO: I tell thee, Kate, 'twas burnt and dried away;
And I expressly am forbid to touch it,
For it engenders choler, planteth anger;
And better 'twere that both of us did fast,
Since, of ourselves, ourselves are choleric,
Than feed it with such over-roasted flesh.
Be patient; to-morrow 't shall be mended,
And, for this night, we'll fast for company:
Come, I will bring thee to thy bridal chamber.

(Exeunt.)

(Re-enter Grumio and Servants.)

NATHANIEL: Peter, didst ever see the like?

GRUMIO: Where is he?

CURTIS: In her chamber, making a sermon of continency to her;
And roars, and swears, and rants, that she, poor soul,
Knows not which way to stand, to look, to speak,
And sits as one new-risen from a dream.
Away, away for he is coming hither!

(Exeunt.)

(Re-enter PETRUCHIO.)

PETRUCHIO: Thus have I politicly begun my reign,
And 'tis my hope to end successfully.
My falcon now is sharp and passing empty;
And till she stoop she must not be full-gorged,
For then she never looks upon her lure.
Another way I have to man my haggard,
To make her come and know her keeper's call,
That is, to watch her, as we watch these kites
That bate and beat and will not be obedient.
She eats no meat to-day, nor none shall eat;
Last night she slept not, nor to-night shall she;
As with the meat, some undeserved fault
I'll find about the making of the bed;
And here I'll fling the pillow, there the bolster,
This way the coverlet, another way the sheets:
Ay, and amid this hurly I do swear
That all is done in reverend care of her;
And in conclusion she shall wake all night:
And if she chance to nod I'll shout and brawl
And with the clamour keep her still awake.
This is a way to kill a wife with kindness;
And thus I'll curb her mad and headstrong humour.
He that knows better how to tame a shrew,
Now let him speak: 'tis charity to show.

(Exit.)

(The Taming of the Shrew **Act 4, Scene 1)**

Schemes and plots (1)
Falstaff and the robbery, from *Henry IV Part 1*

Some background

King Henry's son, Prince Hal, is involved with some disreputable characters, much to his father's annoyance. The Prince enjoys the company of some of the London low-life, but he also thinks it will help him to understand his people when he becomes King. His involvement sometimes puts him in a difficult position, such as when his friends plan a highway robbery. With Poins, he sees a way to keep out of trouble and to have some fun at the same time. He knows that Falstaff is a cheat, a coward and a liar and sees a way of using his nature to trap him into something that will give them all 'laughter for a month'. Falstaff was a popular comic character among Shakespeare's audience, and Shakespeare included him in the two parts of *Henry IV*, in *Henry V* and in *The Merry Wives of Windsor.*

Parts and the whole

Plot and character

This is the last time we see the Prince in his irresponsible, low-life role. He is soon to show himself worthy to be a King, and Falstaff is soon to show himself in a less amusing light.

Audience appeal

The farce-like playing of the second robbery, and Falstaff's dramatic re-enactment of his pretended role as heroic fighter, demonstrating energetic swordplay in the close confines of an inn.

What's so good about this scene:

- comedy of character – Falstaff is an unashamed rogue and liar; his mixture of bravado and cowardice, craftiness and naivety makes him amusing even though we know we should disapprove of him
- comedy of situation – the planned robbery is a comic affair as Falstaff robs the travellers and is then robbed by the disguised prince and Poins is visual and active
- dramatic irony – as Falstaff tells his story of the robbery, we know the truth of it and appreciate the way Hal prompts him to further lies and exaggerations.

Getting involved

- **edit** text – how much has already been cut from the original?
- **rework** text – is it necessary to keep all the characters Bardolph, Peto and Gadshill?
- **elaborate** text – would a narrator help?
- **translate** text – what are the modern equivalents of 'vizards', 'arrant', 'doublet' and 'buckler'?
- **improvise** text – how does Falstaff demonstrate his claimed role in the fight?
- **perform** text – for an audience or to camera
- **compare** texts – different group performances and/or different screened performances e.g. BBC Shakespeare and The English Shakespeare Company.

Scene 1: The highway, at night

BARDOLPH: On with your vizards: there's money of the king's coming down the hill; 'tis going to the King's Exchequer.

FALSTAFF: You lie, ye rogue; 'tis going to The King's Head.

PRINCE: You four shall front them in the narrow lane; Ned Poins and I will walk lower: if they 'scape from your encounter, then they light on us.

PETO: How many be there of them?

GADSHILL: Some eight or ten.

FALSTAFF: 'Zounds, will they not rob us?

PRINCE: What, a coward, Sir John Paunch?

FALSTAFF: Indeed, I am no coward, Hal.

PRINCE: Well, we leave that to the proof. *(Aside) Ned, where are our disguises?*

POINS: *Here, hard by: stand close.*

(Exeunt PRINCE and POINS.)

FALSTAFF: Now, my masters, every man to his business.

(Enter the Travellers.)

Ist Traveller: Come, friend: the boy shall lead our horses down the hill; we'll walk afoot awhile, and ease our legs.

THIEVES: Stand!

TRAVELLERS: Jesus bless us!

FALSTAFF: Strike; down with them; cut the villains' throats! Ah - whoreson caterpillars! Bacon-fed knaves! They hate us youth. Down with them: fleece them.

TRAVELLERS: O, we are undone, both we and ours for ever!

FALSTAFF: Undone, ye gorbellied knaves? No, ye fat chuffs: On, ye aged knaves! Young men must live.

(They rob them and bind them. Exeunt.)

(Re-enter PRINCE and POINS, disguised.)

PRINCE: The thieves have bound them. Now could thou and I rob the thieves and go merrily to London, it would be argument for a week, laughter for a month and a good jest for ever.

POINS: Stand close; I hear them coming.

(Enter the Thieves again.)

FALSTAFF: Come, my masters, let us share, and then to horse before day. If the Prince and Poins be not two arrant cowards, there's no equity stirring: there's no more valour in that Poins than in a wild-duck.

(As they are sharing, the Prince and Poins set upon them.)

PRINCE: Your money!

POINS: Villains!

(They all run away; and Falstaff, after a blow or two, runs away too, leaving the money bags behind.)

PRINCE: Got with much ease. Now merrily to horse:
The thieves are all scatter'd and possess'd with fear.
Away, good Ned. Falstaff sweats to death,
And lards the lean earth as he walks along:
Were 't not for laughing, I should pity him.

POINS: How the rogue roar'd! *(Exeunt.)*

Scene 2: The King's Head tavern, Eastcheap

(Enter Prince and Poins.)

Landlord: My lord, old Sir John and some others are at the door: shall I let them in?

PRINCE: Let them alone awhile, and then open the door.

(Exit Landlord.)

PRINCE: Poins! Falstaff and the rest of the thieves are at the door: shall we be merry?
Call in ribs, call in tallow.

(Enter Falstaff, Gadshill, Bardolph, Peto and Landlord.)

POINS: Welcome, Jack: where hast thou been?

FALSTAFF: A plague on all cowards, I say, and a vengeance too!
Give me a cup of sack, boy. A plague on all cowards!
Give me a cup of wine, rogue. Is there no virtue extant?
(He drinks.)

FALSTAFF: You rogue, here's lime in this wine: there is nothing but roguery to be found in villainous man: yet a coward is worse than a cup of wine with lime in it. A villainous coward! A plague on all cowards, I say.

PRINCE: How now, wool-sack! What mutter you? What's the matter?

FALSTAFF: A king's son! You Prince of Wales! Are not you a coward?
Answer me to that: and Poins there?

POINS: 'Zounds, ye fat paunch, you call me coward, by the Lord, I'll stab thee.

FALSTAFF: Call thee coward? I would give a thousand pound to run as fast as thou. You care not who sees your back: call you that backing of your friends? A plague upon such backing. Give me a cup of wine: I am a rogue, if I drunk to-day. *(Drinks.)*

PRINCE: O villain! thy lips are scarce wiped since thou drunkest last.

FALSTAFF: A plague on all cowards, still say I.

PRINCE: What's the matter?

FALSTAFF: What's the matter! There be four of us here have ta'en a thousand pound this day morning.

PRINCE: Where is it, Jack? Where is it?

FALSTAFF   Where is it! Taken from us: a hundred upon poor four of us.

PRINCE: What, a hundred?

FALSTAFF: I am a rogue, if I were not at half-sword with a dozen o them two hours together. I have 'scaped by miracle. I am eight times thrust through the doublet, four through the hose; my buckler cut through and through; my sword hacked like a hand-saw. I never dealt better since I was a man. A plague on all cowards! Let them speak: if they speak more or less than truth, they are villains.

PRINCE: Speak, sirs; how was it?

GADSHILL: We four set upon some dozen –

FALSTAFF: Sixteen at least, my lord.

GADSHILL: And bound them. Then some six or seven fresh men set upon us...

FALSTAFF: And unbound the rest, and then come in the other.

PRINCE: What, fought you with them all?

FALSTAFF: All! I know not what you call all; but if I fought not with fifty of them, I am a bunch of radish: if there were not two or three and fifty upon poor old Jack, then am I no two-legged creature.

PRINCE: Pray God you have not murdered some of them.

FALSTAFF: Nay, that's past praying for: I have peppered two of them; two I am sure I have paid, two rogues in buckram suits. I tell thee what, Hal, if I tell thee a lie, spit in my face, call me horse. Four rogues in buckram let drive at me –

PRINCE: What, four? Thou said'st but two even now.

FALSTAFF: Four, Hal; I told thee four. These four came all a-front, and thrust at me. I made me no more ado but took all their seven points in my target, thus.

PRINCE: Seven? why, there were but four even now.

FALSTAFF: Seven, by these hilts, or I am a villain else.

PRINCE: *(Aside.)* Prithee, let him alone; we shall have more anon.

FALSTAFF: Dost thou hear me, Hal? These nine in buckram that I told thee of –

PRINCE: So, two more already.

FALSTAFF: Began to give me ground: but I followed me close, came in foot and hand; and with a thought seven of the eleven I paid.

PRINCE: O monstrous! Eleven buckram men grown out of two!

FALSTAFF: But, as the devil would have it, three misbegotten knaves in Kendal green came at my back and let drive at me; for it was so dark, Hal, that thou couldst not see thy hand.

PRINCE: These lies are like their father that begets them; gross as a mountain, open, palpable. Why, thou clay-brained guts, thou knotty-pated fool, thou whoreson, obscene, grease tallow-catch, –

FALSTAFF: What, art thou mad? Art thou mad? Is not the truth the truth?

PRINCE: Why, how couldst thou know these men in Kendal green, when it was so dark thou couldst not see thy hand? Listen to him! Hear this sanguine coward, this bed-presser, this horseback-breaker, this huge hill of flesh!

FALSTAFF: 'Sblood, you starveling, you elf-skin, you dried neat's tongue, you bull's pizzle, you stock-fish!

PRINCE: Well, breathe awhile, and hear me speak but this.

POINS: Mark, Jack.

PRINCE: We two saw you four set on four and bound them, and were masters of their wealth. Mark now, how a plain tale shall put you down. Then did we two set on you four; and, with a word, out-faced you from your prize, and have it; yea, and can show it you here in the house: and, Falstaff, you carried your guts away as nimbly, with as quick dexterity, and roared for mercy and still ran and roared, as ever I heard bull-calf. What a slave art thou, to hack thy sword as thou hast done, and then say it was in fight! What trick, what device, what starting-hole, canst thou now find out to hide thee from this open and apparent shame?

POINS: Come, let's hear, Jack; what trick hast thou now?

FALSTAFF: By the Lord, I knew ye as well as he that made ye.
           Why, thou knowest I am as valiant as Hercules.
           Why, hear you, my masters: was it for me to kill the
           heir-apparent? Should I turn upon the true prince?
           But, by the Lord lads, I am glad you have the money.
           Hostess, clap to the doors: What, shall we be merry? Shall we have a play extempore?

PRINCE: Content; and the argument shall be thy running away.

FALSTAFF: Ah, no more of that, Hal, if thou lovest me!

                                                    (*Henry IV Part 1* **Act 2, Scene 4**)

SCHEMES AND PLOTS (2)
Falstaff the great lover, from
The Merry Wives of Windsor

Some background

Falstaff is an idle, drunken rogue who is always scheming to make some easy money. Here he is staying at an inn in Windsor, where he has heard there are many rich, bored wives who could fall for his charms. He chooses two local married women and writes each of them a love letter, flattering them for their beauty and declaring his love. If one fails, he thinks, the other may work out. What he doesn't realise is that the two women to whom he sends an identical letter are very close friends, and they decide to get their revenge on this would-be two-timer.

Parts and whole

Plot and character

The latest in a series of events where Falstaff's plans to fool others come adrift, and succeed only in making the women of Windsor (and the men) united in stopping his pranks.

Audience appeal

Dramatic irony as we realise that Mistress Page has seen through Falstaff's cunning and arranged her own cunning plan – much potential for farcical humour as Page may search the room and perhaps sit on the basket before it is carried away to be tipped into the river. A comic example of the way men and women deal with each other.

What's so good about this scene:

- comedy of character – another show of Falstaff's unashamed cheek and cunning in trying to keep money in his purse
- comedy of situation – farcical elements as Falstaff tries to hide and squeezes himself into a laundry basket while the angry husband searches for him
- comedy of theme – Falstaff thinks that he knows how to manage women by flattery and cunning, yet Mistress Page is much cleverer in that she has outwitted and out-tricked him.

Getting involved:

- **edit** text – how much of Mistress Page's opening speech is necessary to set the scene?
- **rework** text – should the lines provided for Mistress Ford and Mistress Page be kept or re-distributed?
- **elaborate** text – should there be any additional business added about Mistress Ford's concealment on stage?
- **translate** text – should the term 'there's sympathy' be changed to something more modern? Does the bawdy humour of 'boarding' and 'hatches' work or does it need re-wording in a modern context?
- **improvise** text – should the Falstaff poem be read by Mistress Page? How? Or should it be read as a voice-over by Falstaff? How? What humour can be derived from the entry of the husband and Falstaff's concealment in the basket?
- **perform** text – for groups or to camera
- **compare** texts – between groups or between screened performances.

Scene I: Mistress Page's house

(Enter Mistress PAGE, with a letter.)

MISTRESS PAGE: What, have I scaped love-letters in the holiday-time of my beauty, and am I now a subject for them? Let me see. *(Reads.)*

> 'Ask me no reason why I love you: but if you must, 'tis
> plain: you are not young, no more am I. Go to then,
> there's sympathy between us: you are merry, so am I; ha,
> ha! Then there's more sympathy: you love wine, and so do
> I; would you desire better sympathy? Let it suffice thee,
> Mistress Page, at the least, if the love of soldier can
> suffice, that I love thee. I will not say, pity me; 'tis
> not a soldier-like phrase: but I say, love me.
> By me,
> Thine own true knight,
> By day or night,
> Or any kind of light,
> With all his might
> For thee to fight,   JOHN FALSTAFF'

What a wicked man is this! O wicked world! One that is well-nigh worn to pieces with age to show himself a gallant young lover! In the devil's name, what hath this drunkard picked out of my conversation, that he dares to think I favour him? Why, he hath not been thrice in my company! What should I say? Heaven forgive me! I'll call for a law in parliament for the putting down of men. How shall I be revenged on him? For revenged I will be, as sure as his guts are made of puddings.

(Enter MISTRESS FORD.)

MISTRESS FORD: O Mistress Page, give me some counsel!

MISTRESS PAGE: What's the matter, woman?

MISTRESS FORD: O, if it were not for one trifling respect, I could come to such honour!

MISTRESS PAGE: Hang the trifle, woman! Take the honour. What is it?

MISTRESS FORD: If I would but risk going to hell I could be knighted.

MISTRESS PAGE: What? Sir Alice Ford!

MISTRESS FORD: Here, read, read; perceive how I might be knighted. Tis from Sir John Falstaff. I think the best way were to entertain him with hope, till the wicked fire of lust have melted him. Did you ever hear the like?

MISTRESS PAGE: Here's the twin-brother of thy letter: Letter for letter, but that the name of Page and Ford differs!

MISTRESS FORD: Why, the very same; the very hand, the very words. What doth he think of us?

MISTRESS PAGE: I warrant he hath thousand of these letters, writ with blank space for different names. I will find you twenty lecherous turtle doves before you find me one chaste man.

MISTRESS PAGE: Nay, I know not: it makes me almost ready to wrangle with mine own decency. Sure, unless he know some weakness in me, that I know not myself, he would never have boarded me so.

MISTRESS FORD: 'Boarding,' call you it? Be sure to keep him above deck.

MISTRESS PAGE: So will I: if he come under my hatches, I'll never to sea again. Let's be revenged on him: let's appoint him a meeting; lead him on with a fine-baited delay, till he hath spent his all and pawned his horses to mine host at the inn.

MISTRESS FORD: I will consent to act any villainy against him, that may not sully our honesty. O, that my husband saw this letter! It would give eternal food to his jealousy.

MISTRESS PAGE: Let's consult together against this greasy knight. Come hither. *(They retire.)*

Scene 2: A room in the inn

(Enter Robin.)

ROBIN: Sir, here's a woman would speak with you.

FALSTAFF: Let her approach.

(Enter Mistress Quickly.)

MISTRESS QUICKLY: Your worship good morrow.

FALSTAFF: Good morrow, good wife.

MISTRESS QUICKLY: Shall I vouchsafe your worship a word or two?

FALSTAFF: Two thousand, fair woman: and I'll vouchsafe thee the hearing.

MISTRESS QUICKLY: There is one Mistress Ford, sir; I pray, come a little nearer this ways.

FALSTAFF: Well, Mistress Ford; what of her?

MISTRESS QUICKLY: Marry, this is the short and the long of it; There has been knights, and lords, and gentlemen, with their coaches, I warrant you, coach after coach, letter after letter, gift after gift; smelling so sweetly, I warrant you, in silk and gold; and in such alligant terms; that would have won any woman's heart; and, I warrant you, they could never get an eye-wink of her: all is one with her.

FALSTAFF: But what says she to me? be brief.

MISTRESS QUICKLY: Marry, she hath received your letter, for the which she thanks you a thousand times; and she gives you to notify that her husband will be away from his house between ten and eleven.

FALSTAFF: Ten and eleven?

MISTRESS QUICKLY: Ay, forsooth; Master Ford, her husband, will be from home. Alas! the sweet woman leads an ill life with him: he's a very jealous man.

FALSTAFF: Ten and eleven. Woman, commend me to her; I will not fail her.

MISTRESS QUICKLY: Why, you say well. But I have another messenger to Your Worship. Mistress Page sends her hearty commendations to you too: she bade me tell your worship that her husband is seldom from home; but she hopes there will come a time. Surely I think you have charms, yes, in truth.

FALSTAFF: But, I pray thee, tell me this: has Ford's wife and Page's wife acquainted each other how they love me?

MISTRESS QUICKLY: That were a jest indeed! That were a trick! Each thinks herself alone the secret cause of your worship's passion.

Scene 3: A room in Ford's house

MISTRESS FORD: John! Robert! Quickly! Is the laundry-basket ready?

MISTRESS PAGE: I warrant. What, Robin, I say! *(Enter Servants with a basket.)* Come, come, come. Here, set it down.

MISTRESS FORD: John and Robert, be ready hard by in the brew-house: and when I suddenly call you, come forth, and without any pause or staggering take this basket on your shoulders; that done, carry it in all haste to the Thames side, and there empty it in the muddy ditch close by. Be gone, and come when you are called. *(Exeunt Servants.)*

(Enter Robin.)

ROBIN: My master, Sir John, is at your back-door, Mistress Ford, and requests your company.

MISTRESS PAGE: Have you been true to us?

ROBIN: Ay, I'll be sworn. My master knows not of your being here.

MISTRESS PAGE: Thou'rt a good boy: I'll go hide me in the next room.

MISTRESS FORD: Do so. Go tell thy master I am alone.

(Exit Robin.)

MISTRESS FORD: Go to, then: we'll use this gross watery pumpion; we'll teach him a thing or two. *(Exit Mistress Page.)*

(Enter Falstaff.)

FALSTAFF: Have I caught thee, my heavenly jewel? Why, now let me die, for I have lived long enough: this is the peak of my ambition: O this blessed hour!

MISTRESS FORD: O sweet Sir John!

FALSTAFF: Mistress Ford, I cannot cog, I cannot prate, Mistress Ford. I would thy husband were dead: I'll speak it before the best lord; I would make thee my lady.

MISTRESS FORD: I your lady, Sir John! Alas, I should be a pitiful lady!

FALSTAFF: Let the court of France show me such a lady. I see how thy eye doth sparkle like a diamond: thou hast the right beauty of the brow that becomes the best in Venice.

MISTRESS FORD: O Sir John: my brows become nothing that well.

FALSTAFF: By the Lord, thou art a traitor to say so: thou wouldst make an absolute Lady in any court in Spain; Come, thou canst not hide it.

MISTRESS FORD: Believe me, there is no such thing in me.

FALSTAFF: Some such thing made me love thee. Something extraordinary in thee. Come, I cannot say thou art this and that, like a many of these lisping rhymers that come like women in men's apparel, and smell like a perfume-house; I cannot: but I love thee and no-one but thee.

MISTRESS FORD: Do not betray me, sir. I fear you love Mistress Page.

FALSTAFF: Thou might as well say I love to walk by the public sewer which is as hateful to me as the stench of the Thames-side drain.

MISTRESS FORD: Well, heaven knows you shall one day find how I feel for you.

FALSTAFF: Keep in that mind; I'll deserve it.

ROBIN: *(Within.)* Mistress Ford, Mistress Ford! Here's Mistress Page
                     at the door, sweating and blowing and looking wildly,
                     and would needs speak with you presently.

FALSTAFF: She shall not see me: I will ensconce me behind the arras.

MISTRESS FORD: Pray you, do so: she's a very tattling woman.

(Falstaff hides himself.) (Re-enter Mistress Page and Robin.)

                     What's the matter? How now!

MISTRESS PAGE: O Mistress Ford, what have you done? You're
                     shamed, you're overthrown, you're undone for ever!

MISTRESS FORD: What's the matter, good Mistress Page?

MISTRESS PAGE: Your husband's coming hither, woman, with all the officers in Windsor, to
                     search for a gentleman that he says is here now in the house by your
                     consent, to take an ill advantage of his absence: you are undone.

MISTRESS FORD: 'Tis not so, I hope.

MISTRESS PAGE: Pray heaven it be not so but 'tis most certain your husband's coming,
                     with half Windsor at his heels, to search for such a one. If you know
                     yourself clear, why, I am glad of it; but if you have a friend here convey,
                     convey him out. Call all your senses to you; defend your reputation, or bid
                     farewell to your good life for ever.

MISTRESS FORD: What shall I do? There is a gentleman my dear friend; and I fear not mine
                     own shame so much as his peril: I had rather than a thousand pound he
                     were out of the house.

MISTRESS PAGE: Never stand 'you had rather' and 'you had rather:' your husband's here,
                     bethink you of some conveyance: in the house you cannot hide him.
                     Look, here is a basket: if he be of any reasonable stature, he may creep
                     in here; and throw foul linen upon him, as if it were going to the laundry.

MISTRESS FORD: He's too big to go in there. What shall I do?

FALSTAFF: *(Coming forward)* Let me see't, let me see't, O, let me see't! I'll in, I'll in.

FALSTAFF: Let me creep in here. I'll never –
                     (Gets into the basket; they cover him with foul linen.)

MISTRESS FORD: What, John! Robert! John!

(Exit Robin.) (Re-enter Servants.)

                     Go take up these clothes here quickly. Carry them to the laundress in
                     Datchet; quickly.

(Enter Ford, Page.)

FORD: Where is the man? If I suspect without cause, why then make sport at
                     me; then let me be your jest; I deserve it. How now! Whither bear you
                     this?

SERVANT: To the laundress, forsooth. *(Exeunt Servants with the basket.)*

                     (*The Merry Wives of Windsor* Act 2, Scenes 1 and 2; Act 3, Scene 3)

SCHEMES AND PLOTS (3)
Getting his garters in a twist, from *Twelfth Night*

Some background

Malvolio is the steward who runs the Lady Olivia's household. He thinks he is superior to most people and dislikes Sir Toby Belch and Sir Andrew Aguecheek because he thinks they are coarse and stupid drunkards. Sir Toby and Sir Andrew decide to make him look foolish, with the help of Maria, the maid. It is not very difficult to make Malvolio look foolish: his vanity and his belief – that he is so attractive that his employer may fall in love with him – does most of the work.

Parts and the whole

Plot and character

Malvolio has been insulting to Sir Toby and Sir Andrew, giving them good reason to seek revenge. This scene sets him up to make a fool of himself and then be locked in a cell, to be tormented by Feste.

Audience appeal

The theme of Puritan hypocrisy made to look ridiculous with the visual spectacle of Malvolio dressed in wholly unsuitable clothing, practising and performing manners that he thinks will make him seem attractive.

What's so good about these scenes:

- comedy of character – Malvolio is a pompous, self-deluding character who treats others with contempt and whose vanity causes him to make a fool of himself
- comedy of situation – Maria's cunning plan gulls him into believing that Olivia loves him, causing him to speak his thoughts aloud, unaware of the fact that those who have tricked him are listening to every word
- dramatic irony – we know that Olivia has no romantic feelings for Malvolio and that she will be outraged that he thinks that she would fall for a servant. We have heard Maria's plan developed and watch it succeed.

Getting involved:

- **edit** text – this is already a much-edited text – compare it with the original and judge what decisions have already been made and why?
- **rework** text – does the script need all the characters or could lines be distributed?
- **translate** text – there has already been some turning into modern English – what examples are there?
- **improvise** text – what scope is there for comedy in the drinking song and in Sir Andrew's attempt to dance?
- **perform** text – for other groups or to camera
- **compare** texts – between groups or between screened performances.

Scene 1: The Lady Olivia's house

(It is one o'clock in the morning. Maria is half-asleep in a chair in the kitchen.)

MARIA: Where can he be until this time of night? It's the same each time he goes out drinking.

(There is a noise outside, then a knock. Another, louder knock follows as Maria goes to open the door.)

MARIA: Sir Toby! Shh! Where have you been? Shh! Oh! What a state! Come in and keep your voice down.

SIR TOBY: I have... I have been... out... with my good friend.

MARIA: Sir Toby, you must come in earlier at night. My Lady takes exception to your hours.

SIR TOBY: Well, let her.

MARIA: You must try to keep a good appearance.

SIR TOBY: Appearance! Ha! These clothes are good enough to drink in, and these boots. Give 'em a pull!

MARIA: Why do you go round with that foolish knight? He's a scoundrel and always in trouble and drunk every night in your company.

SIR TOBY: He has raised his glass to drink my niece's health... He is a scholar and a gentleman. He can play the flute and... dance... and speak in French ... and he's got thirty grand a year!

(There is a noise at the door, then a crash, then a knock.)

SIR TOBY: Ah, that'll be him now.

SIR ANDREW: Psssst! Sir Toby!

SIR TOBY: Sweet Sir Andrew!

MARIA: Shhh! Both of you! You'll wake my Lady!

SIR TOBY: My niece's chambermaid, Sir Andrew. Greet her!

SIR ANDREW: Ah! Erhem! Good evening, Greta. *(Bows.)*

MARIA: Enough of this, now, gentlemen. 'Tis late.

SIR TOBY: Nay! To be up late... is to be... up late. It's not too late for a little drink. What says Sir Andrew?

SIR ANDREW: A drink? O yes, a drink and then a song!

MARIA: A song! At this time of night? You'll have us all in trouble. For the love of God, hold thy peace!

SIR TOBY: Yes, there's a song. 'Hold thy Peace'.
              (Sings. Sir Andrew joins in, singing a round.)

MARIA: Now you've done it. You've woken Malvolio. *(Enter.)*
              Oh, Malvolio, Sir Toby's... er... a little tired.

MALVOLIO: My masters, are you mad? Have you no sense or manners to be caterwauling at this hour? Do you make an alehouse of my Lady's dwelling? She is sad and grieving for the death of her brother. Have you no respect for place or person or time?

SIR TOBY: We kept time in our singing! Go on, sup up! *(Offers him a drink.)* A bit of cake and ale will do you good, you old misery.

MALVOLIO: How dare you! I shall report you to my Lady in the morning. You've not heard the last of this.

(Malvolio strides out, followed by Sir Andrew, copying his walk.)

MARIA: Go shake your ears! O, what a pompous ass!

SIR ANDREW: Who does he think he is, to treat us so?

SIR TOBY: God's gift, he thinks. The trouble is, he has the trust of my niece, and she'll believe him.

MARIA: Tis true. So let us make her trust him not.

SIR TOBY: What wilt thou do? How can we shame this ass?

MARIA: I can write very like my Lady Olivia. I will drop in his way some note that seems to prove that she's in love with him. We'll have some sport, I'll warrant.

SIR TOBY: Excellent! And we can watch to see him take the bait.

MARIA: And get him to wear something outrageous when he meets her next – remember she's in mourning.

SIR ANDREW: What a good wench! Well done, Greta! Well done!

(He does a skipping dance in a circle. Sir Toby claps his hands, calling out 'Higher! Higher!' and Sir Andrew tries to lift his knees higher until he collapses, out of breath.)

Scene 2: Olivia's garden

SIR TOBY: Come this way, Master Fabian. Would you like to see Mr. Perfect make a fool of himself?

FABIAN: I would, man. Let me be boiled to death rather than miss this. You know he got me into trouble with my Lady because he saw me in the betting shop.

SIR ANDREW: Well, I'll bet we get the better of him. Hee hee!

MARIA: Get ye all three into the box-tree. Malvolio's coming this way. He's been practising putting on his manners for the last half hour. I'll drop the letter here.

(All four hide and watch Malvolio talking to himself, practising handshakes and bowing. He carries a pocket mirror.)

MALVOLIO: If only I could be Lord Malvolio.

SIR TOBY: What! The rogue!

FABIAN: Shh!

MALVOLIO: I would wear my velvet gown and call my servants about me. You, Andrew Thingy, fetch me some paper...

SIR ANDREW: Oh, what a cheek!

MALVOLIO: And you, Sir Toby, leave the house, you drunken sot.

SIR TOBY: I'll cudgel him!

FABIAN: SHH! He's seen the letter.

MALVOLIO: Ah! What's this? This looks like Olivia's writing. 'I cannot stop thinking about my darling M——. I love to hear his voice and I love the way he walks. I dream about him in his (purple corduroy jacket.) But my love must stay a secret in this diary. If only he felt for me the way I feel for him. O my dearest M—— One smile from him would...' 'Tis torn; there is no more. She loves me! Thanks, God! I will smile indeed.

(Malvolio puts the paper next to his heart and walks off, muttering, 'Lord and Lady Malvolio... His worship, Malvolio and his wife, Olivia', followed by the plotters.)

Scene 3: Olivia's study

OLIVIA: Maria! Where is Malvolio?

MARIA: He's coming, madam, but in a very strange manner.

OLIVIA: Why, what's the matter?

MARIA: He does nothing but smile, your Ladyship. You'd best be careful, for I'm sure he's lost his wits.

OLIVIA: Go call him hither. Ah, how now, Malvolio?

MALVOLIO: Sweet Lady, Ho, ho! *(He winks at her.)*

OLIVIA: Ho ho? I sent for you because I needed you.

MALVOLIO: Needed me? You needed me? I'm here, my dearest.

OLIVIA: My dearest!

MALVOLIO: Yes darling! *(Moving towards her.)*

OLIVIA: Darling!!! *(Backing away.)*

MALVOLIO: You see what I'm wearing? I know what you like...

OLIVIA: Are you mad?

MALVOLIO: Mad for your love. 'One smile from him would...' What would it do for you, my love, my sweet?

OLIVIA: I don't know what to say. Words fail me!

MALVOLIO: Dearest, let your sweet lips do all the talking.

OLIVIA: This is ridiculous boldness! You should go to bed.

MALVOLIO: To bed, my love? Oh yes, at any time!

(Olivia tries to keep the table between them but he follows her round. She looks for help. He has her trapped against the wall.)

MALVOLIO: Some are born great...

OLIVIA: What?

MALVOLIO: Some achieve greatness...*(He kneels in front of her.)*

OLIVIA: What are you saying?

MALVOLIO: And some have greatness thrust upon them...

(Malvolio tries to embrace her. She escapes from his clutch and runs out. Malvolio pauses to admire himself in the mirror. He picks up her pen and kisses it.)

MALVOLIO: She loves me! She's mine, all mine, the lucky girl!

(*Twelfth Night* Act 2, Scenes 3 & 5; Act 3, Scene 4)

WIT AND WITLESSNESS (1)
Life, death, some dreadful jokes and a song in a graveyard, from *Hamlet*

Some background

This is the beginning of the last act of a play in which Hamlet's father has been poisoned, Hamlet has killed the Prime Minister in mistake for the new King, the Prime Minister's daughter Ophelia (Hamlet's lover) has killed herself and the Norwegian army is threatening to invade. Hamlet, just returned to Denmark from a seafight and rescued by some pirates, comes across a gravedigger at work. Not many playwrights would turn the beginning of the last act into this collection of comic interchanges. (PS Hamlet doesn't know that Ophelia is dead, and that this grave is being dug for her.)

Parts and whole

Plot and character

Hamlet does not know about Ophelia's death because Claudius sent him away to England and he has only recently returned. Discovering Ophelia's funeral, and fighting with her brother, Laertes, leads to the duel in which Claudius tries to poison Hamlet and Hamlet kills Laertes and Claudius, the Queen drinks the poison, Hamlet dies and the play ends.

Audience appeal

Wit, pathos, irony, thoughts on Life, Death and the Hereafter, a tragic corpse on stage, a fight in the grave and the emergence of a dastardly plot.

What's so good about this scene:

- comedy of character and comedy of language – comic relationship between the two gravediggers and the comedy of the gravedigger's response to Hamlet's questions
- the range of emotions as Hamlet passes from scholarly observations to the shock of realising that the skull is Yorick's, the jester who made him laugh when he was a child
- dramatic irony – we know that the grave is for Ophelia, whose suicide is on Hamlet's account and which he does not know has happened.

Getting involved:

- **edit** text – should the discussion of Christian burial ethics stay? Should the explanation of suicide stay? Should the riddle between the two gravediggers stay?
- **rework** text – should the lines of the two gravediggers be merged into one?
- **elaborate** text – how much scope is there to make the digging comic or tragic?
- **translate** text – should words like 'hath' and 'dost' and 'sconce' and 'prithee' be turned into modern expressions or cut?
- **improvise** text – what is the scope for humour in the gravedigger's song?
- **perform** text – should it be comic or tragic or both?
- **compare** texts – between groups and between screened versions.

Scene in graveyard

1ST GRAVEDIGGER: Is she to be buried in Christian burial that wilfully takes her own life?

2ND GRAVEDIGGER: I tell thee she is: the coroner hath judged it a Christian burial.

1ST GRAVEDIGGER: How can that be, unless she drowned herself by accident?

2ND GRAVEDIGGER: Why, 'tis found so.

1ST GRAVEDIGGER: Give me leave. Here lies the water; good: here stands the man; good; if the man goes to the water, and drowns himself, he takes his own life; but if the water comes to him and drowns him, he drowns not himself: therefore, he does not take his own life. If he takes his own life, it cannot be a Christian burial.

2ND GRAVEDIGGER: But is this law?

1ST GRAVEDIGGER: Ay, 'tis; coroner's inquest law.

2ND GRAVEDIGGER: Will you have the truth? If this had not been a gentlewoman, she would not have a Christian burial.

1ST GRAVEDIGGER: Why, there thou say'st: 'tis always so. Great folk have more rights in this world even when it's drowning or hanging themselves. Come, my spade. Gentlefolk, ha! Your true gentlemen be gardeners, ditchers, and grave-makers: they hold up Adam's profession.

2ND GRAVEDIGGER: Adam? Was he a gentleman?

1ST GRAVEDIGGER: He was the first that ever bore arms.

2ND GRAVEDIGGER: Why, he had none.

1ST GRAVEDIGGER: What, art a heathen? How dost thou understand the Scripture? The Scripture says 'Adam digged': could he dig without arms? I'll put another question to thee.

2ND GRAVEDIGGER: Go on.

1ST GRAVEDIGGER: What is he that builds stronger than the mason, the shipwright, or the carpenter?

2ND GRAVEDIGGER: Aye, now I can tell.

1ST GRAVEDIGGER: Go on.

2ND GRAVEDIGGER: Nay, I cannot tell.

1ST GRAVEDIGGER: I'll put it thee again. What is he that builds stronger than the mason, the shipwright, or the carpenter?

2ND GRAVEDIGGER: Now I can tell – the gallows-maker; for his frame outlives a thousand tenants.

1ST GRAVEDIGGER: I like thy wit well: the gallows does well; but how does it well? It does ill to its tenants. Try again.

2ND GRAVEDIGGER: 'Who builds stronger than a mason, a shipwright, or a carpenter?'

1ST GRAVEDIGGER: Cudgel thy brains no more about it, for your dull ass will not mend his pace with beating; when you are asked this question next, say 'a grave-maker: the houses that he makes last till doomsday'. Go, get thee to the inn: fetch me a flagon of liquor.

(Exit.) (Enter Hamlet and Horatio.)

(He digs and sings.)

> A pick-axe, and a spade, a spade,
> For and a shrouding sheet:
> O, a pit of clay for to be made
> For such a guest is meet.

HAMLET: Has this fellow no feeling, that he sings at grave-making?

HORATIO: Custom hath made him at ease with his work.

HAMLET: 'Tis so: the hand of little employment hath the daintier sense.

(Throws up a skull.)

HAMLET: That skull had a tongue in it, and could sing once: how the knave casts it to the ground! It might be the pate of a politician, which this ass now o'er-reaches. Or of a courtier; who could say 'Good morrow, sweet lord! How dost thou, good lord?' And now knocked about the mazzard with a sexton's spade.

(Throws up another skull.)

HAMLET: There's another: why may not that be the skull of a lawyer? Where be his cases and his tricks now? Why does he suffer this rude knave now to knock him about the sconce with a dirty shovel, and not tell him of his action of battery? I will speak to this fellow. Whose grave's this, sirrah?

1ST GRAVEDIGGER: Mine, sir.

HAMLET: I think it be thine, indeed; for thou liest in't.

1ST GRAVEDIGGER: You lie out of it, sir, and therefore it is not yours: for my part, I do not lie in't, and yet it is mine.

HAMLET: Thou dost lie in it, to be in it and say it is thine: 'tis for the dead, not for the living; therefore thou liest. What man dost thou dig it for?

1ST GRAVEDIGGER: For no man, sir.

HAMLET: What woman, then?

1ST GRAVEDIGGER: For none, neither.

HAMLET: Who is to be buried in it?

1ST GRAVEDIGGER: One that was a woman, sir; but, rest her soul, she's dead.

HAMLET: How absolute the knave is! We must speak by the card, or equivocation will undo us. How long hast thou been a grave-maker?

1ST GRAVEDIGGER: Of all the days in the year, I came to it the very day that young Hamlet was born; he that is mad, and sent into England.

HAMLET: Ay, marry, why was he sent into England?

1ST GRAVEDIGGER: Why, because he was mad: he shall recover his wits there; or, if he do not, it's no great matter there.

HAMLET: Why?

1ST GRAVEDIGGER: 'Twill, not be seen in him there; there the men are as mad as he.

HAMLET: How came he mad?

1ST GRAVEDIGGER:	Very strangely, they say.
HAMLET:	How strangely?
1ST GRAVEDIGGER:	Faith, by losing his wits.
HAMLET:	Upon what ground?
1ST GRAVEDIGGER:	Why, here in Denmark.
HAMLET:	How long will a man lie in the earth ere he rot?
1ST GRAVEDIGGER:	In faith, if he be not rotten before he die – we have many pocky corses now-a-days, that will scarce last the funeral – he will last some eight or nine year: a tanner will last you nine year.
HAMLET:	Why he more than another?
1ST GRAVEDIGGER:	Why, sir, his hide is so tanned with his trade, that he will keep out water a great while; and your water is a sore decayer of your whoreson dead body. Here's a skull now has lain in the earth three and twenty years.
HAMLET:	Whose was it?
1ST GRAVEDIGGER:	A whoreson mad fellow's it was: a mad rogue! He poured a flagon of wine on my head once. This same skull, sir, was Yorick's skull, the king's jester.
HAMLET:	This?
1ST GRAVEDIGGER:	Even so.
HAMLET:	Let me see. *(Takes the skull.)* Alas, poor Yorick! I knew him, Horatio: a fellow of infinite jest, of most excellent fancy: he hath borne me on his back a thousand times; and now, so abhorrent my throat gags at it. Here hung those lips that I have kissed I know not how oft. Where be your jokes now? your songs? your flashes of merriment, that set the table on a roar? Now get you to my lady's chamber, and tell her, let her paint an inch thick, to this favour she must come; make her laugh at that. Prithee, Horatio, tell me one thing.
HORATIO:	What's that, my lord?
HAMLET:	Dost thou think Alexander the Great looked thus in the earth?
HORATIO:	Even so.
HAMLET:	And smelt so? Pah! To what base uses we may return, Horatio! Alexander died, Alexander was buried, and returneth into dust; the dust is earth; of earth we make clay; and with that clay, might we not stop a beer-barrel or fill a gap? *Imperious Caesar, dead and turn'd to clay,* *Might stop a hole to keep the wind away.* But soft! but soft! aside: here comes the king.

(*Hamlet* Act 5, Scene 1)

WIT AND WITLESSNESS (2)
Maintaining law and order, from
Much Ado About Nothing

Some background

The Watch is the title of the men paid to keep order in the town – a sort of local community guardian force. Unfortunately, the recruits are not the most youthful, energetic, brave or effective people for the task. They are led by Dogberry, who sees himself as an important and successful operator with good knowledge of the law and how to manage people. In fact, he has very little understanding, and his grasp of language doesn't help. In the first scene he is explaining their duties to his men. Then, by accident, he discovers some criminals at work. Finally, he decides that he can be detective, judge, jury and anything else when he takes charge of law and order.

Parts and the whole

Plot and character

The Prince John subplot involving Borachio will result in disaster if it succeeds in making Hero seem unworthy of marrying Claudio. The inefficiency of Dogberry and the Watch creates suspense as he fails to understand what is going on.

Audience appeal

The main plot is a romantic one based on the relationship between Beatrice and Benedick, contrasted with a potentially tragic sub-plot. The comic additional sub-plot of Dogberry and the Watch gives variety to the play, creating a triangle of Romance, Tragedy and Comedy – something for everyone.

What's so good about this scene:

- comedy of character – Dogberry is a self-important official who thinks he impresses others by his authority and his speech
- comedy of situation – the Watch that he imagines to be his efficient police force is composed of people who are elderly, feeble, lazy, afraid of thieves and wholly unsuited to the task. Everything they do is clumsy and incompetent
- dramatic irony – we know that Borachio is part of Don John's nasty scheme to disrupt the marriage of Hero and Claudio, and know it needs to be exposed, but we also know how incapable the Watch is to do what is necessary and how Dogberry fails to recognise what is happening.

Getting involved

- **edit** text – will a modern audience understand some of the errors in Dogberry's speech?
- **rework** text - should some of the lines of members of the Watch be combined?
- **elaborate** text – what additional lines could be added to show how unsuited the member of the Watch are for their role?
- **translate** text – any words need modern substitutes?
- **improvise** text – what stage effects could reinforce the incompetence of the Watch? (uniforms, weapons, parade drill?)

- **perform** text – with miserable, bullied watch, with cheerful, enthusiastic but hopeless Watch? Dogberry confident or Dogberry struggling to put on show of being in charge?
- **compare** texts – with Branagh screen version?

Scene 1: A street

DOGBERRY: Are you good men and true?

VERGES: Yea, or else they shall suffer everlasting salvation of their soul.

DOGBERRY: Nay, that be small punishment if they fail their duty as the Prince's Watch.

VERGES: Well, give them their charge, neighbour Dogberry.

DOGBERRY: First, who think you the most disqualified man to be constable?

1ST WATCH: Hugh Oatcake, sir, or George Seacoal, for they can write and read.

DOGBERRY: Come hither, neighbour Seacoal. God hath blessed you with a good name and fortune hath blessed you with good looks: but to write and read comes by your nature.

SEACOAL: Both which, Master Constable –

DOGBERRY: You have. I knew it would be your answer. You are the most senseless and fit man for the constable of the Watch, therefore bear you the lantern. This is your charge: first, you must comprehend all fragrant men. You are to bid any man stand, in the Prince's name.

SEACOAL: What if he will not so?

DOGBERRY: Why, then, let him go; and thank God you are rid of a knave.

VERGES: If he will not stand in the name of the Prince, he is no true subject of the Prince.

DOGBERRY: True, and they are to meddle with none but the Prince's subjects. Second, you shall also make no noise in the streets; for, for the Watch to babble and talk is most tolerable and not to be endured.

1ST WATCH: We will rather sleep than talk. We know what belongs to a Watch.

DOGBERRY: Why, you speak like an honest watchman, for I cannot see how sleeping can offend, only have a care that your weapons be not stolen. Fourth, you are to call at all the ale-houses and bid those that are drunk get them to bed.

SEACOAL: What if they will not?

DOGBERRY: Why, let them alone till they are sober; if they make you not a better answer then, you may say they are not the men you took them for.

SEACOAL: Well sir.

DOGBERRY: Third, if you meet a thief, you may suspect him to be no true man. And, for such kind of men, the less you meddle with them, why the more it is gain for your honesty.

SEACOAL: If we know him to be a thief, shall we lay hands on him?

DOGBERRY: Truly, you may, but I think that they who touch pitch will be defiled. The most peaceable way, if you do take a thief, is to let him show himself for what he is and 'steal' away from you.

VERGES: You have always been called a merciful man, partner.

DOGBERRY: Truly, I would not hang a dog by my will, much more a man with any honesty in him.

VERGES: Lastly, if you hear a child cry in the night, you must call to the nurse and bid her still it.

SEACOAL: What if the nurse be asleep and will not hear us?

DOGBERRY: Why, then, depart in peace and let the child wake her, for you can take a leopard to the trough but you can't make it change its spots.

VERGES: True, True. Very true, very true.

DOGBERRY: This is the fifth of your charge: you, constable will reprehend the Prince himself. If you meet anyone, you may stop them on behalf of the Prince.

SEACOAL: What if I meet the Prince?

DOGBERRY: You are to stop him in the name of the Prince.

SEACOAL: And what if he say he will not stop?

DOGBERRY: You are to report him for not stopping to himself.

VERGES: Nay, by'r Lady, that I think you cannot do.

DOGBERRY: Five pounds upon it, any man who knows his Law may tell you.

VERGES: Ah, by'r Lady, then I think it so.

DOGBERRY: Well, masters, good night. Any matter of weight chances, wake me up. Good night, be vigitant, I pray you.

Scene 2: Outside Leonato's house

(The Watch arrests a man they suspect to be a wrong-doer and Dogberry takes charge. Hoping for praise and reward, he brings the suspect to Leonato.)

LEONATO: What would you with me, honest neighbour?

DOGBERRY: I would have some conference with you about a matter that discerns you closely.

LEONATO: Briefly, I pray you. It is a busy time with me.

DOGBERRY: Well, sir, this it is, sir.

VERGES: Yes, sir, in truth it is, sir.

LEONATO: What is it, good friends?

DOGBERRY: Goodman Verges, sir, speaks a little off the matter – an old man, sir, and his wits are not so blunt as they should be, but he's as honest as the next man.

VERGES: Yes I thank God I am as honest as any man as honest as I am, or any man next to me.

DOGBERRY: Your comparisons are odorous, neighbour Verges.

LEONATO: Neighbours, you are tedious.

DOGBERRY: My thanks to your worship for saying so, we do our best. For my part, if I were as tedious as a king, I would bestow all my tediousness of your worship, sir.

VERGES: And I also, sir, too, as well.

LEONATO: I would like to know what you have to say.

VERGES: Sir, our watch tonight hath taken an arrant knave.

DOGBERRY: A good man, sir, but he will be always talking. As they say, 'When the age is in, the wit is out', God help us. Well said, neighbour Verges, but if two men ride a horse, then one must sit behind. He's an honest man, sir, but you see how it goes... All men cannot be the same.

LEONATO: I must leave.

DOGBERRY: But our watch hath comprehended this auspicious person, and we have brought him here to be examined.

LEONATO: You must examine him yourself. I am now in great haste.

DOGBERRY: It shall be suffigent.

LEONATO: Drink some wine before you go. Farewell.

DOGBERRY: We must examinate this man.

VERGES: And we must do it wisely.

DOGBERRY: I shall. As fine a wine as I have tasted. Let us set to.

Scene 3: A prison

DOGBERRY: Is our whole dissembly appeared?

VERGES: A stool and a cushion for the Sexton.

SEXTON: Which be the malefactors?

DOGBERRY: That am I and my partner.

VERGES: Yea, that's certain. We are ready to examine.

SEXTON: No, sir. I mean which are the offenders. Let them come forth.

DOGBERRY: Yea, let them come before me. What is your name?

BORACHIO: Borachio.

DOGBERRY: Pray write down Borachio. And yours, fellow?

CONRADE: I am a gentleman, not a fellow. It is Conrade.

DOGBERRY: Write down this fellow's name as Conrade. Masters, it is proved that you are false knaves and soon this will be alleged. How answer you?

CONRADE: We are not false knaves.

DOGBERRY: Well, Borachio, I say you are false knaves.

BORACHIO: We are not!

DOGBERRY: Well, they cling to their tale! Write that down.

SEXTON: Master constable, you do not go about it the right way. You must call forth the Watch that are the accusers.

DOGBERRY: Yes that's the way. Let the Watch come forth. Masters, accuse these men.

1ST WATCH: He, sir, said that Prince John was a villain.

DOGBERRY: A villain! Burglary! As bad as was ever committed. O villain, thou wilt be condemned into everlasting redemption for this.

SEXTON: Master constable, let these men be bound and brought to Leonato's for examination.

DOGBERRY: Come let them be opinionated

VERGES: Yes, let their hands be opinioned.

BORACHIO: Off, you oaf!

DOGBERRY: An oaf. Write down he calls me an oaf. Thou naughty varlet!

CONRADE: Away, you ass. You are an ass.

DOGBERRY: Dost thou not suspect my position? Dost thou not suspect my office? So, I am an ass. Write down I am an ass.

VERGES: Master constable Dogberry is an ass...

DOGBERRY: Bring him away. Thou villain, varlet, knave: I am a wise fellow, and, what is more, an officer; and, which is more, a houseowner, and, which is more, as pretty a piece of flesh as is in the city, and one who knows the law, and one that hath riches and gowns and everything handsome about him. And I am an ass! It is written down and may be used in evidence.

*(**Much Ado About Nothing** Act 3, Scenes 3 & 6; Act 4, Scene 2)*

GETTING ON IN POLITICS (1)
How to get elected: the art of politics from *Coriolanus*

Some background

Coriolanus is a young general who has become a Roman hero after defeating Rome's enemies in battle. He decides he would like to give up soldiering and become a Consul. He thinks he deserves the post because of what he has done for Rome, but his advisers tell him that he has to get the Roman citizens to vote for him if he wants to be a Consul, and wear The Gown of Humility. Coriolanus doesn't think much of this democratic idea because he thinks the people are stupid, lazy and cowardly, and he doesn't conceal his opinions. Patiently, his advisers explain to him that if he wants to be elected, he has to learn some lessons about people and how to make them vote for him. He finds it hard at first, but then surprisingly easy, as long as he thinks one thing but says another…

Brutus and Sicinius are Tribunes, who are supposed to represent the people of Rome. They do not trust Coriolanus. He does not trust them, either. Shakespeare shows here his understanding of politicians and of politics.

Parts and whole

Plot and character

Coriolanus has to change his behaviour and ideas through the play as he realizes that the roles of soldier and politician require different skills. This scene shows him adapting but also shows the parts of his nature that cause conflict later on.

Audience appeal

Humour in the way he first fails to suppress his natural thoughts and feelings, then discovers how easy it is to fool people once you've learned the skills of dishonesty – understanding how this scene has much to say about politics and politicians in Shakespeare's time and in our time.

What's so good about this scene:

- political insight – showing the process whereby people wanting political power can influence voters by putting on a false display of caring for the ordinary people and wishing to serve them, rather than rule them
- psychological insight into the mind of a character who despises the common people but has to abide by a system that gives them the right to choose their leader, so that he has to suppress his usual ideas and feelings. He has to learn how to put aside his soldier's mentality and develop a different public persona
- dramatic irony in seeing Coriolanus adopt the robe and manner of humility to conceal his arrogance.

Getting involved

- **edit** text – how much should be cut without losing the script's concern with how to win people's votes?
- **rework** text – are all the minor parts necessary?
- **elaborate** text – should there be a narrator or some context such as a general election campaign?

- **translate** text – do any words need modern substitutes?
- **improvise** text – how does the wearing of the gown of humility create comedy or a sense of Coriolanus' character?
- **perform** text – is there scope for exaggerating the doing it wrong/doing it right parts of the text?
- **compare** texts – with other groups or with a screened performance (BBC).

Scene 1: The Capitol

(Enter two Officials, to arrange the seating.)

1ST OFFICIAL:　Come, come, they are almost here. How many stand for consulships?

2ND OFFICIAL:　Three, they say: but 'tis thought of every one Coriolanus will carry it.

1ST OFFICIAL:　He's a brave fellow; but he's very proud, and loves not the common people.

2ND OFFICIAL:　Faith, there had been many great men that have flattered the people, who ne'er loved them. Coriolanus cares not whether they love or hate him and out of his noble carelessness lets them plainly see't.

1ST OFFICIAL:　But, sure, to stir the malice and displeasure of the people is as bad as to flatter them for their love.

2ND OFFICIAL:　He thinks his honour and his deeds hath deserved the respect of all, and need not beg it from them.

1ST OFFICIAL:　No more of him; he is a worthy man: make way, they are coming.

Scene 2: The Forum

(Trumpets. Enter Cominious the consul, Menenius, Coriolanus, Senators, the Tribunes, Sicinius and Brutus. Coriolanus stands.)

MENENIUS:　　Remains the point of this our meeting to report the worthy work perform'd by Caius Marcius Coriolanus.

(To the Tribunes.)
　　　　　　　Masters o' the people, we do request your kindest ears, and after, yield what passes here toward the common body.

BRUTUS:　　　Which we shall be pleased to do, if he remember a kinder value of the people than he hath prized them at thus far.

MENENIUS:　　That's off, that's off; I would you rather had been silent. He loves your people, but tie him not to be their bedfellow. Worthy Cominius, speak.

(Coriolanus offers to go away.)
　　　　　　　Nay, keep your place. Sit, Coriolanus; never shame to hear what you have nobly done.

CORIOLANUS:　Your honour's pardon: I had rather have my wounds again than hear report of how I got them.

BRUTUS:　　　Sir, I hope my words disbench'd you not.

CORIOLANUS:　No, sir: yet oft, I fled from words when blows have made me stay. As to your people, I love them as they weigh. *(Exit.)*

MENENIUS: Masters of the people, how can he flatter?
             He had rather venture all his limbs for honour
             Than bear to hear it told. Proceed, Cominius.

COMINIUS: I shall lack voice: the deeds of Coriolanus
             Should not be utter'd feebly. It is held
             That valour is the chiefest virtue, and
             Most dignifies the haver: if it be,
             The man I speak of cannot in the world
             Be singly counterpoised. At sixteen years,
             When Tarquin led his troops to Rome, he fought
             Beyond the mark of others. That day he slew
             three of his opposers: Tarquin's self he met,
             And struck him to his knees. His pupil age
             Man-enter'd thus, he waxed like a sea,
             And in the brunt of seventeen battles since
             He proved best man i' the field. For this last,
             At Corioli, he stopp'd the fliers;
             And by his rare example made the coward
             Turn terror into sport so men obey'd.
             Alone he enter'd the gate of Corioli, aidless,
             And till we call'd both field and city ours,
             He never stood to ease himself with breath.

MENENIUS: Worthy man!

1ST SENATOR: He's right noble: Let him be call'd for.

(Re-enter Coriolanus.)

MENENIUS: The senate, Coriolanus, are well please to make thee consul.

CORIOLANUS: I do owe them still my life and services.

MENENIUS: It then remains that you do speak to the people.

CORIOLANUS: I do beseech you,
             Let me o'erleap that custom, for I cannot
             Put on the gown, stand naked and entreat them,
             For my wounds' sake, to give their suffrage: please you
             That I may pass this doing.

SICINIUS: Sir, the people must have their voices; neither will they bate
             One jot of ceremony.

CORIOLANUS: It is a part
             That I shall blush in acting. I cannot
             Brag unto them 'Thus I did, and thus;'
             Show them my scars as if I had received them
             For the hire of their breath only!

MENENIUS: Think again and be not rash: 'tis the end that matters, not the means by
             which you gain it. We will advise you.

SENATORS: To Coriolanus all joy and honour!

(Flourish of cornets. Exeunt all but Sicinius and Brutus.)

BRUTUS: You see how he intends to use the people.

SICINIUS: May they see it clear! He will request them in contempt of what they have to
             give.

BRUTUS: Come, we'll inform them of our proceedings here.

(Exeunt.)

Scene 2: The Forum

(Enter some Citizens.)

1ST CITIZEN: Once, if he do require our voices, we ought not to deny him.

2ND CITIZEN: We may, though, deny him, if we will do so.

3RD CITIZEN: But if he show us his wounds and tell us his noble deeds, we must tell him our noble acceptance of them. Ingratitude is monstrous, and for the multitude to be ungrateful, were to make a monster of the multitude.

2ND CITIZEN: I say, if he would incline to the people, there was never a worthier man. Here he comes, and in the gown of humility: mark his behaviour.

(They withdraw.)

(Enter Coriolanus in a gown of humility, with Menenius.)

MENENIUS: O sir, you are not right: do you not know
The worthiest men before have done this thing?

CORIOLANUS: What must I say?
'I Pray, sir' – Plague upon't! I cannot bring
My tongue to such a pace: – 'Look, sir, my wounds!
I got them in my country's service, when
Some certain of your brethren roar'd and ran
From the noise of our own drums.'

MENENIUS: O me, the gods!
You must not speak of that: you must desire them
To think upon you.

CORIOLANUS: Think upon me! hang 'em!

MENENIUS: You'll mar all: I'll leave you now: I pray you, speak to them in wholesome manner. *(Exit.)*

CORIOLANUS: *Bid them wash their faces and keep their teeth clean.*

(The Citizens come forward.)
So, here comes a brace.
You know the cause, sirs, of my standing here.

1ST CITIZEN: We do, sir; tell us what hath brought you to't.

CORIOLANUS: Mine own desert.

2ND CITIZEN: Your own desert!

CORIOLANUS: Ay, but not mine own desire.

3RD CITIZEN: How not your own desire?

CORIOLANUS: 'Twas never my desire yet to trouble the poor with begging.

3RD CITIZEN: You must think, if we give you anything, we hope to gain by you.

CORIOLANUS: Well then, I pray, your price o' the consulship?

1ST CITIZEN: The price is to ask it kindly.

CORIOLANUS: Kindly! Sir, I pray, let me ha't: I have wounds to show you, which shall be yours to see in private. Your good voice, sir; what say you?

2ND CITIZEN: You shall ha' it, worthy sir.

CORIOLANUS: A match, sir. There's two worthy voices begged. I have your alms: adieu.

(Exeunt Citizens.) (Enter other Citizens.)

CORIOLANUS: Pray you now, if it may stand with the tune of your voices that I may be consul. I have here the customary gown.

4TH CITIZEN: You have deserved nobly of your country, and you have not deserved nobly.

CORIOLANUS: Your meaning?

4TH CITIZEN: You have been a scourge to her enemies, but you have been a rod to her friends; truth is, you have not loved the common people.

CORIOLANUS: You should account me the more virtuous that I have not been 'common' in my love. I will, sir, flatter the people, to earn a dearer estimation of them: *[And since the wisdom of their choice is rather to have my hat than my heart, I will practise the insinuating nod and be off to them most counterfeitly.]* Therefore, sirs, I beseech you I may be consul.

5TH CITIZEN: We hope to find you our friend; and therefore give you our voices heartily.

(Exeunt.)

CORIOLANUS: Most sweet voices!
　　　　　　　　　Better it is to die, better to starve,
　　　　　　　　　Than crave the hire which first we do deserve.
　　　　　　　　　Why in this woolvish toge should I stand here,
　　　　　　　　　To beg of Hob and Dick, that do appear?
　　　　　　　　　Custom calls me to't. Rather than fool it so,
　　　　　　　　　Let the high office and the honour go
　　　　　　　　　To one that would do thus. I am half through;
　　　　　　　　　The one part suffer'd, the other will I do.

(Re-enter three Citizens more.)
　　　　　　　　　Here come more voices.
　　　　　　　　　Your voices: for your voices I have fought;
　　　　　　　　　Watch'd for your voices; for Your voices bear
　　　　　　　　　Of wounds two dozen odd; battles thrice six
　　　　　　　　　I have seen and heard of; for your voices have
　　　　　　　　　Done many things, some less, some more your voices:
　　　　　　　　　Indeed I would be consul.

6TH CITIZEN: He has done nobly, and cannot go without any honest man's voice.

7TH CITIZEN: Therefore let him be consul: the gods give him joy, and make him good friend to the people!

ALL CITIZENS: Amen, amen. God save thee, noble consul! *(Exeunt.)*

CORIOLANUS: Worthy voices!

Scene 3: The Forum

Re-enter Menenius, with Brutus and Sicinius.)

MENENIUS: You have stood your limitation; and the tribunes note the people's voice.

SICINIUS: The custom of request you have discharged: the people do admit you.

CORIOLANUS: Is this done? May I change these garments?

SICINIUS: You may, sir.

CORIOLANUS: That I'll straight do; and, knowing myself again, repair to the Senate-house.

(Exeunt Coriolanus and Menenius.)

BRUTUS: With a proud heart he wore his humble weeds. Will you dismiss the people?

(Re-enter Citizens.)

SICINIUS: How now, my masters! Have you chose this man?

1ST CITIZEN: He has our voices, sir. He has deserved our voices.

BRUTUS: We pray the gods he may deserve your loves.

2ND CITIZEN: Amen, sir: it seemed to me he mock'd us when he begg'd our voices.

1ST CITIZEN: No,'tis his kind of speech: he did not mock us.

3RD CITIZEN: He said he had wounds, which he could show in private;
And with his hat, thus waving it in scorn,
'I would be Consul,' says he: 'But aged custom,
Permits me office, only by your voice;
Your voice, therefore, I beg.' That granted here was,
'I thank you for your voices: now, I have no further with you.'
Was not this mockery?

SICINIUS: Why either were you ignorant to see't or, seeing it, of such childishness to yield your voices?

BRUTUS: Did you perceive
He did solicit you in free contempt
When he did need your loves, and do you think
That his contempt shall not be bruising to you,
When he hath power to crush?
Get you hence instantly, and tell those friends,
They have chose a consul that will from them take
Their liberties; make their voice no more than that
Of dogs that are as often beat for barking
As kept to do so.

3RD CITIZEN: He's not confirm'd; we may deny him yet.

2ND CITIZEN: And will deny him: I'll have five hundred voices of that sound.

1ST CITIZEN: I twice five hundred and their friends.

SICINIUS: Let them assemble,
And on a safer judgment all revoke
Your ignorant election. Speak of his pride,
And his old hate unto you; besides, forget not
With what contempt he wore the humble gown,
And how in his manner he seemed to scorn you.

BRUTUS: Lay
            A fault on us, your tribunes; that we laboured,
            No impediment between, but that you must
            Cast your election on him.

SICINIUS: Say, you chose him
            More after our commandment than as guided
            By your own true affections, and that your minds,
            Preoccupied with what you rather must do
            Than what you should, made you against the grain
            To voice him consul: lay the fault on us.

BRUTUS: Ay, spare us not. Say we read lectures to you.
            How youngly he served his country.

SICINIUS: But you have found, weighing his present manner with his past,
            That he's your enemy, and revoke your hasty judgment.

BRUTUS: Say, you would never have done it but for our urging you;
            And quickly repair to the Capitol.

ALL: We will so: almost all repent in their election.

(Exeunt Citizens.)

SICINIUS: To the Capitol, come:
            We will be there before the stream o' the people;
            And this shall seem, as partly 'tis, their own,
            Which we have goaded onward.

(Exeunt.)

(*Coriolanus* Act 2 Scenes 2 & 3)

GETTING ON IN POLITICS (2)
How to do it/How not to do it:
Roman public relations from *Julius Caesar*

Some background

Julius Caesar, the greatest man in Rome, has been assassinated. The group who assassinated him was led by Brutus, who had been Caesar's friend, but he thought that Caesar had plans to make himself a dictator, and agreed with others to stop him the only way they could. Brutus said they should not cause any more bloodshed, and so they did not kill Mark Antony, who was Caesar's closest supporter. In order to explain why they took such extreme measures, Brutus decides to speak to the Roman people in the Forum. He also agrees to let Mark Antony follow him and say a few words as part of Caesar's funeral. Mistake!

Brutus thinks the people will be reasonable and accept his statement of what had to be done. Mark Antony thinks that people are not ruled by reason. He uses other means to influence them.

Parts and the whole

Plot and character

We see Mark Antony develop from a youthful friend of Caesar's to a mature political leader, and Brutus change from a respected public figure to a fugitive from the public's rage.

Audience appeal

Physical action of an mob growing sorrowful then angry on stage; display of powerful feelings and language from Mark Antony and sense of relevance to the ways that people can be manipulated in Roman, Elizabethan and modern times.

What's so good about this scene:

- political insight – showing how the public can be influenced by emotional manipulation, appeal to nationalism and economic self-interest
- psychological insight – into the way an honest, decent and principled man can fail to make an impact on people because he thinks honesty, decency and principle are enough, and the way a devious, scheming and unprincipled man can make an impact because he has a less flattering view of the people
- dramatic irony – we know from what Mark Antony said earlier that he intends to stir up trouble – and use Brutus' decency in letting him speak second, after Brutus has gone, to whip up the crowd against him.

Getting involved

- **edit** text – is it important to keep Brutus' speech before Mark Antony's speech? Should the comments of the citizens be kept?
- **elaborate** text – should the scene by presented as a public one or as a TV broadcast?
- **translate** text – do the details of Caesar's will need to be made more modern?
- **improvise** text – what would be the three most important moments to represent in stills or a tableau? How can the changing mood of the people be made dramatic?
- **perform** text – to groups or to camera
- **compare** texts – between groups or between screened versions.

Scene 1: Rome, the Forum

(Enter Brutus and Cassius, and a throng of Citizens.)

CITIZENS: We will be satisfied! Let us be satisfied!

BRUTUS: Then follow me and give me audience, friends.
           Cassius, go you into the other street
           And part the numbers.
           Those that will hear me speak, let 'em stay here;
           Those that will follow Cassius, go with him;
           And public reasons shall be rendered
           Of Caesar's death.

CITIZEN 1: I will hear Brutus speak.

CITIZEN 2: I will hear Cassius and compare their reasons,
            When severally we hear them rendered.

(Exit Cassius, with some Citizens. Brutus goes into the pulpit.)

CITIZEN 3: The noble Brutus is ascended. Silence!

BRUTUS: Be patient till the last.
           Romans, countrymen, and lovers! Hear me for my cause, and be silent, that you
           may hear. Believe me for mine honour, and have respect to mine honour, that you
           may believe. Censure me in your wisdom, and awake your senses, that you may
           the better judge. If there be any in this assembly, any dear friend of Caesar's,
           to him I say that Brutus' love to Caesar was no less than his. If then that friend
           demand why Brutus rose against Caesar, this is my answer: Not that I loved
           Caesar less, but that I loved Rome more. Had you rather Caesar were living and
           die all slaves, than that Caesar were dead to live all free men? As Caesar loved
           me, I weep for him; as he was fortunate, I rejoice at it; as he was valiant,
           I honour him; but as he was ambitious, I slew him. There is tears for his love, joy
           for his fortune, honour for his valor, and death for his ambition. Who is here so
           base that would be a bondman? If any, speak, for him have I offended. Who is
           here so rude that would not be a Roman? If any, speak, for him have I offended.
           Who is here so vile that will not love his country? If any, speak, for him have I
           offended. I pause for a reply.

ALL: None, Brutus, none.

BRUTUS: Then none have I offended. I have done no more to Caesar than you shall do to
           Brutus. The question of his death is enrolled in the Capitol, his glory not
           extenuated, wherein he was worthy, nor his offences enforced, for which he
           suffered death.

(Enter Antony and others, with Caesar's body.)
           Here comes his body, mourned by Mark Antony, who, though he had no hand in
           his death, shall receive the benefit of his dying, a place in the commonwealth, as
           which of you shall not? With this I depart – that, as I slew my best lover for the
           good of Rome, I have the same dagger for myself, when it shall please my
           country to need my death.

ALL: Live, Brutus, live, live!

CITIZEN 1: Bring him with triumph home unto his house.

CITIZEN 2: Give him a statue with his ancestors.

CITIZEN 3: Let him be Caesar.

CITIZEN 4: Caesar's better parts shall be crown'd in Brutus.

CITIZEN 1: We'll bring him to his house with shouts and clamors.

BRUTUS: My countrymen –

CITIZEN 2: Peace! Silence! Brutus speaks.

CITIZEN 1: Peace, ho!

BRUTUS: Good countrymen, let me depart alone,
And, for my sake, stay here with Antony.
Do grace to Caesar's corse, and grace his speech
Tending to Caesar's glories, which Mark Antony,
By our permission, is allow'd to make.
I do entreat you, not a man depart,
Save I alone, till Antony have spoke. *(Exit.)*

CITIZEN 1: Stay, ho, and let us hear Mark Antony.

CITIZEN 3: Let him go up into the public chair;
We'll hear him. Noble Antony, go up.

ANTONY: For Brutus' sake, I am beholding to you. *(Goes into the pulpit.)*

CITIZEN 4: What does he say of Brutus?

CITIZEN 3: He says, for Brutus' sake, He finds himself beholding to us all.

CITIZEN 4: 'Twere best he speak no harm of Brutus here.

CITIZEN 1: This Caesar was a tyrant.

CITIZEN 3: Nay, that's certain. We are blest that Rome is rid of him.

CITIZEN 2: Peace! Let us hear what Antony can say.

ANTONY: You gentle Romans –

ALL: Peace, ho! Let us hear him.

ANTONY: Friends, Romans, countrymen, lend me your ears!
I come to bury Caesar, not to praise him.
The evil that men do lives after them,
The good is oft interred with their bones;
So let it be with Caesar. The noble Brutus
Hath told you Caesar was ambitious;
If it were so, it was a grievous fault,
And grievously hath Caesar answer'd it.
Here, under leave of Brutus and the rest –
For Brutus is an honourable man;
So are they all, all honourable men –
Come I to speak in Caesar's funeral.
He was my friend, faithful and just to me;
But Brutus says he was ambitious,
And Brutus is an honourable man.
He hath brought many captives home to Rome,
Whose ransoms did the general coffers fill.
Did this in Caesar seem ambitious?
When that the poor have cried, Caesar hath wept;
Ambition should be made of sterner stuff:
Yet Brutus says he was ambitious,

> And Brutus is an honourable man.
> You all did see that on the Lupercal
> I thrice presented him a kingly crown,
> Which he did thrice refuse. Was this ambition?
> Yet Brutus says he was ambitious,
> And sure he is an honourable man.
> I speak not to disprove what Brutus spoke,
> But here I am to speak what I do know.
> You all did love him once, not without cause;
> What cause withholds you then to mourn for him?
> O judgement, thou art fled to brutish beasts,
> And men have lost their reason. Bear with me;
> My heart is in the coffin there with Caesar,
> And I must pause till it come back to me.

CITIZEN 1:   Methinks there is much reason in his sayings.

CITIZEN 2:   If thou consider rightly of the matter, Caesar has had great wrong.

CITIZEN 3:   Has he, masters? I fear there will a worse come in his place.

CITIZEN 4:   Mark'd ye his words? He would not take the crown;
Therefore 'tis certain he was not ambitious.

CITIZEN 1:   If it be found so, some will dear abide it.

CITIZEN 2:   Poor soul, his eyes are red as fire with weeping.

CITIZEN 3:   There's not a nobler man in Rome than Antony.

CITIZEN 4:   Now mark him, he begins again to speak.

ANTONY: But yesterday the word of Caesar might
Have stood against the world. Now lies he there,
And none so poor to do him reverence.
O masters! If I were disposed to stir
Your hearts and minds to mutiny and rage,
I should do Brutus wrong and Cassius wrong,
Who, you all know, are honourable men.
I will not do them wrong; I rather choose
To wrong the dead, to wrong myself and you,
Than I will wrong such honourable men.
But here's a parchment with the seal of Caesar;
I found it in his closet, 'tis his will.
Let but the commons hear this testament –
Which, pardon me, I do not mean to read –
And they would go and kiss dead Caesar's wounds
And dip their napkins in his sacred blood,
Yea, beg a hair of him for memory,
And, dying, mention it within their wills,
Bequeathing it as a rich legacy
Unto their issue.

CITIZEN 4:   We'll hear the will. Read it, Mark Antony.

ALL: The will, the will! We will hear Caesar's will.

ANTONY: Have patience, gentle friends, I must not read it;
It is not meet you know how Caesar loved you.
You are not wood, you are not stones, but men;
And, being men, hearing the will of Caesar,

It will inflame you, it will make you mad.
'Tis good you know not that you are his heirs,
For if you should, O, what would come of it!

CITIZEN 4: Read the will; we'll hear it, Antony.
You shall read us the will, Caesar's will.

ANTONY: Will you be patient? Will you stay awhile?
I have o'ershot myself to tell you of it.
I fear I wrong the honourable men
Whose daggers have stabb'd Caesar; I do fear it.

CITIZEN 4: They were traitors. Honourable men!

ALL: The will! The testament!

CITIZEN 2: They were villains, murtherers. The will! Read the will!

ANTONY: You will compel me then to read the will?
Then make a ring about the corse of Caesar,
And let me show you him that made the will.
Shall I descend? And will you give me leave?

ALL: Come down.

CITIZEN 2: Descend.

(He comes down from the pulpit.)

CITIZEN 3: You shall have leave.

CITIZEN 4: A ring, stand round.

CITIZEN 1: Stand from the hearse, stand from the body.

CITIZEN 2: Room for Antony, most noble Antony.

ANTONY: Nay, press not so upon me, stand far off.

ALL: Stand back; room, bear back!

ANTONY: If you have tears, prepare to shed them now.
You all do know this mantle. I remember
The first time ever Caesar put it on;
'Twas on a summer's evening, in his tent,
That day he overcame the Nervii.
Look, in this place ran Cassius' dagger through;
See what a rent the envious Casca made;
Through this the well-beloved Brutus stabb'd;
And as he pluck'd his cursed steel away,
Mark how the blood of Caesar follow'd it,
As rushing out of doors, to be resolved
If Brutus so unkindly knock'd, or no;
For Brutus, as you know, was Caesar's angel.
Judge, O you gods, how dearly Caesar loved him!
This was the most unkindest cut of all;
For when the noble Caesar saw him stab,
Ingratitude, more strong than traitors' arms,
Quite vanquish'd him. Then burst his mighty heart,
And, in his mantle muffling up his face,
Even at the base of Pompey's statue,
Which all the while ran blood, great Caesar fell.

O, what a fall was there, my countrymen!
Then I, and you, and all of us fell down,
Whilst bloody treason flourish'd over us.
O, now you weep, and I perceive you feel
The dint of pity. These are gracious drops.
Kind souls, what weep you when you but behold
Our Caesar's vesture wounded? Look you here,
Here is himself, marr'd, as you see, with traitors.

CITIZEN 1: O piteous spectacle!

CITIZEN 2: O noble Caesar!

CITIZEN 3: O woeful day!

CITIZEN 4: O traitors villains!

CITIZEN 1: O most bloody sight!

CITIZEN 2: We will be revenged.

ALL: Revenge! About! Seek! Burn! Fire! Kill!
         Slay! Let not a traitor live!

ANTONY: Stay, countrymen.

CITIZEN 1: Peace there! Hear the noble Antony.

CITIZEN 2: We'll hear him, we'll follow him, we'll die with him.

ANTONY: Good friends, sweet friends, let me not stir you up
         To such a sudden flood of mutiny.
         They that have done this deed are honourable.
         What private griefs they have, alas, I know not,
         That made them do it. They are wise and honourable,
         And will, no doubt, with reasons answer you.
         I come not, friends, to steal away your hearts.
         I am no orator, as Brutus is;
         But, as you know me all, a plain blunt man,
         That love my friend, and that they know full well
         That gave me public leave to speak of him.
         For I have neither wit, nor words, nor worth,
         Action, nor utterance, nor the power of speech,
         To stir men's blood. I only speak right on;
         I tell you that which you yourselves do know;
         Show you sweet Caesar's wounds, poor dumb mouths,
         And bid them speak for me. But were I Brutus,
         And Brutus Antony, there were an Antony
         Would ruffle up your spirits and put a tongue
         In every wound of Caesar that should move
         The stones of Rome to rise and mutiny.

ALL: We'll mutiny.

CITIZEN 1: We'll burn the house of Brutus.

CITIZEN 3: Away, then! Come, seek the conspirators.

ANTONY: Yet hear me, countrymen; yet hear me speak.

ALL: Peace, ho! Hear Antony, most noble Antony!

ANTONY: Why, friends, you go to do you know not what.
            Wherein hath Caesar thus deserved your loves?
            Alas, you know not; I must tell you then.
            You have forgot the will I told you of.

ALL: Most true, the will! Let's stay and hear the will.

ANTONY: Here is the will, and under Caesar's seal.
            To every Roman citizen he gives,
            To every several man, seventy-five drachmas.

CITIZEN 2: Most noble Caesar! We'll revenge his death.

CITIZEN 3: O royal Caesar!

ANTONY: Hear me with patience.

ALL: Peace, ho!

ANTONY: Moreover, he hath left you all his walks,
            His private arbors, and new-planted orchards,
            On this side Tiber; he hath left them you,
            And to your heirs forever – common pleasures,
            To walk abroad and recreate yourselves.
            Here was a Caesar! When comes such another?

CITIZEN 1: Never, never. Come, away, away!
            We'll burn his body in the holy place
            And with the brands fire the traitors' houses.
            Take up the body.

CITIZEN 2: Go fetch fire.

CITIZEN 3: Pluck down benches.

CITIZEN 4: Pluck down forms, windows, anything.

(Exeunt Citizens with the body.)

ANTONY: Now let it work. Mischief, thou art afoot
            Take thou what course thou wilt.

                                        (*Julius Caesar* Act 3, Scene 2)

4. The screened Shakespearience in the classroom

The range of digital and screen resources

Studying performances of Shakespeare's scripts is as important as reading them – probably more important for most students, at both ends of the ability range. Certainly, a first encounter with the text on the page will not motivate the less academic, though this book's Shakespeariences will have made that encounter more congenial. Fortunately, there is a wealth of material available, ranging from the (mostly) rather staid BBC Shakespeare to more enterprising and classroom-friendly screen versions, such as Lurhmann's 1995 *Romeo + Juliet* and Woolcock's 1997 *Macbeth on the Estate*. Even if some screen versions are less than gripping, comparing them with others that *are* gripping allows students to make personal and critical comparison, developing their own rationale for preference and engaging with dramatic conventions and tradition. Apart from making them more confident with the plays as performative texts, this use of different versions can be a major part of GCSE study in years 10 and 11. (See Chapter 7: Shakespearience and Examinations.)

This section is devoted to live action recordings, but there are other ways in which digital and screen resources can support study and engage students critically and creatively. There are useful adaptations, re-creations and transformations of the plays, such as the BBC's *Shakespeare: The Animated Tales*. These engage students with key issues of textual adaptation for different audiences and different media, and hence with editorial and directorial choices as well as comparison with the original text to judge fidelity to Shakespeare's insights and concerns. They are not only a strong basis for studying interpretation, they are also a quality stimulus for students' own creativity though their own multi-modal media adaptations and re-creations. Students working towards creative options in GCSE – for example, Edexcel's English Studies – will have plenty of scope for Controlled Assessment activities. Solo and/or group work activities will also provide real contexts for students' Speaking and Listening profiles. Again, see Chapter 6 for specific requirements.

Focus and use

When using screened versions of Shakespeare's playtext, it is important to focus on a small part of the play and to prepare students for observing differences in the way that the text has been realised for public performance.

Purposeful and effective use of screened Shakespeare means directing students to the following:

a) **Editing:** preparing the raw print text resource – conscious choices of cuts in the published text and substitutions to make meaning clearer to a modern audience, usually referred to as 'screenplay'.

b) **Directing:** interpreting the whole edited resource, locating the play in a social or historical context to help coherence and relevance – supporting meaning and appeal by choices in setting, dress, movement, grouping or action – and making structural choices of scene re-sequencing or amplification.

c) **Producing:** delivering the final product to the audience, including ways in which the technical resources of the medium are used support interpretation and performance – such as sound, lighting, or other effects to gain and sustain audience interest and understanding – by use of camera angles and transitions such as cuts, fades and dissolves, insertions such as flashbacks and overlays such as sound effects and musical score – includes editing the media text.

d) **Acting:** making a fictional character believable by human resources of intonation, posture, gesture, facial expression, volume, pause and emphasis.

If students are simply screen-watching to follow the story, the most compelling engagement is with the acting – which is why actors become celebrities – but if they are to develop their study and appreciation, it's directing that needs emphasis. Directing involves editing, presenting and influencing a large part of what actors do. Students need to understand that directors shape and twist Shakespeare's script to give it an appeal and a significance that previous productions have not. This is usually a matter of making the play fit a topical issue, or match the spirit of a particular political or philosophical view. It is direction which constantly renews and refreshes a script to the point where someone who knows it intimately is surprised, delighted or infuriated by new ways of interpreting it. Creatively-directed productions do not fix a text in a theatrical museum case, but allow it to take on tones and hues that may not have been manifest in the late sixteenth century. Modern Shakespeare production owes much to the 1960s work of the Polish writer Jan Kott, whose book *Shakespeare Our Contemporary* emphasised what was relevant today rather than what was relevant when the plays were written. This view is enthusiastically endorsed by Michael Bogdanov in his statement that Shakespeare is 'our greatest living playwright'.

Some great art is great because it is fixed in time and medium – Greek statues, for example. Other art forms are fixed at the time of completion. Great paintings can be cleaned to remove accumulated dirt but they can't be re-painted. Scraping the colour off parts of the Mona Lisa would destroy the original. Music is more adaptable. Great music can be adapted, arranged, played on different instruments, edited and taken at a different tempo. Drama is even more adaptable; it can be appreciated for what it was in its time but it can also be appreciated for the way it is updated. Updating can mean keeping all the words but using modern costume and setting. It can mean editing and substituting the words. It can mean cutting and re-arranging the text. Drama script is capable of infinite modification, adaptation and transformation. Drama script only comes to life when it's performed, so performance allows the option of playing it as it would have been played in Shakespeare's day (the museum approach) or playing it as if it was written for today (the living approach).

Modernising the text is what makes it refreshed each time it is played.

Romeo and Juliet

Baz Luhrmann's *Romeo + Juliet* was a huge success not only because of the idiomatic modernisation such as branding the revolvers as 'Sword' and making the Prologue a TV newsflash, but because of the thematic modernisation, by setting the play in a context of urban drug-fuelled gang-feuds.

Here is the beginning of *Romeo and Juliet* as Shakespeare wrote it. Following it is the filmscript used in filming Baz Lurhmann's film of the play. Compare the two to see how it has been edited, adapted, produced and interpreted by the director, producer and actors.

 The original:
Romeo and Juliet **Act I, Scene I Verona. A public place**

PROLOGUE: Two households, both alike in dignity,
　　　　　In fair Verona, where we lay our scene,
　　　　　From ancient grudge break to new mutiny,
　　　　　Where civil blood makes civil hands unclean.
　　　　　From forth the fatal loins of these two foes
　　　　　A pair of star-cross'd lovers take their life;
　　　　　Whose misadventured piteous overthrows
　　　　　Do with their death bury their parents' strife.

The fearful passage of their death-mark'd love,
And the continuance of their parents' rage,
Which, but their children's end, nought could remove,
Is now the two hours' traffic of our stage;
The which if you with patient ears attend,
What here shall miss our toil shall strive to mend.

Enter SAMPSON and GREGORY, of the house of Capulet, armed with swords and bucklers.

SAMPSON: Gregory, o' my word, we'll not carry coals.

GREGORY: No, for then we should be colliers.

SAMPSON: I mean, an we be in choler, we'll draw.

GREGORY: Ay, while you live, draw your neck out o' the collar.

SAMPSON: I strike quickly, being moved.

GREGORY: But thou art not quickly moved to strike.

SAMPSON: A dog of the house of Montague moves me.

GREGORY: To move is to stir; and to be valiant is to stand: therefore, if thou art moved, thou runn'st away.

SAMPSON: A dog of that house shall move me to stand: I will take the wall of any man or maid of Montague's.

GREGORY: That shows thee a weak slave; for the weakest goes to the wall.

SAMPSON: True; and therefore women, being the weaker vessels, are ever thrust to the wall: therefore I will push Montague's men from the wall, and thrust his maids to the wall.

GREGORY: The quarrel is between our masters and us their men.

SAMPSON: 'Tis all one, I will show myself a tyrant: when I have fought with the men, I will be cruel with the maids, and cut off their heads.

GREGORY: The heads of the maids?

SAMPSON: Ay, the heads of the maids, or their maidenheads; take it in what sense thou wilt.

GREGORY: They must take it in sense that feel it.

SAMPSON: Me they shall feel while I am able to stand: and 'tis known I am a pretty piece of flesh.

GREGORY: 'Tis well thou art not fish; if thou hadst, thou hadst been poor John. Draw thy tool! Here comes two of the house of the Montagues.

SAMPSON: My naked weapon is out: quarrel, I will back thee.

GREGORY: How! turn thy back and run?

SAMPSON: Fear me not.

GREGORY: No, marry; I fear thee!

SAMPSON: Let us take the law of our sides; let them begin.

The adaptation:
Romeo + Juliet, Act 1 Scene 1, screenplay by Baz Lurhmann

EXT. HIGHWAY. AFTERNOON.

A ribbon of freeway stretching into a blue and pink late afternoon sky. A huge dark sedan, windows tinted gold, powers directly for us.
CUT TO: A heavy, low-slung pickup truck travelling toward the sedan.
WIDE SHOT: Sky, freeway, the cars closing.
TIGHT ON: The sedan.
TIGHT ON: The pickup.
Like thunderous, jousting opponents, the cars pass in a deafening cacophony of noise.

INT. TRUCK. AFTERNOON.

TIGHT ON: The fat face of Gregory, yelling at the disappearing sedan.
GREGORY: *A dog of the house of Capulet moves me!*
He and the pimply-faced front seat passenger, Sampson, explode with laughter. The red-haired driver, Benvolio, keeps his eyes on the road.

INT. TV STUDIO. DAY.

An Anchorwoman: behind her the faces of two middle-aged men. The caption reads 'Montague; Capulet. The feud continues.' She speaks to camera.
Anchorwoman: *Two households, both alike in dignity.*
                    (In fair Verona, where we lay our scene)
                    From ancient grudge break to new mutiny,
                    Where civil blood makes civil hands unclean.

EXT. GAS STATION. AFTERNOON.

The truck is in the busy driveway of a large gas station, being filled with gas. The surrounding walls are painted with murals of blue sky and palm trees.

INT. TRUCK. AFTERNOON.

Inside the truck, Gregory and Sampson are boasting outrageously. The driver's seat is empty.
GREGORY: *I will take the wall of any man or maid of Capulets.*

EXT. GAS STATION. AFTERNOON.

SAMPSON: *I will show myself a tyrant: when I have fought with the men, I will be civil*
                    with the maids. I will cut off their heads.
GREGORY: (mock outrage) *The heads of the maids?*
Sampson leers lecherously at a minibus full of Catholic schoolgirls next to them.
SAMPSON: *Ay, the heads of the maids, or their maidenheads. Take it in what*
                    sense thou wilt.
GREGORY: *They must take it in sense that feel it.*
GREGORY and SAMPSON pump up the song on the sound system while gyrating crudely at the girls.
GREGORY & SAMPSON, singing:
                    I am a pretty piece of flesh
                    I am a pretty piece of flesh
                    Me they shall feel while I am able to stand:
                    I am a pretty piece of flesh.

EXT. GAS STATION. MINIMART. AFTERNOON.

The teacher nun from the minibus returns to the vehicle.
GREGORY'S POV: the girls' minibus pulls away revealing... a tough-looking Latino boy, ABRA, leaning against the huge dark sedan.

INT. TRUCK. AFTERNOON.

GREGORY suddenly stops gyrating.
CLOSE ON:
SAMPSON: *Here comes of the House of Capulet.*

EXT. GAS STATION. AFTERNOON.

ABRA stares coldly towards the boys. His goateed sidekick PETRUCHIO takes notice.

INT. TRUCK. AFTERNOON.

CLOSE ON: Gregory; eyes locked to the Capulets. With fake bravado, he pulls back his
                 shirt to reveal a handgun. He nudges SAMPSON.
GREGORY: *Quarrel! I will back thee.*
CUT TO: ABRA. He unfolds his arms to reveal an even more ferocious holstered gun
CLOSE ON: SAMPSON. Trying to quell his rising panic. He nervously unbuttons his shirt to
clear his sidearm.
SAMPSON: *Let us take the law of our sides. Let them begin.*

Prompt students to probe adaptation and interpretation for performance.

a)   What reasons would Lurhmann have for cutting parts out?
b)   How far does his screenplay preserve the letter and the spirit of the original?
c)   How has the medium and the audience shaped the editorial decisions and presentation?

Let's take two other examples that can be used with students, either as an introduction to Shakespeare in performance or the basis for a free-standing scheme of learning with an assessment outcome.

Twelfth Night

In John Siddall's 1981 filmed version of *Twelfth Night* with Sir Alec Guinness as Malvolio and set in a Tudor/Elizabethan context, the directorial interpretation is clear in the cover blurb: 'a delightfully gentle and lyrical romantic comedy'. A later BBC version, with Donald Sinden as Malvolio, was set in an Edwardian context. Both used the gulling scene to maximise ironic humour by showing what happens on both sides of the box-tree concealment device. One used a hedge; the other a Christmas tree. Both offered the play as a comic diversion for post-Christmas delight, with the only sombre note (and that not very sombre) being the tormenting of the caged Malvolio. Both began with unadorned use of Shakespeare's opening where Viola laments her brother's loss in a shipwreck and adopts a male persona to survive in a foreign country. And both versions do the business well.

When Tim Supple directed *Twelfth Night* in 2003 for Channel 4, it was with a wish to use Shakespeare's contrived opening as more than a simple convenience for starting the plot. Supple wanted to put the play in a compelling and relevant modern context, and sought for something in the opening that would explain motivation and add an extra dramatic dimension to the mainly light-hearted plot. Hence the film opens with realistic and frightening scenes of house-burning, panic escape from murderous enemies and stowing away on a ship. This struck chords with an audience painfully and recently familiar with ethnic cleansing, the brutalities of fundamentalist faith and the trade in people-smuggling aboard unseaworthy vessels. The echoes of illegal immigration and asylum-seeking made it all too clear why Viola (played by Leicester-born Parminder Nagra) lamented her brother's apparent loss, and why she decided to disguise herself in order to survive in a foreign country. This aligning of the play with topical issues and events makes the play a more complex production, interweaving the comic and the serious in a way that matches Shakespeare's penchant for that blend. This made-for-TV production substituted CCTV observation of Malvolio rather than concealment behind a box-tree, as a way of modernising the details, but modernising the context and relevance is more than bringing details up to date. In this sense, Supple's *Twelfth Night* is similar to Lurhmann's *Romeo + Juliet*.

Richard III

Any attempt to make interpretation and direction understandable to students is going to make use of the work of a number of major actors, some of them actor-directors – Olivier, Branagh and McKellen, for example. Olivier's 1954 Richard III, placed in a Tudor context, set a standard for the role that made it hard for others to follow. Olivier's mannered vocal delivery and equally mannered limping gait made the character of the bunch-backed toad visually and aurally unforgettable. Perhaps only Antony Sher on the Stratford stage matched and even exceeded Olivier's physical performance by his tarantulan use of crutches. On screen, Olivier's performance is a good starting point as it presents the play in a believably Tudor context, establishing historical credentials and exploiting the dramatic device of the aside in confidential straight-to-camera delivery. It was, as with most of Olivier's work, the drama of personality, intricately, painstakingly researched, practised and performed.

McKellen's 1995 Richard III was also a vivid character presentation with some underplaying of the physical disabilities and a similar use of the lens for asides, but it gave a powerful twist to the play by the directorial choice of context. As a modern dress production it was securely placed within the twentieth century by military uniforms and military technology. This was more than costume: the whole play's political drama was sharpened by making Richard's takeover seem a modern English civil war coup – a toppling of monarchy to impose a fascist rule. All of this is instantly visible and understandable from the first five minutes of the opening, before the credits.

The screen version begins with a realistic scene of a military communications room, with the King and the Prince receiving bad news of Richard's advance. The King goes to bed, and the Prince retreats to his study for a late supper. There follows an extraordinarily intense few minutes of silence, broken by amplified diegetic sounds of the fire's crackle, the dog's bone-chewing and the clink of fork on plate. These tiny details make the audience unusually attentive to sound. Then the dog, with its superior hearing, looks up. The wine glass trembles, the Prince looks up. We hear nothing other than what is happening in the room. The prince returns to his supper, then there is a violent crashing, auditorium-deafening roar as, sensationally, a tank bursts through the wall. What follows is cinematic, theatrical, historical and political, as well as personal. Richard enters wearing a gas-mask, his breathing dominating the soundtrack, again, amplified, as he shoots the Prince and makes his way to the room where the King is praying. As he fires the bullets that end the Plantagenet reign, the screen fills with Red lettering – RICHARD – in a cinematic borrowing from early Bond movie intros.

It's a stunning opening, and it does more than set the character of Richard ruthlessly in pursuit of his ambition: it reminds us, politically, of other twentieth-century coups and, morally, of the phenomenon of the twentieth century hero whose prowess and expertise do not include a moral or spiritual dimension, but whom we dangerously or guiltily admire, like Bond or the various film identities of Clint Eastwood. This crafting of an ambivalent interest in a complex character is authentic to Shakespeare's original and, relocated to a modern historical and political context, sharpens the play's significance for a modern audience.

So, getting students to see the macro-dimension of direction which leads to the micro-direction of language, dress and behaviour, is part of the wider English agenda based on keeping sight of the Whole and the Parts throughout Reading, Speaking and Listening, Writing – and, of course, Thinking.

Using multiple screen versions

For classroom purposes, chosen parts of the play need to be fairly short: watching too long tends to engage students only at the level of story, so there needs to be a focus on the craft of the extracts, linked eventually to the craft of the original writing. The most discriminating judgements will come from a comparison of three or even four versions of the chosen scene, but two versions closely observed will be enough to show a published text transformed into a multi-sensory experience. Some of the plays are available in numerous quality versions. The following section uses two plays to show how they can be used, followed by some pointers to similar work with other plays. The comments are not intended to be a thorough analysis – merely a starting point for teachers and students to do their own observation, comparison and evaluation of how the text has been realised and how they impact on an audience.

Hamlet

The choice is almost too rich – there are so many high-quality productions ideally suited. These are the ones which have never let me down:

1946 starring Laurence Olivier (Dir. Olivier)

1969 starring Nicol Williamson (Dir. Richardson)

1990 starring Mel Gibson (Dir. Zeffirelli)

1996 starring Kenneth Branagh (Dir. Branagh).

There is also a very good BBC version with Derek Jacobi repeating his Old Vic performance as Hamlet – an interesting background to his playing of Claudius in Branagh's production. Jacobi's 1978 Old Vic Hamlet delivered the speech directly to Ophelia, with his back to the audience – a feature not carried forward into the film version.

Any pairing from these will provide excellent classroom material, prompting responses to differences in time, audience and medium. There is ample scope here for some technical Media Studies work, as well as Drama, focusing not only on the different conventions of stage and cinema, but also on the way the moving image medium has developed over half a century.

'TO BE OR NOT TO BE' – *HAMLET* ACT 3 SCENE 1, LINES 56-88

This is a very good stand-alone scene that needs little prior knowledge of the play because most students will have some awareness of it. Much of the interest in it is in the nature of Hamlet's feelings and thoughts revealed in a soliloquy, but the study interest is in the way that the soliloquy has been realised on the screen – it's hard to avoid the effects of director and actor choice. One of the major differences is in playing the scene as a private soliloquy or as an overheard soliloquy. Whilst the first holds psychological interest, the second adds dramatic irony and an extra dimension of Elsinorian deviousness.

| **Olivier** | (4 min 10 sec running time); | **Gibson** | (3 min 45 sec running time); |
| **Williamson** | (2 min 30 sec running time); | **Branagh** | (3 min 5 sec running time) |

a) Editing

All play the full text.

- The Olivier is an early (black and white) version of an Old Vic performance and very substantially cut – there is no Fortinbras to compare with Hamlet and provide an ironic twist at the play's conclusion, for example.
- The Olivier, Williamson and Gibson versions cut Ophelia from the scene, losing the poignancy of Ophelia's dilemma as she is used by Polonius, her father, to entrap Hamlet into talk which can be overheard by himself and Claudius concealed behind the arras.
- The Gibson is made on location for cinema and is cut and glossed for a wider audience
- The Branagh is an unusually uncut text , running the play at four and a half hours, as in the original stage production. Ophelia is present in the background in the Branagh, but in no way a part of the speech.

b) Directing

- In the Olivier version, Olivier directed himself and the result is a very Hamlet-focused performance, with little development of the roles of others. The young Dane, morosely at odds with the moods and mores of Elsinore, renders the speech alone, unheard by Claudius and Polonius.

- In the Williamson version, Hamlet is lying on his bed, thinking aloud in private, engaged in an academic debate, as befitting a scholar from Wittenberg. Claudius and Polonius are not present: the speech is a private soliloquy.

- In the Gibson version, Hamlet is moved to these thoughts by wandering into the family vault and confronting the coffin of his father and his ancestors, reminding the audience of his princely role and obligations, rather than his scholarly Wittenberg interests. Claudius and Polonius are not present. The speech is a private soliloquy.

- In the Branagh version, Hamlet is in a mirrored hall inside a palace. Ophelia can hear what he is saying. Claudius and Polonius hear and see every part of what he says, providing a sharp dramatic irony in this unwittingly public soliloquy.

c) Producing

- In the Olivier version, the scene is set by rushing up a spiral staircase to the top of the castle tower, overlooking a long drop to the waves below – creating a sombre, dizzy context of suicidal intent. An over-explicit soundtrack melodramatically accentuates the pace and urgency, and, as if the lines need explicit orchestral emphasis, breaks in again after 'to sleep' and before 'perchance to dream'. Foaming waves below the rock illustrate the 'sea of troubles', and the camera cuts between Hamlet and the sea below, moving into close-up of Hamlet's torso, face, then forehead before merging swirling waves with an apparent swirl of thoughts inside his head. Some of the speech is done as a voice-over.

- In the Williamson version, most of the speech is delivered in a single shot of Hamlet's head and upper chest, giving a static, meditative quality. There is no visual embellishment of seascape, daggers or tombs.

- In the Gibson version, there is use of light and shadow to contrast the living and the dead, and to illuminate some expressive facial gestures. There is some apt use of descent into the tomb at the start, and ascent at the end of the speech, perhaps over-literally evoking depths and emergence as the spirit of the speech.

- In the Branagh version, Hamlet speaks the lines to a mirror which, unknown to him, is two-way, allowing the concealed Claudius and Polonius to see and hear all. This allows the speech to be shot from both sides of the mirror, so that the audience sees and hears the speech from the point of view of Claudius and Polonius, who want to know if Hamlet is mad or bad, to be ignored or feared, and be alarmed at the reference to a dagger. The device emphasises Hamlet's introspective self-scrutiny, and Claudius' skilful, devious manipulation, protecting the roles he has usurped.

d) Acting

- Olivier makes much of his essential prop, the dagger, throughout. He draws it at 'end them', contemplates it at 'bare bodkin', and drops it after 'makes us rather bear those ills we have than fly to others that we know not of', giving the following line, 'Thus conscience doth make cowards of us all' some explicit pointing.

- Williamson makes no use of props: his meditative delivery is changed half-way through when he shifts from horizontal to vertical, indicating some resolution and decision.

- Branagh, too, makes some play with his dagger: at the moment of pointing it at the mirror the camera switches to Claudius behind it, flinching. There is very little added to the soundtrack, which makes strong use of diegetic (part of the action) sound, as in Hamlet's heels on the hall floor, and the click as the blade touches the mirror.

- Zeffirelli also preferred diegetic sound to added score, exploiting the echo of the tomb location, as the scene also exploits the props of tomb effigies and bones at 'from whose bourn no traveller returns'. Gibson's tone is of anger and disgust as he lists the vicissitudes of so long life, giving more vocal and facial emphasis to doubt, questioning and despair than others in the role

THE GRAVEDIGGER SCENE – ACT 5 SCENE 1, LINES 1-210

This is a very rich scene which needs little prior knowledge of the play. It has scope for character humour, tragedy, irony, verbal wit, let alone reflections upon destiny, morality, mortality and the eccentricities of the English.

Olivier   (4 min 15 sec running time);   **Gibson**   (3 min 40 sec running time);

Williamson   (4 min running time);   **Branagh**   (8 min running time)

a) Editing

- The Olivier, Williamson and Gibson versions cut the second gravedigger. All include the jokes about 'not a man or a woman but one who was a woman, but now she's dead' and Hamlet's madness not being noticeable in England, but there are various cuts and glosses involving the puns based on 'lie'. Olivier's edited text includes 'speak by the card or equivocation will undo us'.

- The Williamson version includes the wider consideration of how Alexander looked in the ground, with the witty verse about great men ending up as draught-excluders.

- Branagh uses an uncut text, so the scene begins with the two gravediggers and talk of legal and religious aspects of suicide and some arcane jokes, as well as speculations about death and commerce, politics and the law.

b) Directing

- In the Olivier version, Hamlet and Horatio approach the gravedigger in a gloomy grave-yard, dressed as gentlemen; this helps to make them superior to the gravedigger, whose disrespectful ripostes are barely tolerated.

- In the Gibson version, Hamlet appears on horseback in informal clothing from a daytime Scottish landscape until he arrives at a roadside burial place.

- In the Williamson version, there is good-humoured laughter and appreciation of the gravedigger's wit to create a light-hearted mood in contrast with the solemnity intro-duced by Yorick's skull.

- In the Branagh version the scene is set at night, illuminated by a lantern. The full text gives Horatio more to do and includes the thoughts about Death as a leveller and Hamlet's thoughts about the gravedigger's insensitivity.

c) Producing

- In the Olivier version, there is clever use of Hamlet's head-shadow over the cast-aside Yorick's skull, suggesting his own mortality.

- In the Gibson version, the landscape includes sea and mountains, providing a healthy contrast to the gloomy business of burial. There is strong diegetic sound of horse-hooves, spadework and gulls.

- In the Williamson version, Hamlet's opening lines are spoken over the singing of the gravedigger, creating a sense of realism. Little use is made of the setting – the scene is constructed from intercut facial shots of speakers with some reactions shots.

- In the Branagh version, a vivid flashback to a merry court scene with young Hamlet as a child on Yorick's back conveys the reality of Yorick's previous life and the affection the young Hamlet had for him. A musical score accompanies the 'Alas poor Yorick' section.

d) Acting

- Olivier's delivery is as sternly staid here as it is elsewhere. He shows no joy in the gravedigger's wit and his use of the skull prop conveys a sense of gloom.

- Williamson's delivery is more richly varied. He enjoys the gravedigger's wit, laughing at his puns. His use of the skull prop generates a contrasting solemnity which culminates in a cheek-by-cheek delivery of 'Get thee to my lady's chamber', indicating some empathy with the skull.

- Gibson's delivery is also more varied than Olivier's. He appreciates the quirkiness of the gravedigger and uses the skull prop interestingly by laying it on a mound, getting down on his front and talking to it, with a close-up of conversational gestures that make it appear a genuine conversation.

- Branagh makes his irritation with the gravedigger and his disgust at the skull clear by voice and facial gesture.
- (It is worth comparing the performance of the gravedigger in each. Possibly the richest gravedigger performance of the four is in the Williamson version, and the weakest in the Gibson version.)

Othello

There are some excellent screen versions well suited to classroom study:

1964 Directed by Olivier – Olivier as Othello, Frank Finlay as Iago.
1981 Directed by Miller, BBC's version – Anthony Hopkins as Othello and Bob Hoskins as Iago.
1990 Directed by Trevor Nunn – Willard White as Othello and Ian McKellen as Iago.
1995 Oliver Parker's film version – Laurence Fishburne as Othello and Kenneth Branagh as Iago.

Any pairing of these screened versions will provide interesting and motivating classroom material. Study can focus on Othello or Iago or Desdemona or Emilia as individuals but there's more scope for students' judgements in studying relationships: the relationships between Othello and Iago, and Othello and Desdemona are obvious choices, but the relationship between Iago and Emilia is also worth study as a sometimes neglected part of the dramatic richness of the play.

(Also worth watching is the 1952 film – directed by Orson Welles with Welles as Othello – and various re-workings such as the Delmer Daves' western *Jubal*, the British jazz movie *All Night Long* and the American *O* set in a US Deep South prep school.)

IAGO SEEDING SUSPICION – ACT 3 SCENE 3, LINES 90-241

This is a scene which can be studied with little prior knowledge of the play. Students will understand that it shows one character working subtly, insidiously, to plant suspicion in another's mind. His method of working – indirection, apparent reluctance to speak, protestations of loyalty – make it an interesting example of duplicity and manipulations. The way Othello reacts to these prompts and hints, and the difference between what he says and what he feels, is good material for exploring implicit cues and what makes men – strong, successful, contented men – vulnerable to doubt, suspicion and jealousy.

a) Editing

All of these play the scene entirely with only very minor cuts or glosses. This makes the performances very suitable for study of details of interpretation and performance.

- **Finlay and Olivier**: two lines cut – two words substituted.
- **Hoskins and Hopkins**: three lines cut.
- **McKellan and White**: cut text.
- **Branagh and Fishburne**: uncut text.

b) Directing

Finlay and Olivier (9 min playing time)

- Taking a cue from references to the 'thicklips' and Brabantio's racist objection to him as a suitor for his daughter, the production made Othello's blackness central to the role, not just as an alien in Venice, but as temperamentally, physically and emotionally, non-European. 'This is the cause' was delivered pointing to his facial skin colour. The assumptions innocently underpinning this portrayal would now be seen as unacceptably stereotyped. Desdemona a cultivated, sedately controlled mature woman. Little to suggest a sexual dynamic.
- This scene set amid tall stone pillars on a very spare, unfurnished set.

Hoskins and Hopkins (9 min 47 sec playing time)

- Miller thought the ethnicity of Othello was a limitation on the play's concern with a universal human dimension of jealousy and wanted to avoid the suggestion that blackness and savage jealousy were necessarily linked. Hence the casting of Hopkins as an urbane, aristocratic Mediterranean – North African/Spanish Moorish, as per the play's title.
- This scene is set indoors, at a desk – Iago busy with paper-work, indicative of civil administration rather than warfare.

McKellen and White (8 min 48 sec playing time)

- The setting is boldly innovative – a nineteenth century American colonial fort with McKellen and others dressed remarkably like post-civil war Union soldiers – including a genuinely black Othello – an apt way of reinforcing the sense of Othello as an unusually accepted outsider in Venice in the original.
- This scene set indoors, both at desk, side by side, jointly dealing with administrative matters but presumably of a military kind.

Branagh and Fishburne (6 min 40 sec playing time)

- Again, Othello played by a genuinely black Fishburne. Othello a confident, macho figure, at ease with martial arts and weaponry. Desdemona cast as younger woman, with evident sexual rapport between the two.
- This scene set in warrior context of single combat practice and weaponry maintenance in the armoury.

c) Producing

Finlay and Olivier

- The film is a record of the stage performance – filmed on a set that appears like a theatre set. Elizabethan costume.

Hoskins and Hopkins

- Miller made much of the ornate and voluptuous interiors, doors and windows to suggest Venetian opulence and the civilised Othello's being at ease in such surroundings. The sets were based on the Renaissance paintings of De La Tour and Tintoretto, and a palace in Urbino. Elizabethan costume.

McKellen and White

- Soundtrack features bugle calls and hymns.

Branagh and Fishburne

- In this version, made for cinema, there is strong use of the flashback insert, not to record events that have actually taken place, but to show the vivid quality of Othello's imagining of Desdemona's sexual encounters with Cassio. Although the audience realises that these scenes are only what Othello imagines, they help to explain and partly to gain sympathy for his outrageous behaviour prompted by such self-torturing thoughts.
- Scene shot over changing locations – 'Perdition catch my soul' delivered to Desdemona on a balcony, after practising close combat with Iago (and beating him). Cuts to locker-room type location as they swill down and towel after exercise. Cuts to armoury, where Othello is oiling and cleaning a pistol, surrounded by weapons. The loaded pistol pointed at Iago is the prompt to make him say what he means.
- Sound track features musical score starting at 'good name' with menacing notes at 'beware the green-eyed monster'.

d) Acting

Finlay and Olivier

- In this version, Finlay's performance is relatively low-key, a kind of heavy-lidded, unblinking cunning based on calm confidence and malice. Presenting himself as a man of substance, not an underling, his voice and gestures were those of a high ranking official, which helped the motivation to revenge when Cassio was appointed over him.

- Olivier's acting, famously, is the result of practising what he took to be the loose-limbed rolling gait of a Negro, with vocal effects created by a thickening of the lips achieved by stuffing cotton wool between his cheeks and teeth. The black make-up allowed him to roll his eyes so the whites were a flashing contrast in moments of anger. Olivier's conscientious attempt to get into the physical and psychic frame of a negro in the Venetian court was disparaged by some as a stereotype, hence the rude description of the production as 'Hello Golly'.

Hoskins and Hopkins

- Hopkins avoided any temptation to play an ethnically 'authentic' role. His Othello is a white, faintly Arabian character, justified by the term Moor which suggests North African/Spanish origins. His Othello is a civilised courtier, socially adept in speech and movement, at ease among the aristocrats of Venice, immaculately dressed in an elegant ruff.

- Bob Hoskins played Iago as a lower-class East End chancer, half in love with the danger of the game, not just motivated by revenge – eloquently captured in his gesture of pinching the flame of a candle to see if he could avoid getting his fingers burnt.

McKellen and White

- Willard White needed no make-up to present himself as the black outsider. There was something of Olivier's wildness of movement in his agonised gestures and tone of voice.

- McKellen was superbly insidious as the man's man, an army man, quick to quip with the soldiery, his pocket full of cigars to pass out in drinking camaraderie. His elaborate gestures, pauses and shifts of glance to indicate reluctance to tell the truth or avoidance of causing offence, and his attention to details of his maps, uniform, brief-case and papers, all amount to one of the most subtly crafted acting performances in the role.

Branagh and Fishburne

- Branagh plays Iago as a deeply sincere brother-in-arms, pained at having to warn Othello and only willing to do so when Othello holds a pistol to him.

- Fishburne maintains a confident resistance to Iago's speech until 'Look to your wife...'

EMILIA AND IAGO – ACT 3 SCENE 3, LINES 289-317

As usual, there is very little explicit stage direction in the printed text, and what there is may not be Shakespeare's own. Whether it is Shakespeare or someone else, we do have a stage direction in this brief scene – 'He takes it' (the handkerchief) which most directors and players assume to mean 'he takes it from her, rather than wait for her to give it to him'. The manner of his taking is a good starting point for comparison.

This short scene where Emilia tries to gain her husband's interest and affection by telling him she has Desdemona's handkerchief is a major part of the plot development but it is also revealing of the relationship between them. It's a very short scene and presents few difficulties to the initial reader. This makes it suitable for use *before* seeing a screened version, so that students can probe and theorise Emilia's motives, and what the scene reveals about the relationship between her and Iago. Students who have already arrived at some conclusion will then be better able to judge the nature and success of the various versions they then watch. Iago's attitude at the beginning of the scene is altogether less than affectionate, referring to having a foolish wife. Earlier in the play Iago claims to have a suspicion that Othello has 'done his office' with Emilia between the sheets and this has warped their relationship and provided a motive for revenge on Othello, but Shakespeare makes little more of this.

Emila's feelings are suggested by her reproach 'Do not chide' – giving students scope to judge how far she is successful in winning a more positive response from Iago. How much she is moved to provide the handkerchief for Iago by duty, or by wanting to please him, or by desperately winning him back, is a matter for actors to explore and students to think about.

a) Editing

All four versions play this scene uncut.

b) Directing

Frank Finlay and Joyce Redman (1 min 47sec playing time)

This production attempted little elaboration of a context through scenery – most of the action occurs in the open space of a tall-columned castle-like building – very much what would have been on stage in the original production. The scene is directed more as a stage in the evolution of the plot than as an exploration of character or relationship.

Bob Hoskins and Rosemary Leach (2 min 36 sec playing time)

Emilia is dressed and presented as a mature lady of the court, her manner more wistful than yearning. It's not directed to engage much audience interest in the role – Hoskins being the main interest.

Ian McKellen and Zoe Wanamaker (Dir. Nunn 1990) (3 min 23 sec playing time)

Emilia is directed and played as an older woman, partly jealous of Desdemona's love for Othello and partly disapproving of her youthful skittishness. This is the most interesting version of Emilia, as the direction puts her and her motives and her feelings more centrally than most.

Branagh and Jacob (2 min 27 sec playing time)

There is more physical rapport between the two in this version – Emilia and Iago being in bed and his pleasure in winning the handkerchief expressed in some rough tumble. The relationship does not convey the agonised loneliness of Emilia: she is more of a realist, taking her cue from her earlier reference to men as stomachs belching women when they are done with them.

c) Producing

Frank Finlay and Joyce Redman

As a recording of a stage production, there's not much to exploit the technology of the camera and the film medium. There is straight-to-camera address for soliloquies, but generally the camera follows the speaker.

Bob Hoskins and Rosemary Leach

The setting is the same as in the earlier scene with Othello – a sumptuous room with a desk covered with documents.

Ian McKellen and Zoe Wanamaker

The camera is often positioned behind Emilia, filming Desdemona over Emilia's shoulder so that we see her as Emilia sees her. Her implied attitude to Desdemona is skilfully created by being mutely in shot, observing the action between Othello and Desdemona.

Branagh and Jacob

The scene ends with Iago's line 'trifles light as air' visually reinforced by a slow-motion shot of the handkerchief descending after Iago has thrown it up.

d) Acting

Frank Finlay and Joyce Redman

Joyce Redman's delivery is impeccably post-war, 'received pronunciation' drama school in enunciation, making Emilia seem a genteel lady of the upper class, though dressed as a retainer. Hints of motive and relationship are in the kiss she gives Iago as he takes the handkerchief, and again after. There is some wistfulness as she ends the speech with 'I nothing but to please his fantasy'. Iago's snatching provokes her agitated expression of concern about Desdemona's feelings about losing it.

Bob Hoskins and Rosemary Leach

Leach's fond smile as she handles the handkerchief and reminisces about Othello and Desdemona suggests no calculated purpose or jealousy. Her facial expression as she says she does not know what Iago will do with it also suggests a motiveless naivety, consistent with the role within the play in this version. Hoskins indicates that the relationship is a cool one, impatiently asking why she is there and muttering the 'foolish wife' line, his attention being more on his desk and papers than on his wife. Her plea against chiding does not seem hurt or angry, though there is an audible sigh. The appearance of the handkerchief prompts a change in Iago – he kisses Emilia and she smiles. There is some teasing – Emilia flutters the handkerchief in front of him, and then with a non-textual 'Ah – Ah – Ah' as she withdraws it well behind her, smiling. There is a mock embrace from Iago and a snatch – but she appears unresentful and goes off happy, thinking that the handkerchief has done some good. This appears to be a consistent part of her naivety – or a missing of some of the poignancy of her role.

Ian McKellen and Zoe Wanamaker

Wanamaker's speech is expressive of her strong feelings – wistful as she touches the handkerchief as she says 'kiss and talk', and wearily hurt at 'Do not chide'. Her emphasis in denying that she stole it displays Emilia's sense of propriety – there is nothing here to suggest otherwise. McKellen kisses her fiercely at the end of the scene, with some potential for passion, but then abruptly dismisses her and lights his pipe, leaving her gesturing hurt and disappointment.

Branagh and Jacob

Branagh's rendering of the 'foolish wife' line is less dismissive than others as he is half asleep – there is a more intimate relationship suggested as Emilia caresses him into wakefulness. Her tone lacks pleading, hurt or reproach.

Conclusion

These notes on *Hamlet* and *Othello* should be enough to exemplify the focus of teaching and learning – and tempt teachers to their own study and observation in these and other plays. Other plays lend themselves well to the approach, and most teachers will have done something similar with the Zeffirelli and Lurhmann versions of *Romeo and Juliet*. Particularly worth study are the many productions and versions of versions of *Macbeth*, as below.

Macbeth – Director Polanski, Finch and Annis 1971; RSC McKellen and Dench Thames TV 1978; RSC Sher and Walter 2001; *Macbeth on the Estate* Director Penny Woolcock BBC 1997; *Shakespeare Re-Told* BBC Malinowski 2005. Try also, if you can get hold of it: *Joe McBeth* 1954.

Other possibilities are: ***Henry V*** – Olivier and Branagh; ***The Taming of the Shrew*** – John Cleese and Richard Burton; ***Henry IV*** – BBC and ESC; ***Much Ado about Nothing***; ***Antony and Cleopatra***.

Useful (if not essential) resources

These are all excellent, providing in various combinations visual materials such as production stills, student activities, texts and notes:

Cambridge School Shakespeare Picture Collection CD-ROMs: *Much Ado About Nothing; The Tempest; Romeo and Juliet; Macbeth; Twelfth Night; As You Like It; The Merchant of Venice*

Oxford School Shakespeare OxBox: *Romeo and Juliet; As You Like It*

Longman School Shakespeare CDROMs: *Much Ado about Nothing; Macbeth; Romeo and Juliet*

BFI Education *Macbeth on Film*

Film Education *Screening Shakespeare* Video & Teacher's Notes, Jill Poppy

Constructing Shakespeare on Screen Ed. Bechervaise, Phoenix

5. Alternative Shakespearience

Hamlet variations

Shakespeare's developing stagecraft: textual variants

Here is the beginning of the opening scene of Hamlet, from the 1603 Quarto text and the later 1605 Quarto.

1603		**1605**	
1.	Stand: who is that?	*(Enter Barnardo and Franciso, two sentinels.)*	
2.	Tis I.	BARNARDO:	Who's there?
1.	O you come most carefully upon your watch.	FRANCISCO:	Nay, answer me: stand, and unfold yourself.
2.	And if you meet Marcellus and Horatio, the partners of my watch, bid them make haste.	BARNARDO:	Long live the king!
		FRANCISCO:	Barnardo?
1.	I will. See who goes there.	BARNARDO:	He.
(Enter Horatio and Marcellus.)		FRANCISCO:	You come most carefully upon your hour.
HORATIO:	Friends to this ground.	BARNARDO:	'Tis now struck twelve; get thee to bed, Francisco.
MARCELLUS:	And liegemen to the Dane. O farewell honest soldier, who hath relieved you?	FRANCISCO:	For this relief much thanks: 'tis bitter cold, And I am sick at heart.
1.	Barnardo hath my place, give you good night.	BARNARDO:	Have you had quiet guard?
MARCELLUS:	Holla, Barnardo. Say is Horatio there?	FRANCISCO:	Not a mouse stirring.
HORATIO:	A piece of him.	BARNARDO:	Well, good night. If you do meet Horatio and Marcellus, The rivals of my watch, bid them make haste.
2.	Welcome Horatio, welcome good Marcellus.	FRANCISCO:	I think I hear them. Stand, ho! Who's there?
MARCELLUS:	What hath this thing appeared again tonight?	*(Enter Horatio and Marcellus.)*	
2.	I have seen nothing.	HORATIO:	Friends to this ground.
MARCELLUS:	Horatio says 'tis but our fantasy And will not let belief take hold of him Touching this dread sight twice seen by us.	MARCELLUS:	And liegemen to the Dane.
		FRANCISCO:	Give you good night.
HORATIO:	Tut. 'Twill not appear.	MARCELLUS:	O, farewell, honest soldier: Who hath relieved you?
		FRANCISCO:	Barnardo has my place. Give you good night. *(Exit.)*
		MARCELLUS:	Holla! Barnardo!
		BARNARDO:	Say, what, is Horatio there?
		HORATIO:	A piece of him.
		BARNARDO:	Welcome, Horatio: welcome, good Marcellus.
		MARCELLUS:	What, has this thing appeared again to-night?
		BARNARDO:	I have seen nothing.
		MARCELLUS:	Horatio says 'tis but our fantasy, And will not let belief take hold of him Touching this dreaded sight, twice seen of us: Therefore I have entreated him along With us to watch the minutes of this night; That if again this apparition come, He may approve our eyes and speak to it.
		HORATIO:	Tush, tush, 'twill not appear.

The first version is probably a faulty one, composed from memory or an early performance. It is known as the Bad Quarto. The second, the Good Quarto, seems derived from a more authentic source. However, it is useful for students to read the 1603 version as an early draft, and the 1605 version as an improvement. Students can then be prompted to test the second version for its more developed stagecraft. Specifically, prompt them to note:

a)   greater interplay between characters on stage

b)   more specific cueing of actors and audience as to setting and mood

c)   effectiveness in suggesting what is to follow.

Here are some prompts which help students to understand the difference between the two versions:

• What is added by Francisco's counter-challenge at line 2?

• How do lines 7, 8 and 9 help set the scene and give the actors more to do?

• Which line of Horatio's suggests more disbelief and dismissal of the reports of a ghost – 'Tut. 'Twill not appear.' or 'Tush, tush. 'Twill not appear.'?

• Why, in both versions, is Horatio, the educated man from Wittenburg university, made to seem so certain that these soldiers are imagining something? (Show students what happens when the ghost does appear.)

More drafting and improvement

Here is one of Shakespeare's most famous scenes – Hamlet's soliloquy from Act 3 Scene 1 – in two versions, again taken from the 1603 Bad Quarto and the 1605 Good Quarto. Again, it helps to consider the first as an early draft and the second as a final version for performance.

Get students to test which one is better for an actor to remember and deliver (because of rhythm and sound cues) and which is better for an audience to grasp ideas and feelings through the imagery of language.

1603

To be, or not to be, ay that's the point,
To Die, to sleepe, is that all? Ay all:
No, to sleepe, to dreame, I marry, there it goes,
For in that dreame of death, when wee awake,
And borne before an Everlasting Judge,
From whence no passenger ever returned,
The undiscovered country, at whose sight
The happy smile, and the accursed damned.
But for this, the joyfull hope of this,
Who'd bear the scornes and flattery of the world,
Scorned by the right rich, the rich cursed of the poor?
The widow being oppressed, the orphan wronged,
The taste of hunger, or a tyrant's reign,
And thousand more calamities besides,
To grunt and sweat under this weary life,
When that he might his full quietus make
With a bare bodkin. Who would this endure
But for a hope of something after death?
Which puzzles the brain, and doth confound the sense,
Which makes us rather bear those evils we have
Than fly to others that we know not of.
Ay that, O this conscience makes cowards of us all.

1605

To be, or not to be – that is the question.
Whether 'tis nobler in the mind to suffer
The slings and arrows of outrageous fortune,
Or to take arms against a sea of troubles,
And, by opposing, end them? To die – to sleep –
No more; and by a sleep to say we end
The heart-ache, and the thousand natural shocks
That flesh is heir to; 'tis a consummation
Devoutly to be wished. To die – to sleep –
To sleep! perchance to dream. Ay, there's the rub;
For in that sleep of death what dreams may come
When we have shuffled off this mortal coil
Must give us pause. There's the respect
That makes calamity of so long life.
For who would bear the whips and scorns of time,
The oppressor's wrong, the proud man's contumely,
The pangs of despised love, the law's delay
The insolence of office, and the spurns
That patient merit of the unworthy takes,
When he himself might his quietus make
With a bare bodkin? Who would fardels bear,
To grunt and sweat under a weary life,
But that the dread of something after death –
The undiscovered country from whose bourn
No traveller returns – puzzles the will,
And makes us rather bear those ills we have
Than fly to others that we know not of?
Thus conscience doth make cowards of us all,
And thus the native hue of resolution
Is sicklied o'er with the pale cast of thought;
And enterprises of great pitch and moment,
With this regard, their currents turn awry,
And lose the name of action.

Textual adaptation: ancient and modern

The famous 'To be' soliloquy is richly packed with imagery which helped the audience of Shakespeare's day to visualise ideas and feelings but this imagery uses references which may not be familiar to a modern audience. For example, a modern audience may not immediately connect with 'slings and arrows' as it does not have daily use of catapults and bows, just as 'whips and scorns' are too technical in reference to instruments of torture. We simply do not have the Elizabethan audience's familiarity with everyday objects like bodkins and the obstacle in bowls known as the rub. As well as unfamiliar references, unfamiliar vocabulary can be an obstacle. Most modern readers need explanations for words like 'fardels', 'bourn', 'contumely', 'quietus' and 'coil'.

This problem of unfamiliar reference and vocabulary has resulted in various attempts to turn Shakespeare's text into more familiar, modern English. Here is an example of the same speech:

HAMLET: To live or not to live. That is the issue. Is it more noble to endure the blows of fickle fortune, or to fight an unwinnable battle against overwhelming odds and be overcome by them?

To die is to sleep: nothing more. And if – by a sleep – we could end the heartaches and the thousand everyday anxieties that humans suffer, it would be an outcome to be cordially welcomed.

To die... to sleep... to sleep and perhaps to dream... Yes, there's the snag! Those dreams that we might have during that sleep of death – after we've cast off the hurly-burly of mortal life – must make us hesitate. That's what makes us tolerate suffering so long

Who would bear the torments of the world we live in – the tyrant's injustice, the arrogant man's rudeness, the pangs of unrequited love, the slow process of the law, the insolence of men in authority and the insults that the humble suffer – when he could settle everything himself with a mere dagger?

Who would be a beast of burden, grunting and sweating with fatigue, if it were not that the dread of something after death – the unexplored country from whose territory no traveller returns – boggles the mind, and makes us choose to bear the troubles that we have rather than fly to others that we know nothing about.

That's why our intelligence makes us all cowards, and why our determination – normally so healthy-looking – takes on a sickly pallor through thinking over-much about precise details. This process causes ventures of the highest importance to go astray and lose their impetus.

(Alan Durband, *Shakespeare Made Easy*, **Nelson Thornes 1987)**

Getting students to compare the original (1605) version and the modern one immediately gets into issues of quality and, more importantly, of suitability for audience and performance. More able students can be engaged with the difference between the literal and the literary conveying of meaning. Students can be prompted to comparison by the following questions.

- How far is the modern version a useful clarifying of meaning?
- How much does it gain and how much does it lose?
- Which is the better crafted for performance by an actor?

Modern compared with modern

Similar issues and others can be discussed by comparing the modern version above with the one below.

HAMLET: The question is: is it better to be alive or dead? Is it nobler to put up with all the nasty things that luck throws your way, or to fight against all those troubles by simply putting an end to them once and for all?

Who would put up with all life's humiliations – the abuse from superiors, the insults of arrogant men, the pangs of unrequited love, the inefficiency of the legal system, the rudeness of people in office, and the mistreatment good people have to take from bad – when you could simply take out your knife and call it quits? Fear of death makes us all cowards.

(Crowther, John, ed. *No Fear Hamlet*. SparkNotes.com. SparkNotes LLC. 2005)

Reduced versions of *Hamlet* for performance

A play as well-known as *Hamlet* may interest an audience because of its comic scenes, its action scenes, its suspense, philosophy or interplay between characters. Playing the whole text as written takes about four and a half hours, so most directors cut the play to fit the more usual three hours of a theatre performance. So, the issue is, what to cut and what to keep. Everyone will have a different idea of what is essential in the play.

Here are two very different reduced versions of the essential *Hamlet*. This first can be performed in only a few minutes. Get students to compare the two versions, finding agreement between the two adapters on what seems essential, and the differences in what they have chosen to keep.

1. A reduced version of the *Hamlet* already edited by Charles Marowitz (published by Marion Boyars publishers Ltd, 1978)

	Act.Scene.Line ref.
HAMLET (*coming off rope*) I did love you once.	III.i.115
OPHELIA (*At left of HAMLET*) Indeed my Lord, you made me believe so.	III.i.116
HAMLET You should not have believed me. For virtue cannot so inoculate our old stock but we shall relish of it.	III.i.117
OPHELIA I have remembrances of yours, That I have longed long to redeliver. I pray you now, receive them.	III.i.93
HAMLET No, I never gave you aught.	III.i. 96
OPHELIA My honour'd Lord, you did, And with them words of so sweet breath compos'd As made the things more rich.	III.i.97
HAMLET (*To Ophelia*) Are you honest?	III.i.103
QUEEN O Hamlet, speak no more; Thou turn'st mine eyes into my very soul, And there I see such black and grained spots As will not leave their tinct.	III.iv.89
HAMLET (*To Ophelia*) Are you fair?	III.i.105

QUEEN
These words like daggers enter in mine ears.   III.iv.96

HAMLET.
Get thee to a nunnery. Why wouldst thou be   III.i.121-122
a breeder of sinners?

GRAVEDIGGER
Cannot you tell that? Every fool can tell that.   V.i.149

OPHELIA
Thou hast cleft my heart in twain.   III.iv.157 (Queen)

POLONIUS
My Lord, the Queen would speak with you, and presently.   III.ii.338

HAMLET
Do you see that cloud that's almost in shape like a camel?   III.ii.339

POLONIUS (*Studying it*)
By the mass, and it's like a camel indeed.   III.ii.340

HAMLET
Methinks it is like a weasel.   III.ii.341

OPHELIA
I was the more deceived.   III.i.118

HAMLET
If thou dost marry, I'll give thee this plague for thy   III.i.131
dowry. Be thou as chaste as ice, as pure as snow ...
(*To QUEEN*)
Go not to my uncle's bed,   III.iv.160
Assume a virtue if you have it not!
(*To OPHELIA*)
Thou shalt not escape calumny.   III.i.132
Get thee to a nunnery. Or if thou wilt needs marry, marry
a fool: for wise men know what monsters you make of
them.

POLONIUS (*Still studying the cloud*)
It *is* back'd like a weasel.   III.ii.342

HAMLET
Or like a whale?   III.ii.343

POLONIUS
Very like a whale.   III.ii.344

HAMLET
(*Facetiously, of POLONIUS*)
O what a noble mind is here o'erthrown.   III.i.144 (Ophelia)
(*The corpses, still stretched out, begin derisive laughter.*)
My thoughts be bloody or be nothing worth.   IV.iv.66
(*Corpses, laughing hysterically, mock HAMLET with jeers,
whistles, stamping and catcalls, till final fade out.*)

The full version of *The Marowitz Hamlet* lasts 90 minutes and was originally staged by the Royal Shakespeare Company, directed by Marowitz and Peter Brooks, before touring in Europe. The production provoked some positive and some negative comments in the press and among audiences. This article gives some flavour of what he was doing and how it was received at the time. Abler students can be prompted to take sides on the basis of the question:

'Is it alright to take liberties with Shakespeare in order to bring him to a wider audience?'

TO BE OR NOT TO BE IN LAKEWOOD? MAROWITZ IS THERE

What has come to be known as 'The Marowitz Hamlet' is Shakespeare's *Hamlet* cut up in little pieces and pasted back together. Speeches appear out of order or are spoken by different characters. The man responsible for this seeming jigsaw is Charles Marowitz who arrived from London the other day to direct his play at the Great Lakes Shakespeare Festival where it will open Aug. 9.

'I always wanted to express the essence of *Hamlet* without telling that tired old story,' Marowitz explained as he recounted the history of his play. Marowitz is a New Yorker who has been involved with the London theater since 1958. That involvement included the Royal Shakespeare Company with English director Peter Brooks.

'In 1965 Brooks and I were working with an experimental group of about 10 people within the Royal Shakespeare Company,' he continued. 'In the course of this Peter suggested I ought to do a Hamlet experiment, which is something I always wanted to do. I pieced it together and it ran about 30 minutes. It was done as part of the Royal Shakespeare Company's Theater of Cruelty season in London.

'At that point I was unhappy with it. It was only a pastiche, a charade of *Hamlet*. I worked on it some more and in its new form, about an hour long, it was done at the Berlin Festival of Experimental Theater. It had an interesting reaction. People booed or screamed or applauded. It was a success or failure depending at what part of the house you looked. The leading critic in Berlin attacked it. A group of students then attacked the critic. He also was reviewing on radio and they demanded equal time. Then it toured Italy, played the Rome Festival and played in Parma and Aquila. I had added 10 minutes more to it by then. After that it went back to London.

'The play is not set. It's always subject to revision. One never gets it right. It's never been done to my satisfaction. It's like taking on the heavyweight champion. You're always losing but sometimes you get a better edge. The advantage of doing something like this in London is that the tradition is so solid that it's possible to get more interest. In the United States extremity in experimental theater is often for its own sake. In England they're more serious and there's a point of reference. The less you know about the play. the more confusing it will be.

'I have some qualms about doing it here. I don't know how well they know 'Hamlet' in Lakewood. I have a theory, however. I don't know that it's true but I think people know 'Hamlet' even without ever having seen it. Most people know it's about a man who couldn't make up his mind.

'I didn't write anything in this version. Every word is Shakespeare's. It's just that they have been completely rearranged and are out of sequence.'

By Tony Mastroianni
Cleveland Press July 28 1972
See http://www.clevelandmemory.org/mastroianni/tm009.shtml

2. *Oor Hamlet* ballad by Adam McNaughtan

This second reduced version is a poem, written to be sung to the tune of 'The Mason's Apron'. The words are by Adam McNaughtan – a Scottish folksinger, songwriter and researcher – who was also a teacher for many years and wrote the first part of *Oor Hamlet* in an attempt to engage his students with the play.

You can listen to the ballad on the Internet in various forms. This site has Adam McNaughtan himself singing: http://www.scotslanguage.com/articles/view/669. A CD is available to buy from Greentrax (http://www.musicscotland.com/).

OOR HAMLET

There was this king sitting in his gairden a' alane,
When his brither in his ear poured a wee tait o' henbane.
Then he stole his brither's crown an' his moaney an' his widow
But the deid king walked an' goat his soan an' said, 'Hey listen, kiddo,
A've been killed an' it's your duty to take revenge oan Claudius,
Kill him quick an' clean an' show the natioan what a fraud he is'
The boay says, 'Right, Ah'll dae it but Ah'll need to play it crafty
So that naeb'dy will suspect me, Ah'll kid oan that I'm a dafty.'

So wi a' excep' Horatio – an' he trusts him as a friend –
Hamlet, that's the boay, kids oan he's round the bend,
An' because he wisnae ready for obligatory killin',
He tried to make the king think he was tuppence aff the shillin'.
Took the mickey oot Polonius, treatit poor Ophelia vile,
Tellt Rosencrantz an' Guildenstern that Denmark was a jile.
Then a troupe o' travellin' actors like the 7.84
Arrived to dae a special wan-night gig in Elsinore.

Hamlet! Hamlet! Loved his mammy!
Hamlet! Hamlet! Acting balmy!
Hamlet! Hamlet! Hesitatin',
Wonders if the ghost's a cheat
An' that is how he's waitin'.

Then Hamlet wrote a scene for the players to enact
While Horatio an' him wad watch to see if Claudius cracked.
The play was ca'ed 'the Moosetrap' – no the wan that's runnin' noo –
An' sure enough the King walked oot afore the scene was through.
So Hamlet's goat the proof that Claudius gi'ed his da the dose,
The only problem being noo that Claudius knows he knows.
So while Hamlet tells his ma that her new husband's no a fit wan
Uncle Claud pits oot a coantract wi' the English king as hit-man.

Then when Hamlet kilt Poloanius, the concealed corpus delecti
Was the King's excuse to send him for an English hempen neck-tie,
Wi' Rosencrantz an' Guildenstern to make sure he goat there,
But Hamlet jumped the boat an' pit the finger straight oan that pair.
Meanwhile Laertes heard his da had been stabbed thru the arras,
He came racing back to Elsinore toute-suite, hotfoot fae Paris,
An' Ophelia wi' her dad kilt by the man she wished to marry –
Afor saying it wi' flooers, she commitit hari-kari.

Hamlet! Hamlet! Nae no messin'!
Hamlet! Hamlet! Learned his lesson!
Hamlet! Hamlet! Yorick's crust
Convinced him that men, good or bad,
At last must come to dust.

Then Laertes loast the place an' was demandin' retribution,
An' the king says, 'Keep the heid an' Ah'll provide you a solution.'
He arranged a sword-fight for the interestit pairties,
Wi' a bluntit sword for Hamlet an' a shairp sword for Laertes.
An' to make things double sure (the old belt-an'-braces line)
He fixed a poisont sword-tip an' a poisont cup o' wine.
The poisont sword goat Hamlet but Laertes went an' muffed it,
'Cause he goat stabbed hissel, an' he confessed afore he snuffed it.

Hamlet's mammy drank the wine an' as her face turnt blue,
Hamlet says, 'Ah quite believe the King's a baddy noo.'
'Incestuous, treacherous, damned Dane,' he said, to be precise,
An' made up for hesitatin' by killin' Claudius twice.
'Cause he stabbed him wi' the sword an' forced the wine atween his lips,
Then he cried, 'The rest is silence!' That was Hamlet hud his chips.
They firet a volley ower him that shook the topmaist rafter,
An' Fortinbras, knee-deep in Danes, lived happy ever after

Hamlet! Hamlet! A' the gory!
Hamlet! Hamlet! End of story!
Hamlet! Hamlet! Ah'm away
If you think this is borin'
Ye should read the bloody play!

Copyright © Adam McNaughtan

Get students to compare these two or other shortened versions (such as Tom Stoppard's *15-minute Hamlet* of 1995), finding agreement between the adapters on what elements of the story seem essential, and differences in what they have chosen to keep.

Graphic Shakespeares

Much Ado About Nothing

After Balthasar's song, knowing Benedick could hear, Don Pedro loudly asked Leonato if his niece, Beatrice, was in love with Benedick. Leonato replied that she doted[1] on Signor Benedick, even though she pretended not to like him.

Benedick could hardly believe his ears. At first he thought it was a trick, but surely Don Pedro and Leonato were too serious and honourable to play tricks.

Then, Don Pedro and Claudio spoke about Beatrice and her 'love' for Benedick. For example, Hero had told Leonato and Claudio how Beatrice sighed and cried for Benedick and even tried to write love letters to him. Hero was afraid that Beatrice would make herself ill, she was so in love. Then they all wondered (loudly) whether Benedick was good enough for her.

Don Pedro, Claudio and Leonato went to dinner, leaving Benedick to think about what he had overheard.

[1]doted on – loved very much

CLAUDIO:	(to Don Pedro and Leonato) He hath ta'en the infection; hold it up.
DON PEDRO:	Hath she made her affection known to Benedick?
LEONATO:	No, and swears she never will; that's her torment.

Extract from: *Much Ado About Nothing – The Graphic Shakespeare Series*, **Evans Brothers Ltd 2005**

The *Graphic Shakespeare Series* (see previous page) produces re-tellings of the plays as stories in simple English, with illustrations attached to samples of playscript.

Does this re-telling simplify the story as well as the language or does it allow a reader easy grasp of the plot and characters?

What is gained and what is lost when stage dialogue is turned into narrative?

Classical Comics produces three versions of a Shakespeare play, all of them with colour graphics. One of them is in modernised English, another is in simplified English and another uses the authentic Shakespeare text.

What are the benefits or disadvantages of each of them? How do they add to the script as usually performed?

Classical Comics modernised 'Plain Text' version (all original versions are in A4 colour):

Extracts from: *Macbeth – Classical Comics*, © Classical Comics Ltd

Classical Comics simplified 'Quick Text' version for quick and easy reading.

Classical Comics 'Original Text' version, uses Shakespeare's own script.

Timber Frame Publications combine original but edited text as well as a modern English translation in their illustrated versions of Shakespeare plays.

Compare this with the original text from *Twelfth Night* and with the edited version in **The Collaborative Shakespearience** (page 72). What is gained? What is lost?

Daylight and champaign discovers not more! This is open... I do not now fool myself, to let imagination jade me, for every reason excites to this, that my lady loves me. She did commend my yellow stockings of late, she did praise my leg being cross-gartered; and in this she manifests herself to my love, and with a kind of injunction drives me to these habits of her liking. I thank my stars, I am happy. I will be strange, stout, in yellow stockings, and cross-gartered, even with the swiftness of putting on... Here is yet a postscript.

It's as clear as daylight. It's obvious... I'm not fooling myself about all this. Everything points to one thing – Lady Olivia's in love with me. Only the other day she said how much she liked my yellow tights, and my crossed-over-garters. She's showing her love to me and is pushing me to act the way she'd like me to. Good luck has made me this happy. I'll be marching proudly around in my yellow tights and crossed-garters in no time at all... Wait a moment – there's more writing.

Malvolio reads the last part of the letter.

Thou canst not choose but know who I am. If thou entertain'st my love, let it appear in thy smiling. Thy smiles become thee well. Therefore in my presence still smile, dear my sweet, I prithee.

You must know who I am. If you accept my love, show it to me by your smiling. You look lovely when you smile. Please smile whenever you come near me.

Jove, I thank thee. I will smile; I will do everything that thou wilt have me.

Thank you God! I will smile. I'll do everything she wants me to do.

Malvolio leaves as Maria arrives.

Why, thou hast put him in such a dream that when the image of it leaves him, he must run mad.

Why, you've sent him into such a dream world that he'll go mad when he comes out of it.

If you will, then, see the fruits of the sport, mark his first approach before my lady. He will come to her in yellow stockings, and 'tis a colour she abhors, and cross-gartered, a fashion she detests; and he will smile upon her which will now be so unsuitable to her disposition, being addicted to a melancholy as she is, that it cannot but turn him into a notable contempt. If you will see it, follow me.

If you want to see the result of all this fun, just watch him the next time he meets Lady Olivia. He'll be wearing yellow tights – and that's a colour she hates. And he'll be wearing crossed-garters – a fashion she hates. On top of that, he'll be smiling at her and she's so sad at the moment she'll really hate him for that too. If you want to see it, follow me.

Extract from *Twelfth Night*, Timber Frame Publications © Timber Frame

Alternative responses to texts

Ever since Shakespeare became known as a playwright in the late sixteenth century, others have had opinions about him and his work.

Here are two contemporaries expressing their sorrow at Shakespeare's death. Both make the point that he was not just a writer who was successful in his own time, but that his works would be relevant beyond his own time.

> Soule of the Age !
> The applause ! delight ! the wonder of our Stage !...
> Thou art a Moniment, without a tombe,
> And art alive still, while thy Booke doth live,
> And we have wits to read, and praise to give.

> **Ben Jonson (from *The Plays of William Shakespeare*, 1765)**

> Those hands, which you so clapt, go now, and wring
> You *Britaines* brave; for done are *Shakespeares* dayes :
> His dayes are done, that made the dainty Playes,
> Which made the Globe of heav'n and earth to ring.
>
> For though his line of life went soone about,
> The life yet of his lines shall never out.

> **Hugh Holland (from The First Folio, 1623)**

The same idea of Shakespeare's appeal to any age, not just his own, was expressed in the foreword to the first collected edition of the plays, seven years after Shakespeare's death.

> Shake-speare, at length thy pious fellowes give
> The world thy Workes : thy Workes, by which, out-live
> Thy Tombe, thy name must when that stone is rent,
> And Time dissolves thy Stratford Moniment,
> Here we alive shall view thee still. This Booke,
> When Brasse and Marble fade, shall make thee looke
> Fresh to all Ages.

> **Leonard Digges's 'To the Memory of the deceased author Master William Shakespeare' (from the First Folio, 1623)**

Perhaps it is natural for these writers, who knew the author, to be so keen to praise the recently departed. In the years that followed, Shakespeare's plays became less popular as new names and new fashions took over in the theatre. In the eighteenth century, Samuel Johnson wrote about Shakespeare's merits by defining what makes some literature greater than others. He also has some criticism.

> Shakespeare is above all writers the poet of nature; the poet that
> holds up to his readers a faithful mirrour of manners and of life.
> His characters are ...the genuine progeny of common humanity, such
> as the world will always supply, and observation will always find.
> His persons act and speak by the influence of those general passions
> and principles by which all minds are agitated. In the writings of other
> poets a character is too often an individual; in those of Shakespeare
> it is commonly a species.

Other dramatists can only gain attention by hyperbolical or aggravated characters, by fabulous and unexampled excellence or depravity. Shakespeare has no heroes; his scenes are occupied only by men, who act and speak as the reader thinks that he should himself have spoken or acted on the same occasion. This therefore is the praise of Shakespeare, that his drama is the mirrour of life.

Shakespeare's plays are not *either* tragedies or comedies, but compositions of good and evil, joy and sorrow; mingled, and expressing the course of the world, in which the loss of one is the gain of another; in which, at the same time, the reveller is hasting to his wine, and the mourner burying his friend. Out of life's chaos of mingled purposes and casualties the ancient poets turned to two modes of imitation, known by the names of tragedy and comedy, but I do not recollect among the Greeks or Romans a single writer who attempted both.

Shakespeare with his excellencies has likewise faults. His main defect is one that may be imputed to most of the evil in books or in men. He is so much more careful to please than to instruct, that he seems to write without any moral purpose. He makes no just distribution of good or evil, nor is always careful to shew in the virtuous a disapprobation of the wicked; he carries his persons indifferently through right and wrong, and at the close dismisses them without further care, and leaves their examples to operate by chance. This fault cannot be excused for it is always a writer's duty to make the world better.

Dr Samuel Johnson (abridged), from *The Plays of William Shakespeare*, 1765

In the nineteenth century there was something of a revival of Shakespeare's plays on the grounds that he had something to say to all ages. But not everyone shared this view. Dr Johnson may have tried to show Shakespeare's strength and weakness, but others took a more one-sided view.

Shakespeare's name, you may depend on it, stands absurdly too high and will go down. He had no invention as to stories, none whatever. He took all his plots from old novels, and threw their stories into a dramatic shape, at as little expense of thought as you or I could turn his plays back again into prose tales.

(Lord Byron)

I have tried lately to read Shakespeare, and found it so intolerably dull that it nauseated me.

(Charles Dickens)

With the single exception of Homer, there is no eminent writer, not even Sir Walter Scott, whom I can despise so entirely as I despise Shakespeare when I measure my mind against his. The intensity of my impatience with him occasionally reaches such a pitch, that it would positively be a relief to me to dig him up and throw stones at him.

(George Bernard Shaw)

Crude, immoral, vulgar and senseless.

(Leo Tolstoy)

This enormous dunghill.

(Voltaire)

Able students can be prompted to weigh up the different attitudes expressed by these writers, and decide where they stand in the debate. All students can be engaged in some debate about the merits or otherwise of Shakespeare by comparing one of the positive views with the following:

The Anti-Shakespeare Society petition

Created by 10B1 English class, published online at www.petitiononline.com)

To: All world education authorities

Ever since the Elizabethans the works of William Shakespeare have been a famous part of English literature and why not? The man has brought us such gory classics as *Macbeth, Hamlet, Richard III* and heck, even *Romeo and Juliet* had a little violence near the end. Despite the mindless killing and gruesome depictions of some of the most famous and important people of the day, Shakespeare's plays are still read frequently in Schools today, in the way they were written. Though most literature is best left unchanged, that is simply not the case with Shakespeare whose primitive language has baffled school children for generations. Now, at the dawn of the 21st century, we must ask ourselves, 'why do we still read texts at school that were written in a language so hard to understand? I mean, come on, the guy and the words used in his plays have been extinct for 100's of years – why can't they modernise this crap and make it understandable?'

That is what we, the Anti-Shakespeare society aim to achieve. A world where if we have to read this prehistoric mumbo jumbo we can read it in words that at least make sense! If you're baffled by Shakespeare's stupid puns, metaphors, similes and what-not, please sign this petition! If you actually like his work (not many, but there are some out there), but you want it to be updated so that the folk of the 21st century can understand it, please sign this petition, too! Remember, we're not trying to kill Shakespeare – He's already dead! So, it's up to us to make the world a happier place by abolishing Shakespeare for good or at least changing it to English! Sign now or forever annoy school children!

Finding your own Shakespearience

What follows is a personal choice of 36 comments, insights and perceptions put by Shakespeare into personally expressive verse or the mouths of characters. The selection could be organised under various sub-headings but I leave it for teachers to decide how best to use the resource. Here are some suggestions that I have found useful in opening up discussion and making students feel that they can agree with Shakespeare, argue with Shakespeare and measure Shakespeare's aptness by reference to their own lives, thoughts and feelings.

For teachers: find what works for you as the essence of Shakespeare by choosing the ten most appealing, apt or useful quotations to express the range, quality or life-enhancing realism of Shakespeare's thought and feeling.

For students: print out and laminate the quotations as separate items. Get students to select and sort to produce either:

- six quotations that seem to show a similar kind of thinking or feeling *or*
- six quotations that show variety and contrast in thinking and feeling.

If students are given both tasks, they can then be prompted to decide whether Shakespeare's merit is in his consistency or in his ability to adopt different points of view. (It sometimes helps to duplicate the 36 quotations twice or even three times to enable a class to share.)

Other things to do with the list of quotations

Shakespeare the wise counsellor

Choose six examples of good practical advice. Write a brief agony letter that could be replied to by one of the quotations.

Shakespeare the cause of argument

Choose three quotations which appear to give good advice and three which seem to offer or imply a contradictory course. Students should debate the merits of the different views or advice.

Save a Shakespeare fragment

Give each student three quotations and advise them they have to save (memorise) three fragments in case all the works of Shakespeare are lost. Most will have one, two or three that they do not want to keep. Students then mingle and swap their quotations until they have three that they do want to keep. (This can be done as 'Desert Island quotations' or 'Room 101'.)

The quotations are listed in no significant order.

INGREDIENTS FOR THE ESSENCE OF SHAKESPEARE

Love is not love
Which alters when it alteration finds.

(Sonnet 42)

The evil that men do lives after them –
the good is oft interred with their bones.

(*Julius Caesar* Act 3, Scene 2)

I am in blood
Stepped in so far, that should I wade no more,
Returning were as tedious as go o'er.

(*Macbeth* Act 3, Scene 4)

Sleep that knits up the ravell'd sleeve of care,
The death of each day's life, sore labour's bath,
Balm of hurt minds, great nature's second course,
Chief nourisher in life's feast...

(*Macbeth* Act 2, Scene 2)

Man, proud man
Dressed in a little brief authority...
Plays such fantastic tricks ...
As makes the angels weep.

(*Measure for Measure* Act 2, Scene 2)

'Tis one thing to be tempted, Escalus,
Another thing to fall.

(*Measure for Measure* Act 2, Scene 1)

The quality of mercy...
is twice blessed
It blesseth him that gives, and him that takes.

(*The Merchant of Venice* **Act 4, Scene 1**)

If all the year were playing holidays,
To sport would be as tedious as to work.

(*Henry IV Part 1* **Act 1, Scene 2**)

Kingdoms are clay – our dungy earth alike feeds beast as man.

(*Antony and Cleopatra* **Act 1, Scene 1**)

The nature of bad news infects the teller.

(*Antony and Cleopatra* **Act 1, Scene 2**)

All the world's a stage,
And all the men and women merely players
They have their exits and their entrances
And one man in his time plays many parts.

(*As You Like It* **Act 2, Scene 7**)

There's no art to find the mind's construction in the face.

(*Macbeth* **Act 1, Scene 4**)

Use every man after his desert and who should 'scape whipping?

(*Hamlet* **Act 2, Scene 2**)

Thus conscience doth make cowards of us all
And thus the native hue of resolution
Is sicklied o'er with the pale cast of thought.

(*Hamlet* **Act 3, Scene 1**)

Imperious Caesar, dead and turned to clay
Might stop a hole to keep the wind away.

(*Hamlet* **Act 5, Scene 1**)

Out of this nettle, Danger, we pluck this flower, Safety.

(*Henry IV Part 1,* **Act 2, Scene 3**)

The fault, dear Brutus, is not in our stars
But in ourselves, that we are underlings.

(*Julius Caesar* **Act 1, Scene 2**)

The worst is not, so long as we can say, 'This is the worst.'

(*King Lear* **Act 4, Scene 1**)

Wisdom and goodness to the vile seem vile.

(*King Lear* **Act 4, Scene 2**)

The labour we delight in physics pain.

(*Macbeth* **Act 2, Scene 3**)

Life's but a walking shadow, a poor player
That struts and frets his hour upon the stage,
And then is heard no more.

(Macbeth Act 5, Scene 5)

It is excellent
To have a giant's strength but is tyrannous
To use it like a giant.

(Measure for Measure Act 2, Scene 2)

They are as sick that surfeit with too much as they that starve with
nothing.

(The Merchant of Venice Act 1, Scene 2)

Love is blind and lovers cannot see
The pretty follies that themselves commit.

(The Merchant of Venice Act 2, Scene 6)

What's in a name? That which we call a rose
By any other name would smell as sweet.

(Romeo and Juliet Act 2, Scene 2)

Roses have thorns, and silver fountains mud.

(Sonnet 35)

For sweetest things turn sourest by their deeds;
Lilies that fester smell far worse than weeds.

(Sonnet 94)

A little fire is quickly trodden out
Which, being suffered, rivers cannot quench.

(Henry VI, Part 3 Act 4, Scene 8)

There is a tide in the affairs of men which,
Taken at the flood, leads on to fortune;
Omitted, all the voyage of their life
Is bound in shallows and in miseries.

(Julius Caesar Act 4 Scene 3)

Nothing emboldens sin so much as mercy.

(Timon of Athens Act 3 Scene 5)

The fool doth think he is wise, but the wise man knows himself to be
a fool.

(As You Like It Act 5 Scene 1)

There was never yet philosopher
That could endure the toothache patiently.

(Much Ado About Nothing Act 5 Scene 1)

How quickly nature falls into revolt
When gold becomes her object!

(*Henry VI, Part 2* **Act 4, Scene 5***)*

If to do were as easy as to know what were good to do, chapels had
been churches, and poor men's cottages princes' palaces.

(*The Merchant of Venice* **Act 1, Scene 2**)

… you, Gods, will give us
Some faults to make us men.

(*Anthony and Cleopatra* **Act 5, Scene 1**)

The RSC Shakespeare

This section of the book has explored alternatives in texts, performances and preferences. The aim has been to provide a range of options from which teachers and students can choose their own way of owning Shakespeare. *The Complete Shakespearience* is based on my own priorities and preferences as expressed in the teachers' manifesto on page 6. An alternative manifesto, similar but from a more illustrious source, is the RSC manifesto, 'Stand Up for Shakespeare'. The complete document is published online:

http://www.rsc.org.uk/standupforshakespeare/content/manifesto_online.aspx

It includes weblinks which give access to some sample teaching materials and other documents of interest to teachers who believe in active and democratic approaches to Shakespeare.

6. Shakespearience for teachers: the wider picture

Shakespeare the man, his mind and his craft

This part of the book aims to do two things: firstly, it aims to give a wider and deeper understanding of Shakespeare's characteristic ways of looking at human behaviour; secondly, it aims to show that the examples of Shakespeare's craft selected for classroom activity earlier are typical of his way of writing across the range of the plays.

The intention is not to burden teachers with exhaustive scholarship but to boost confidence in practical activities by basing them on some more specialist subject knowledge. What is offered here is the eclectic result of casual noticing, determined digging, accidental discovering and, sometimes, imagining and guessing that have emerged from my own experience of Shakespeare on the stage and in the classroom. Starting from my interest in whatever play I was working on, my curiosity has led to further reading which has then increased my own appreciation, insight, understanding and pleasure. I have tried to represent this personal hoard in relatively short, informal sections which can be read as leisurely stand-alone explorations of Shakespeare's thinking and writing. However, the aspects more widely covered here are all ones which have been part of the preceding activities, so there will be close links between the understanding of the wider album and the closer and more practical snapshots in the earlier parts of this book.

The structure of this part of the book is clear and, I hope, simple. In short, this part covers the man, the man's mind and the man's craft – but these three features are inevitably intertwined and I have not striven to separate them too forcefully.

Firstly, the man. I have tried to glean whatever hints and traces I can from the poems about Shakespeare's personality – his feelings, attitudes and character. This is, inevitably, speculative and cannot be the basis of biography – but I think there is more than enough to get us close to the man himself. Others have, unashamedly, constructed more on such little evidence.

Secondly, the man's mind. I have tried to construct something of a profile of Shakespeare's mind – the ideas and assumptions about society and about history.

Thirdly, the man's craft. I have tried to show the characteristic way in which he communicated feelings, attitudes, and ideas (not just his own) in language for a mixed audience and for public performance.

Shakespeare, himself in his poems

Most biographers of Shakespeare begin with the statement that there is very little documentary evidence to work with. This is true, but does not seem to halt the production of new life portraits. Most of these work on possibilities, probabilities and selectively amplified hints, references and implications in the plays. This creative use of thin evidence sometimes attributes to Shakespeare himself views, attitudes and beliefs that he merely created for his characters. To assume that he believed all – or any – of the things that he expressed through his characters is as false and unfair to him as assuming he was jealously moved to murder his innocent wife, give up his state and cares to his three daughters or shuffle off this mortal coil for an ending devoutly to be wished. He understood what motivated men like Othello, Lear and Hamlet without *being* them. That is what makes art, after all – imaginative empathy.

Shakespeare's sonnets probably get as close as possible to the man himself, as there is a consistently personal voice in them. This voice, and the dedication to Mr W.H., the 'onlie begetter' of the poems, has caused much speculation about a dark lady or an aristocratic young man, and the implications of either for Shakespeare's sexuality. This literary persona may be a literary convention, but I'm willing to join others in making what I can from the sonnets. Sexual orientations apart, it is true that the words 'I' and 'me' and 'my' recur time and time again, as the sonnets grapple with feelings of failure, rejection and devotion.

These themes run through the sonnets, making an interesting pattern if we trust the numbering of the sonnets as a chronological sequence. The pattern is of a continuing battle between insecurity and confidence, in respect of three things: mortality, love and writing.

The early sonnets lament the lack of fortune, fame and progress of a young actor struggling to make it in the metropolis:

> Let those who are in favour with their stars
> Of public honour and proud titles boast,
> Whilst I, whom fortune of such triumph bars...

(Sonnet 25)

Whether in honesty about events now lost to us in time, or in self-pitying exaggeration, there is a strong sense of isolation and failure:

> When, in disgrace with fortune and men's eyes,
> I all alone beweep my outcast state,
> And trouble deaf heaven with my bootless cries,
> And look upon myself, and curse my state...

(Sonnet 29)

These early woes relate to Art as well as Life, expressing frustration with his 'pupil pen' (Sonnet 16) and the limited inspiration of his 'slight Muse' (38) – perhaps, as some have suggested, in contrast with the accomplishments of university-educated (g)literati on the London scene, like Jonson and Marlowe. This lack of confidence in his own poetic skill persists with reference to his 'tongue-tied Muse' (85) or his 'truant Muse' (Sonnet 101) and in self-criticism as one lacking the fashionable tricks of the trend-setters on the literary scene:

> Why is my verse so barren of new pride,
> So far from variation or quick change?
> Why with the time do I not glance aside
> To new-found methods and to compounds strange?

(Sonnet 76)

The historian A. L. Rowse famously decided that, not only was the addressee of the love sonnets the Earl of Southampton, but that both Marlowe and Shakespeare were suitors to him, producing in Shakespeare a modest sense of his own inferior talent:

> I think good thoughts, whilst others write good words,
> And, like unlettered clerk, still cry Amen
> To every hymn that able spirit affords,
> In polished form of well-refined pen.

(Sonnet 85)

This feeling that his merit lies in sincerity rather than in artistry re-occurs when, thinking he may die before developing his literary talent, he consoles himself with the thought that he would continue to be read for his simple, genuine feelings, if not for his literary merit:

> But since he died, and poets better prove,
> Theirs for their style I'll read, his for his love.

(Sonnet 32)

Despite these doubts, Shakespeare finds some magical potency in writing. Aware that some readers regard verse as an indulgence of rhetorical flourishes, he relishes its ability to preserve both life and beauty:

> Who will believe my verse in time to come?
> ...
> But were some child of yours alive that time
> You should live twice, in it and in my rhyme.

(Sonnet 17)

He senses, too, the preservation of feeling as well as beauty, in the durability of quillcraft, the knowledge:

> That in black ink my love may still shine bright.

(Sonnet 65)

It is this trust in ink that, eventually, triumphs over modesty and doubts and the fear that life is swiftly passing. Shakespeare begins to see that writing passes to posterity, and that humble ink may outlast even the most lavishly expensive statuary:

> Not marble, nor the gilded monuments
> Of princes shall outlive this powerful rime;
> But you shall shine more bright in these contents
> Than unswept stone, besmeared with sluttish time.

(Sonnet 55)

Occasionally, his confidence in the power of the word is boundless and a source of contempt for the lesser powers of the rich and titled:

> And thou in this shalt find thy monument
> When tyrants' crests and tombs of brass are spent.

(Sonnet 109)

Literally, and literarily, it's the power of writing to outreach mortality and Time that makes it superior to that ornament that is merely visible. He presents poetry as a means to preserve life and beauty beyond the grave:

> You still shall live – such virtue hath my pen –
> Where breath most breathes, even in the mouths of men.

(Sonnet 81)

Shakespeare's genius has found him immortality in print – or, as he, with puts it with characteristic bold modesty: '*Death to me subscribes/Since, spite of him, I'll live in this poor rhyme.*'

He is resolutely unsentimental in accepting the potential futilities of life and art. There is a persistent theme that art is frail, and human indifference strong. He understands the corrosion of '*time's thievish progress*' and understands that poetry, by attempting elevation, brings on itself mistrust or disbelief. This makes the sonnets more than romantic effusions and glorifications. The lenses through which he peers are not rose-tinted.

Throughout the sonnets he steers away from soggy sentiment: there is a mellowed sharpness that takes the breath away in defining life's essentials:

> Love is not love which alters when it alteration finds.
>
> **(Sonnet 116)**

This understanding that Love is not the same as infatuation or lust, and that genuine love is what survives as those we love change and age, makes him both idealistic and realistic, but with the emphasis on the realistic. That's his strength, as a poet and a playwright. It's a strength that affects the way he writes about poetry as well as life and love:

> If I could write the beauty of your eyes
> And in fresh numbers number all your graces
> The age to come would say, 'This poet lies:
> Such heavenly touches ne'er touched earthly faces.'
>
> **(Sonnet 17)**

It's as if he knew that there was something in the English taste, some culture of unlyrical pragmatism, that snagged the wings of the soaring poetic. He not only understood this but gave it voice in occasionally undermining his own poetic pretensions. He could put words to the beautiful, the precious and the sublime, but his richest virtue is in the realism that keeps such idealism in its place. See how he rejects reliable cliché and derides pathetic fallacy:

> Roses have thorns, and silver fountains mud
> Clouds and eclipses stain both moon and sun
> And loathsome canker lives in sweetest bud.
>
> **(Sonnet 35)**

It's as if he could never rid himself of the Warwickshire down-to-earthiness that called 'a coy conceit in numbers sweet' *'nobbut rime'*.

His ability to match the realities of his love's real features against poeticised incantations of worshipped beauty gives warmth and sanity to the verse:

> My mistress' eyes are nothing like the sun;
> Coral is far more red than her lips' red.
>
> **(Sonnet 130)**

The poem goes on to contrast 'damask cheeks' and snowy breasts with the reality of her pale cheeks and dun coloured embonpoint. He contrasts perfume with her reeky breath and pleasing music with her voice. Then, just when you think he's gone too far and risks a decent slapping, he pulls the trick of synthesising sense and sentiment: it's for what *she is* that he loves her and not for some bogus ethereal grace:

> I grant I never saw a goddess go
> My mistress when she walks treads on the ground.
>
> **(ibid)**

There it is: an elegant verse celebrating the un-adorned, the un-extravagant, the un-hyperbolised. Shakespeare's lover, loved for having her feet on the ground. Shakespeare, poet, writing with his feet on ground. And what is his view of poetic traders in idealising verbal whimsy, rhetoric and flannel?

> And yet, by heaven, I think my love as fair
> As any she belied with false compare.
>
> **(ibid)**

It's the feet-on-ground refusal to accept that 'false compare' does any favours that makes Shakespeare greater than the greatness of his art. The Warwickshire lad was never completely seduced by the scholarly and the fanciful. He knew that every silver lining had its cloud. He knew that, at ground level – Warwickshire ground level – truth was likely to be more rough than beautiful:

> Lilies that fester smell far worse than weeds.

(Sonnet 94)

You can prefer lilies to weeds, if you like, but don't be too disappointed when what was once splendid turns, naturally and inevitably, into something else. If the thought bothers you, forget the lilies and live your life in realistic and 'un-disappointable' acceptance of weeds as weeds, whether plants or people.

The qualities that make Shakespeare's theatrical writing so appealing re-appear in other poems, as well as the sonnets. The same sharp summaries of life's vexations and delights, ironies and inevitabilities are there. There's recognition of the fundamental antagonism built into family and other relationships:

> Crabbed age and youth cannot live together
> Youth is full of pleasance, age is full of care.

('The Passionate Pilgrim')

And there's reassuring consolation that Time the Great Destroyer is also bringer of some good:

> Time's glory is to calm contending kings,
> To unmask falsehood and bring truth to light.

('The Rape of Lucrece')

There's more to Shakespeare as a poet than versified sentiment: what he has left us with is a rich vein of feeling qualified by realism, irony; more sense than sensibility, as another, later, writer would have recognised.

Shakespeare on writing and drama

Holding the mirror up to nature (1): the way we live

Shakespeare knew that drama is an imitation of life, reflecting on the page or stage what happens in the palace, the kitchen, the battlefield or the bedroom. In *Hamlet* he defined the 'purpose of playing' as:

> 'to hold, as 'twere, the mirror up to nature: to show virtue her feature,
> scorn her own image, and the very age and body of the time his form
> and pressure.'

(*Hamlet* Act 2, Scene 3)

Throughout the plays, Shakespeare holds his mirror up to show us what we're like – and without the fashion-floor assistant's aim to flatter and disguise. His view of Life on Earth was Attenborough-like in observation of his own species; a mixture of objectivity, respect and ironic humour.

> Man, proud man
> Dressed in a little brief authority
> Plays such tricks as makes the angels weep.

(*Measure for Measure* Act 2, Scene 2)

...you, gods, will give us
Some faults to make us men.

(***Anthony and Cleopatra** Act 5, Scene 1*)

Drink... provoketh the desire but taketh away the performance.

(***Macbeth** Act 2, Scene 1*)

He was a sharp documentarist in the satirical vein, who, unburdened by the post-modernist's fear of being thought to believe in anything, put a moral gloss on what he saw. When he showed Virtue her feature, it was to recommend and approve, but not to lecture or sermonise:

It is excellent
To have a giant's strength but is tyrannous
To use it like a giant.

(***Measure for Measure** Act 2, Scene 2*)

The quality of mercy...is twice blessed
It blesseth him that gives, and him that takes.

(***Merchant of Venice** Act 4, Scene 1*)

He unleashes a withering scorn on those vices or follies which make the species less than glorious and admirable, like the fickle way in which we blame our own bad luck or bad behaviour on anything rather than ourselves:

This is the excellent foppery of the world: that when we are sick in
fortune – often the surfeit of our own behaviour – we make guilty of
our own disasters the sun, the moon and the stars; as if we were
villains by necessity, fools by heavenly compulsion, knaves, thieves
and teachers by spherical predominance, drunkards, liars and
adulterers by an enforced obedience of planetary influence.

(***King Lear** Act 1, Scene 2*)

Virtue! A fig! Tis in ourselves that we are thus or thus. Our bodies are
our gardens, to the which our wills are gardeners.

(***Othello** Act 1, Scene 3*)

Interestingly, though, he also shows that habitual scorn becomes a moral defect, a cynical contempt for what is good:

Wisdom and goodness to the vile seem vile.

(***King Lear** Act 4, Scene 2*)

To read Shakespeare is to feel the pulse of the age; to detect the tremors of history's seismic shifts; to sniff the stench or fragrance of the winds of social change. When he records 'the form and pressure of the very age', he gets to the very spirit of his time and ours, whether it's recording the decline of old workplace protocols,

Tis the curse of the service,
Preferment goes by letter and affection,
Not by the old gradation, where each second
Stood heir to the first.

(***Othello** Act 1, Scene 1*)

or warning about the perils the young are prey to:

> The canker galls the infants of the spring
> Too oft before their buttons be disclosed,
> And in the morn and liquid dew of youth
> Contagious blastments are most imminent.
> Be wary, then: best safety lies in fear.
> Youth to itself rebels, though none else near.

(*Hamlet* Act 1, Scene 3)

To read him is to sometimes see what we prefer not to see. Four hundred years ago it seemed to him that privilege, wealth, rank and status made it possible to outwit or evade what the rest were subject to:

> In the corrupted currents of this world
> Offence's gilded hand may shove by justice,
> And oft 'tis seen the wicked prize itself
> Buys out the law.

(*Hamlet* Act 3, Scene 3)

He may have presented characters who inspire by their fortitude, generosity or virtue, but he was always wryly aware that economics was as potent as morality in the daily workings of the human scene:

> O what a world of ill-favoured faults
> Looks handsome in three hundred pounds a year!

(*The Merry Wives of Windsor* Act 3, Scene 4)

Holding the mirror up to nature (2): how we speak and write

Shakespeare has the remarkable virtue of adapting his writing style for a range of dramatic purposes. He can do elegant sonnets in rhyming couplets to indicate the stylised romantic exchanges of *Romeo and Juliet*; he can do fractured staccato, disrupted rhythms and thought sequences at times of high emotion (*Hamlet*, *Othello* and *Macbeth*, to name but three); and he can do lyrical flights of whimsy as in Mercutio's Queen Mab speech in *Romeo and Juliet*.

Usually, the purpose of such a distinctive stylistic choice is to express a feature of mood and character. Sometimes, though, his stylistic repertoire goes beyond the needs of characterisation. At some moments, there is a glimpse of Shakespeare as the conscious mocker of kinds of speaking, kinds of writing and kinds of theatre. In his parodic vein, we see his artistry at work in ways that show a sense of humour matched with confidence in turning his hand to lesser, as well as to higher, tasks.

Take Fluellen, for example. He is characterised as hot-tempered, passionate, volatile but with a decent heart, loyal and brave. These things emerge from his actions and his speech, but the speech that Shakespeare gives him is riddled with parodies of accent, pronunciation, rhythm and idiom that make him not only a Welshman, but a karaoke Taff.

FLUELLEN: To the mines! tell you the duke, it is not so good
to come to the mines; for, look you, the mines is
not according to the disciplines of the war: the
concavities of it is not sufficient; for, look you,
the athversary, you may discuss unto the duke, look
you, is digt himself four yard under the
countermines: by Cheshu, I think a' will plough up
all, if there is not better directions.

(*Henry V* Act 4, Scene 7)

The 'look you's, the emphatic repetitions and confusion of singulars and plurals are part of the stock features of the stage (or joke) Welshman, but the pronunciation of the 'd' in 'adversary' as though it were the 'dd' sound (th) in Welsh shows a keener sensitivity to phonetics and phonology. The same play (*Henry V*) has similar representations of a Scot and an Irishman, showing some relish for parodying Celtic fringers. The parody screws some laboured humour from the difficulties of getting English pronunciation and grammar right:

FLUELLEN: What call you the town's name where Alexander the Pig was born?

GOWER: Alexander the Great.

FLUELLEN: Why, I pray you, is not pig great? the pig, or the great, or the mighty, or the huge, or the magnanimous, are all one reckonings, save the phrase is a little variations.

(*Henry V* Act 4, Scene 7)

In a more sophisticated and literary vein, Shakespeare provides a witty parody of the conceits and flourishes of the educated theatrical critic when he has Hamlet introduce the players, and recalls the comments of those appointing themselves as judges of literary merit:

HAMLET: I heard thee speak me a speech once, but it was never acted; or, if it was, not above once; for the play, I remember, pleased not the million; 'twas caviare to the general: but it was – as I received it, and others, whose judgments in such matters cried in the top of mine – an excellent play, well digested in the scenes, set down with as much modesty as cunning. I remember, one said there were no sallets in the lines to make the matter savory, nor no matter in the phrase that might indict the author of affectation; but called it an honest method, as wholesome as sweet, and by very much more handsome than fine.

(*Hamlet* Act 2, Scene 2)

Following this, Shakespeare pulls off a literary double whammy as he reproduces the sort of rhetorical, melodramatic and over-alliterative bombast available at a theatre near you (and possibly one putting on a Marlowe):

HAMLET: 'The rugged Pyrrhus, he whose sable arms,
Black as his purpose, did the night resemble
When he lay couched in the ominous horse,
Hath now this dread and black complexion smear'd
With heraldry more dismal; head to foot
Now is he total gules; horridly trick'd
With blood of fathers, mothers, daughters, sons,
Baked and impasted with the parching streets,
That lend a tyrannous and damned light
To their lord's murder: roasted in wrath and fire,
And thus o'er-sized with coagulate gore,
With eyes like carbuncles, the hellish Pyrrhus
Old grandsire Priam seeks.'

(*Hamlet* Act 2, Scene 2)

The easiest sort of parody is of the ignorant but aspiring, and examples of Shakespeare having fun with the struggles of the unlearned when tangling with language are to be found in Mistress Quickly and Dogberry. Even better is the combination of the same kind of language mangling combined with duff am-dram acting, a subject that must have caused him some annoyance in his time. The mechanicals' rehearsal in *A Midsummer Night's Dream* is a classic of the kind, as lines are delivered with no regard for punctuation for meaning or breath:

PROLOGUE: If we offend, it is with our good will.
                      That you should think, we come not to offend,
                      But with good will. To show our simple skill,
                      That is the true beginning of our end.
                      Consider then we come but in despite.
                      We do not come as minding to contest you,
                      Our true intent is. All for your delight
                      We are not here. That you should here repent you,
                      The actors are at hand and by their show
                      You shall know all that you are like to know.

(A Midsummer Night's Dream Act 5, Scene 1)

You see the same joy in knocking and mocking those at the bottom of the theatrical tree in his parody of over-done dramatic scripting and performance:

PYRAMUS: O grim-look'd night! O night with hue so black!
                     O night, which ever art when day is not!
                     O night, O night! alack, alack, alack,
                     I fear my Thisby's promise is forgot!
                     And thou, O wall, O sweet, O lovely wall,
                     That stand'st between her father's ground and mine!

(A Midsummer Night's Dream Act 5, Scene 1)

See also Hotspur's speech as a soldierly parody of unmanly behaviour, in 'The close Shakespearience' page 34.

The easiest parody is of romantic verse, but Shakespeare doesn't do what's easiest – he parodies both the bluntly unsentimental and the naffly clichéd sentimental vein in verse in Falstaff's amorous endeavours. In *The Merry Wives of Windsor* Mistress Page reads his love letter:

> 'You are not young, no more am I; go to then, there's sympathy: you are
> merry, so am I; ha, ha! then there's more sympathy: you love sack, and so do
> I; would you desire better sympathy? Let it suffice thee, Mistress Page, – at
> the least, if the love of soldier can suffice – that I love thee. I will not say, pity
> me; 'tis not a soldier-like phrase: but I say, love me. By me,
> Thine own true knight,
> By day or night,
> Or any kind of light,
> With all his might
> For thee to fight,
>   John Falstaff'

(The Merry Wives of Windsor Act 2, Scene 1)

Shakespeare the thinker

1. History

The word 'history' occurs 22 times in Shakespeare's works, always as a synonym for story, life-record or series of events, as in 'the history of all her secret thoughts', 'there is a history in all men's lives'; or even, as a verb, 'to repeat and history his loss'. It is never used as an abstract noun related to a process or an academic area of study. History, after all, did not exist as a discipline until long after Shakespeare. For him, history was a story warehouse to be plundered for plots and characters. Accuracy was not the point: factual record alone did not fill a theatre.

Although Plutarch, the source for the Roman plays, had Antony lose the battle of Actium because fickle Cleopatra turned tail and he followed her, this did not suit Shakespeare's interest in Antony as a dramatic character. His Antony chooses, mistakenly and against the advice of supporters, to take on superior naval forces with press-ganged men and un-seaworthy ships, out of provoked, macho, unwise wilfulness – 'because that he dares me to't'. It's the typicality of behaviour that the dramatist mirrors – and that the audience recognises. Shakespeare was looking for characters and events to re-animate on stage, to illustrate arche-typal human emotions at work – ambition, love or jealousy, for example. That's the stuff of popular entertainment. But there are places in the plays where Shakespeare's grasp of history as more than story can be seen.

When Hemings and Cundell published the *Complete Works* in the First Folio of 1623, seven years after Shakespeare's death, they listed the plays under headings of Tragedy, Comedy and History. The History plays, thus grouped, present a nation's rites of passage, illustrating the travails and turmoils by which England became the politically mature world power of Shakespeare's day. They seem, collectively, to dramatise the growth of a nation, so that the true subject of the Histories was England itself.

Shakespeare's grasp of history as a process of social and political change can be seen in the relationships between Kings and subjects – the way kingship can no longer be confident of the automatic obeisance and trust of earlier regimes. In *Henry V*, for example, England goes to war with France, the justice of the cause avowed by senior counsellors. Shakespeare writes a scene before the battle of Agincourt (*Henry V* Act 4, Scene 1) in which the King passes, cloaked and incognito, among his soldiers to sound out their morale. Privates Williams and Bates express their view of their King untouched by worry about his subjects and soldiers, so he reassures them:

HENRY: I think the king is but a man, as I am: the violet smells to him as it doth to me: ... all his senses have but human conditions: his ceremonies laid by, in his nakedness he appears but a man; and though his affections are higher mounted than ours, yet, when they stoop, they stoop with the like wing.

Bates, not impressed by this, declares his view of a better ending to the war:

BATES: Then I would he were here alone; so should he be sure to be ransomed, and a many poor men's lives saved.

Henry, resisting temptation to treat this unheroic attitude as treasonable, as he certainly could, appeals to the justice of the cause rather than to the unquestioning loyalty owed by a subject to his king:

HENRY: Methinks I could not die any where so contented as in the king's company; his cause being just and his quarrel honourable.

Williams does not accept this 'just and honourable' argument:

WILLIAMS: That's more than we know.

He states the responsibilities of the King for injury and death caused to his people if his 'just and honourable' judgement proves baseless:

WILLIAMS: But if the cause be not good, the king himself hath a heavy reckoning to make, when all those legs and arms and heads, chopped off in battle, shall join together at the latter day and cry all 'We died at such a place;' some swearing, some crying for a surgeon, some upon their wives left poor behind them, some upon the debts they owe, some upon their children rawly left.

Momentarily, Henry reacts to Bates' and Williams' insubordinate views by playing the 'unaccountable to inferiors' card:

HENRY: ...the king is not bound to answer the particular endings of his soldiers, the father of his son, nor the master of his servant;

Shakespeare's Henry at this point is interesting as characterisation but, more significantly, is a dramatising of a historical process. Here is a late mediaeval king, speaking (ostensibly) as an equal with his subjects, aware that the old loyalties are no longer automatically enough, reaching for another, moral, authority for support. Shakespeare was writing at a time of crumbling routine obeisance, when Parliament was flexing its muscle and obstinate persistence in the old beliefs in kingship and authority was a recipe for conflict. It was only 13 years after Shakespeare's death that Charles 1st persisted in the old model of kingship, resulting in his trial for treason and execution in 1649.

Shakespeare shows Henry aware that there is more to New Nation thinking than this. Throughout his life he saw both Church and State lose moral authority and be as fallible as anything of mortal making, and he saw the people develop a voice of their own. Spiritually or politically, their sense of independence had to be recognised, as Henry recognises it in a new grasp of citizenship and private conscience:

HENRY: Every subject's duty is the king's; but every subject's soul is his own.

The scene highlights a shift in popular sentiment, social obligation and respect for authority, as well as the fraughtness of leading people where they do not want to go. It's an apt insight into a nation and its history when applied to recent events. In Henry's tone we can hear Tony Blair seeking to carry the people with him in pursuit of a war that may not seem worth the suffering of so many of his vocal citizen soldiers and their parents.

2. Politics

Some things change over time, and some things don't. Look at the scripts earlier in this book featuring relationships between men and women and it would take a good few hours to decide that things have changed, and then to decide that they haven't. It's uncannily the same with politics. Whether he is recording the factional strife of the English Wars of the Roses, or the big moments of Roman history, or the heroics and anti-heroics of the Trojan War, he had the knack of nailing the essentials that still seem with us today. Before blogs and biogs and morning chat-shows and marginal constituency walkabouts and sound-bites, he saw the way the artfully-ambitious use mock-humility to win the hearts and minds of those they aim to rule and how, when successful, they detach themselves from such common contacts:

BRUTUS: But 'tis a common proof
             That lowliness is young ambition's ladder,
             Whereto the climber-upward turns his face;
             But when he once attains the upmost round,
             He then unto the ladder turns his back,
             Looks in the clouds, scorning the base degrees
             By which he did ascend.

(*Julius Caesar* **Act 2, Scene 1**)

Shakespeare, with contacts in theatre and court, saw the actor's craft in both. He understood the politician's ability to put on an act in dealing with those they privately despise:

RICHARD: [We] Observed his courtship to the common people,
             How he did seem to dive into their hearts
             With humble and familiar courtesy;
             What reverence he did throw away on slaves,
             Wooing poor craftsmen with the craft of smiles...
             Off goes his bonnet to an oyster-wench;
             A brace of draymen bid God speed him well,
             And had the tribute of his supple knee...

(*Richard II* **Act 1, Scene 4**)

It's not that Shakespeare revered the role of the citizenry in a participatory democracy. Generally, he portrays 'the people' as ignorant, selfish and fickle, as when manipulated by Mark Antony's funeral oration in *Julius Caesar*. He seems to have been equally sceptical and contemptuous of both rulers and ruled – the one for applied stupidity and the other for misapplied intelligence. This sense of the frailty of mass judgement and the cunning of rulers is astutely portrayed as Claudius gets some spin into a news release of Hamlet's banishment:

CLAUDIUS: He's loved of the distracted multitude,
           Who like not in their judgement but in their eyes,
           And where 'tis so, th' offender's scourge is weighed
           But never the offence. To bear all smooth and even,
           This sudden sending him away must seem
           Deliberate pause.

(*Hamlet* Act 4, Scene 3)

For the sharpest insight into the processes of democracy, it's hard to beat *Coriolanus*. The eponymous hero, fresh from success in battle, now seeks office as Consul, only to be told by the politician Menenius that he has to win approval from the very people he regards as contemptible, and who already owe him for saving them from the enemy. Initially, he cannot bring himself to seek their goodwill;

CORIOLANUS: What must I say?
           'I Pray, sir' – Plague upon't! I cannot bring
           My tongue to such a pace: – 'Look, sir, my wounds!
           I got them in my country's service, when
           Some certain of your brethren roar'd and ran
           From the noise of our own drums.'

(*Coriolanus* Act 2, Scene 3)

Menenius, appalled at this naïve view that honest speaking matters, counsels a more 'wholesome manner'. Coriolanus, then, finding to his surprise that the citizens value flattery and don't detect insincerity, begins to grasp the art of electioneering:

CORIOLANUS: I will, sir, flatter my
           sworn brother, the people, to earn a dearer
           estimation of them... I will practise
           the insinuating nod and be off to them most
           counterfeitly.

(ibid)

Politics is about the institutional protocols and hierarchical structures of the work-place and the community. In *Antony and Cleopatra*, two of Antony's supporters have just won a battle. The younger, Silius, urges Ventidius to press on and destroy the retreating foe, thinking their absent leader would 'set thee on triumphant chariots and put garlands on thy head'. Ventidius, better and more realistically versed in the complex mingling of the public and the personal, the ideal and the real, counsels otherwise. He cites the error of one Sossius who hadn't seen where appreciation of effort gives way to jealous mistrust of another's success:

VENTIDIUS: Learn this, Silius;
           Better to leave undone, than by our deed
           Acquire too high a fame when him we serve's away.
           Sossius, one of my place in Syria, his lieutenant,
           For quick accumulation of renown,
           Which he achieved by the minute, lost his favour.
           Who does i' the wars more than his captain can
           Becomes his captain's captain: and ambition,
           The soldier's virtue, rather makes choice of loss,
           Than gain which darkens him.

(*Antony and Cleopatra* Act 3, Scene 1)

There's a whole Citizenship curriculum here for the youth of the 21st century, though I'm not sure that our political masters would approve.

3. The world without and the world within

A dramatist looking for material to turn into stage spectacular will plunder previous literature and history for tales of nobility, treachery, fortitude and passion. Shakespeare found in English, Greek and Roman history a rich source of characters and events suitable for embellishment in comic, tragic or moralistic vein. Rome, Egypt and Troy provided exotic contexts for the grand play of those passions which stirred in humbler folk in Warwickshire and Cheapside. Your South Bank punter expected some imperial strut and the clash of epic swords in the two hours traffic of the wooden O. He gave the punters the pomp and strut but insistently, he also reminded them that great men and women have the same needs, fears, flaws and dreams as lesser men and women. He portrays 'the world without' not as historians and politicians may wish to see it, exposing the intimate, fallible, characteristically human follies, foibles and ficklenesses that we all share, but some deny.

What's remarkable and delightful about Shakespeare's use of historical sources is his warm and witty embellishment of his source. Free of any laws of copyright, he happily ripped off Plutarch for the details of Cleopatra's Cydnus entry on her ceremonial barge with cloth of gold and crew-boys tarted up like cherubs, upstaging the great Antony who had come to visit this minor queendom:

> 'She was laid under a pavilion of cloth of gold of tissue, apparelled
> and attired like the goddess Venus commonly drawn in picture; and
> hard by her, on either hand, pretty fairboys apparelled as painters do
> set forth god Cupid, with little fans in their hands, with the which they
> fanned wind upon her.'

(Plutarch)

ENOBARBUS: She did lie
               In her pavilion – cloth of gold of tissue –
               O'er-picturing that Venus where we see
               The fancy outwork nature: on either side her
               Stood pretty dimpled boys, like smiling Cupids,
               With divers colour'd fans, whose wind did seem
               To glow the delicate cheeks which they did cool,
               And what they undid did.

(Antony and Cleopatra **Act 2, Scene 2)**

Shakespeare's version is improved, partly by metaphorical extension and partly by rhythm and alliterative emphasis, but this is a matter of text re-working. What's more revealing is the nature of Shakespeare's addition. Plutarch confines himself to the historian's record of fact:

> Antony was left post-alone in the market-place in his imperial seat to
> give audience.

Shakespeare's inspired, witty, humanly realistic addition was that:

ENOBARBUS: Antony,
               Enthroned in the market-place, did sit alone
               Whistling to the air.

(Antony and Cleopatra **Act 2, Scene 2)**

Whistling! To the air! A world-conquering triumvir; a revered pillar of the universe; a military leader who, on campaign, has drunk the stale of horses and eaten the bark of trees, *whistling* through his teeth, on his own, on a throne, in an emptied market-place! It's the humanising of history that makes this so appealing, the hint of the domestic in the panoply of grandeur.

Julius Caesar, larger than life in his own and others' Histories, emblem of great Roman might and reach, was an obvious choice to put on stage though not, with Shakespeare, for long. Act 3, scene 1 and he's gone. So much for the Gallic wars, thrashing the Germans and the conquest of Britain. The lasting impression of the military demi-god is of the husband who agrees to send a sickie to the Senate when his wife urges him to stay at home that day. First he agrees to do what she says with the brash bravado of one who doesn't need to tell a lie,

CAESAR: Have I in conquest stretch'd mine arm so far
          To be afear'd to tell greybeards the truth?

(*Julius Caesar* Act 2, Scene 2)

and then he changes his mind for fear of being thought too much under the wifely thumb,

CAESAR How foolish do your fears seem now, Calphurnia!
          I am ashamed I did yield to them.

(ibid)

Shakespeare relishes the exposure of the domestic realities in the lives of those who bestride the planet. In *Julius Caesar* he takes his audience behind the scenes to see both protagonists, heroically grappling with destiny and conscience, having to deal with the anxieties and feelings of their wives. The dramatist makes us know that Portia and Calphurnia, Imperial Rome's players' wives, were active parts of what is History.

The insistence on the mundane truths of domestic life is there in moments of high tragic tension. Macbeth, whom a lesser dramatist may portray exclusively as the butcher partner of a fiend-like queen, gets into a fluster before the murder of Duncan and this noble thane. This famous ripper of foes from the navel to the chaps has to be told what's what by 'her indoors', down to smearing the faces of the grooms with blood and, later, getting a grip on himself when guests turn up for the dinner party.

Where others have laboured to turn the human into more than it is, Shakespeare's merit is in humanising the epic and historic. There is an art to mythologising, and many writers have excelled in ornamenting myths and making them plausible. Shakespeare goes further: his is the greater art of de-mythologising, and without any loss of plausibility.

In *Troilus and Cressida*, Homer's epic Greeks, those giants of the Trojan War, strut their stuff in pride and honour, seeking and preserving name and reputation, yet Shakespeare has Ajax taunted by Thersites as one,

    whose horse will sooner con an oration than thou learn a prayer without a book.
(*Troilus and Cressida* Act 2, Scene 1)

As for Achilles, his exit from Act 3, Scene 3 is followed by Thersites' remark that:

    I had rather be a tick in a sheep than such a valiant ignorance.

Even when, in approving vein, Shakespeare comes close to hagiography in *Henry V*, where his idealised English king is pious, brave and astute throughout, there is the reminder of the domestic in his stumbling over French and wooing in the (prose) scene with Katharine:

HENRY: Je quand sur le possession de France, et quand vous avez le possession de
            moi – let me see, what then? St Denis be my speed! – donc votre est France,
            et vouse etes mienne. It is as easy for me, Kate, to conquer the kingdom as
            to speak so much more French: I shall never move thee in French, unless it
            be to laugh at me.

(*Henry V* Act 5, Scene 2)

In lighter vein, it's clear that Shakespeare sees the domestic spats that mark the course of marriage as at least as interesting as moments of passion and tenderness. He thought those best left to the young and reckless, like Romeo and Juliet or Ferdinand and Miranda. The mature relationships of those who share a bed and dinner table are more realistically rendered. If domestic life is a matter of give and take, and putting up with foibles, fads and follies, there's scope for stage performance. And it's not just the mortals we're talking about here. In *A Midsummer Night's Dream*, even the immortals, Oberon and Titania, share the mortals' susceptibility to jealousy and acts of petty spite. It's a comic mingling of the light fantastic and the light domestic.

Shakespeare's imagery: using what his audience knew

Some devotees of Shakespeare see his greatest merit in his comprehensive insight. He's very good on both the humdrum practicalities of daily life and on what is the exceptional and profound in the human condition. His gift is for making links between the minor, the parochial and the personal, and the major, the universal and the public.

As Warwickshire born-and-bred, it's not surprising that Shakespeare's plays and poems are full of references to agriculture and wildlife. He constantly reworked his country knowledge in the search for imagery and ideas. For example, he knew about birds and found bird behaviour interesting. He could identify common garden birds:

BOTTOM: The ousel-cock*, so black of hue
                    With orange-tawny bill
                    The throstle** with his note so true,
                    The wren with little quill.

                    (*male blackbird **thrush)

(*A Midsummer Night's Dream* **Act 3, Scene 1**)

He also knew something of their behaviour, whether they were nocturnal songsters or not,

ROMEO: It was the nightingale, and not the lark,
                    That pierced the fearful hollow of thine ear
                    Nightly she sings on yon pomeganate tree.

(*Romeo and Juliet* **Act 3, Scene 5**)

or whether a raptor's diet was fillet or whole,

            Even as an empty eagle, sharp by fast,
            Tires with her beak on feathers, flesh and bone,
            Shaking her wings, devouring all in haste,
            Till either gorge be stuff'd or prey be gone;

(**'Venus and Adonis'**)

When he wrote Duncan's praise for Macbeth's 'pleasant seat', he made it authentic by referring to the 'temple-haunting martlets', referring to the nesting habits of the house-martin, which favours stone-built underledges from which to launch itself in search of its diet of flies.

These general observations of avian life were part of the same ability to notice appearance and behaviour in the human species. Perhaps the most interesting thing here is Shakespeare's sense that we are not so different from the animals. When he describes Beatrice's furtive scuttle along the hedge to overhear the conversation of her friends, his knowledge of the lapwing's gait is doubly apt:

HERO: Look where Beatrice, like a lapwing runs
                Close by the ground.

(*Much Ado About Nothing* **Act 3, Scene 1**)

He also knew that lapwings are precocious creatures, not needing as long in the nest as most to start their reed-bed explorations:

HERATIO: This lapwing (Osric) runs away with the shell on his head.

(*Hamlet* **Act 5, Scene 2**)

He also knew how a brooding lapwing may divert attention from the nest by making a kerfuffle some distance from it:

ADRIANA: Far from her nest the lapwing cries away

(*A Comedy of Errors* **Act 4, Scene 2**)

Hawking was a popular sport in Shakespeare's day, and its terms of training would have been familiar to a wide audience. It provided some apt comparison between human relationships and relationships between hawks and hawkers. Othello's agonised view of Desdemona being restrained or freed says much about his view of marital accord, but also about Shakespeare's confidence that his audience would understand what he meant by the hawking references:

OTHELLO: If I do prove her haggard,
           Though that her jesses were my dear heartstrings,
           I'ld whistle her off and let her down the wind,
           To pray at fortune.

(*Othello* **Act 3, Scene 3**)

In *The Taming of the Shrew*, the idea is expanded as Petruchio plans to make his wife submissive by methods familiar to the falconer, the pun on 'stoop' being crucial:

PETRUCHIO: My falcon now is sharp and passing empty;
             And till she stoop she must not be full-gorged,
             For then she never looks upon her lure.

(*The Taming of the Shrew* **Act 4, Scene 1**)

It wasn't just that Shakespeare saw falconry as a metaphor for patriarchal attitudes in the home. He saw it as a metaphor for much that was deeply human. On the nature of appetite, for example:

    Look, as the full-fed hound or gorged hawk,
    Unapt for tender smell or speedy flight,
    Make slow pursuit, or altogether balk
    The prey wherein by nature they delight;

(**'The Rape of Lucrece'**)

It's not surprising that he found in beak and claw a potent parallel for human affairs. The cunning dispossession of a family from within could have no sharper reference than to the habits of the Easter caller:

EARL OF WORCESTER: And being fed by us you used us so
                     As that ungentle hull, the cuckoo's bird,
                     Useth the sparrow; did oppress our nest;
                     Grew by our feeding to so great a bulk
                     That even our love durst not come near your sight
                     For fear of swallowing;

(*Henry IV, Part One* **Act 5, Scene 1**)

Bird behaviour, clearly, was a useful source of simile and metaphor for a poet and playwright. Notions of fierce family defence against the odds were conveniently summarised by reference to feathered life:

LADY OF MACDUFF: For the poor wren
                    The most diminutive of birds, will fight –
                    Her young ones in the nest – against the owl.

(*Macbeth*, Act 4, Scene 2)

Notions of rank, dignity, power and lofty sufferance of the inferior are aptly conveyed in avian terms:

TAMORA: The eagle suffers little birds to sing
           And is not careful what they mean thereby.

(*Titus Andronicus* Act 4, Scene 4)

The attributes of birds, and the values human put upon them, are conventional tokens of aesthetic value. Traditionally, the lark and nightingale are regarded as the most beautiful in song, but all things are relative, and Shakespeare the pragmatist is feather-light in his realistic challenge to convention:

PORTIA: The crow doth sing as sweetly as the lark
           When neither is attended, and I think
           The nightingale, if she should sing by day,
           When every goose is cackling, would be thought
           No better a musician than the wren.

(*Merchant of Venice* Act 5, Scene 1)

Morality, too, can be given substance by analogy with birds. How better to explain that those already heavily darkened get away with more, unfairly, than those who, new to dirt, stand out when slightly blemished?

> The crow may bathe his coal-black wings in mire,
> And unperceived fly with the filth away;
> But if the like the snow-white swan desire,
> The stain upon his silver down will stay.

('The Rape of Lucrece')

What sometimes seems obscure to us today was, in his day, no more than simple reference to what was common knowledge. Hamlet's denial that he was confused by some insanity is a good example. His apparently cryptic: 'I know a hawk from a handsaw' is a blunt statement that he can see as clearly as anyone. A 'handsaw' is a corruption of 'hernshaw' – a heron. How better to show discernment than to tell the difference between the high hovering and swooping of a kestrel and the trailing-legged low flapping and gliding of a heron?

This ability to use metaphors based on common knowledge to make one thing merge seamlessly with another is functional, not fanciful. You can see him work from the known to the less familiar in some sustained developments of analogy.

Take, for example, the three great extended metaphors in which Shakespeare explores the principles that underlie an orderly society. In *Richard II*, the King's indulgence, indecision and timidity have resulted in a ferment of plotting and disorder. In Act 3, scene 4, two gardeners enter. The experienced one instructs his underling in a basic task of orchard-tending, using a domestic analogy:

GARDENER: Go, bind thou up yon dangling apricocks,
             Which, like unruly children, make their sire
             Stoop with oppression of their prodigal weight:

Having established a situational link between garden maintenance and the toll that wayward offspring take on parents, it is easy to develop the notion of the larger family that is the nation:

> Go thou, and like an executioner,
> Cut off the heads of too fast growing sprays,
> That look too lofty in our commonwealth:

Importing law, justice and the need for all to recognise the rights and obligations of citizenship, the message goes from family to commonwealth to the destructive effects of plants whose uncontrolled growth begins to threaten the stability of the state. The political morality that arises is a matter of tough dealing with those who do not contribute and who take from society what is the entitlement of those who do contribute:

> I will go root away
> The noisome weeds, which without profit suck
> The soil's fertility from wholesome flowers.

There's plenty here to trigger thoughts of social order and social justice in the minds of the subtler audience but something rather schoolmasterly in Shakespeare's Warwickshire head makes him go the extra yard to make the point for those who haven't read their Machiavelli. The apprentice gardener's question makes the link between this garden and the garden that is England:

SERVANT: Why should we in the compass of a pale
Keep law and form and due proportion,
Showing, as in a model, our firm estate,
When our sea-walled garden, the whole land,
Is full of weeds, her fairest flowers choked up,
Her fruit-trees all upturned, her hedges ruin'd,
Her knots disorder'd and her wholesome herbs
Swarming with caterpillars?

This question the expert horticulturalist uses to rub the message in. Dramatically, the power of this is that these humble loppers know more about governance than the King himself. As the gardener might have put it, the principles of effective rule are not exactly horse-cart science:

GARDENER: O, what pity is it
That he had not so trimm'd and dress'd his land
As we this garden! We at time of year
Do wound the bark, the skin of our fruit-trees,
Lest, being over-proud in sap and blood,
With too much riches it confound itself:
Had he done so to great and growing men,
They might have lived to bear and he to taste
Their fruits of duty: superfluous branches
We lop away, that bearing boughs may live:
Had he done so, himself had borne the crown,
Which waste of idle hours hath quite thrown down.

Shakespeare worked this seam of metaphor again in *Henry V*, Act 1, Scene 2. To stress the need for division of labour and respect for social hierarchy and rank, the Archbishop of Canterbury presents social order, not as something man-made, but something rooted in Nature itself, and even Heaven. Explaining the 'divers functions' of the state of man, he sets up a similarity:

CANTERBURY: For so work the honey-bees,
Creatures that by a rule in nature teach
The act of order to a peopled kingdom.

What follows is an analogy of the benefits of rank and role-acceptance in an orderly society, and one with a supreme head at the top of the hierarchy:

> They have a king and officers of sorts;
> Where some, like magistrates, correct at home,
> Others, like merchants, venture trade abroad,
> Others, like soldiers, armed in their stings,
> Make boot upon the summer's velvet buds,

> Which pillage they with merry march bring home
> To the tent-royal of their emperor;
> Who, busied in his majesty, surveys
> The singing masons building roofs of gold,
> The civil citizens kneading up the honey,
> The poor mechanic porters crowding in
> Their heavy burdens at his narrow gate,
> The sad-eyed justice, with his surly hum,
> Delivering o'er to executors pale
> The lazy yawning drone.

What's especially interesting about this is that, rather than representing a feudal view of aristocracy and peasantry, it recognises the status of those who are new specialists: the traders, craftsmen and professionals of an emerging post-feudal society. Perhaps because so many things are changing, Canterbury clings to the message about knowing your place and chopping the parasites.

The most famous example of exploring social order by analogy is in *Troilus and Cressida* Act 1, Scene 3. Years ago, E.M.W.Tillyard constructed an elaborate schema of what Elizabethans believed on the basis of this speech (*The Elizabethan World Picture*, Vintage Books USA, 1959). Whether this was justified is another matter: just as Canterbury had his own political reasons for representing England as ordered on the principles of aristocracy, trade and peasantry, with drones at the bottom of the pile, Ulysses has his own reasons for wanting society to be seen as an expression of fixed cosmic order. In other words, we would be unwise to assume that what Shakespeare wrote for a character necessarily represented what he thought as an author.

The speech begins with reference to the hive and honey:

ULYSSES: The specialty of rule hath been neglected:
> When that the general is not like the hive
> To whom the foragers shall all repair,
> What honey is expected? Degree being vizarded,
> The unworthiest shows as fairly in the mask.

                                                   (*Troilus and Cressida* Act 1, Scene 3)

The theme is then enlarged to show that the same principle of order is evident in scientific knowledge about the whole solar system, bringing in new Copernicus to support old views of order:

> The heavens themselves, the planets and this centre
> Observe degree, priority and place,
> Insisture, course, proportion, season, form,
> Office and custom, in all line of order;

The beauty, for Ulysses, in this is that he is able to link the sun at the centre with the king:

> And therefore is the glorious planet Sol
> In noble eminence enthroned and sphered
> Amidst the other; whose medicinable eye
> Corrects the ill aspects of planets evil,
> And posts, like the commandment of a king,
> Sans check to good and bad:

It's not then difficult to argue that departure from the fixed order will bring about chaos and destruction:

> but when the planets
> In evil mixture to disorder wander,
> What plagues and what portents! what mutiny!
> What raging of the sea! shaking of earth!
> Commotion in the winds! frights, changes, horrors,

> Divert and crack, rend and deracinate
> The unity and married calm of states
> Quite from their fixure! O, when degree is shaked,
> Which is the ladder to all high designs,
> Then enterprise is sick!

Finally, as an example of how widely he plundered the field of reference in the interest of clarifying ideas, look at the way he is willing to approach a similar idea without reference to scientific knowledge of the cosmos, but with reference to something everyone in his audience could understand. Here is Menenius in *Coriolanus*, speaking about the need for discipline, harmony and status:

MENENIUS: There was a time when all the body's members
Rebell'd against the belly, thus accused it:
That only like a gulf it did remain
I' the midst o' the body, idle and unactive,
Still cupboarding the viand, never bearing
Like labour with the rest, where the other instruments
Did see and hear, devise, instruct, walk, feel,
And, mutually participate, did minister
Unto the appetite and affection common
Of the whole body. The belly answer'd –

FIRST CITIZEN: Well, sir, what answer made the belly?

MENENIUS: Sir, I shall tell you. With a kind of smile,
Which ne'er came from the lungs, but even thus –
For, look you, I may make the belly smile
As well as speak – it tauntingly replied
To the discontented members, the mutinous parts
That envied his receipt; even so most fitly
As you malign our senators for that
They are not such as you.

FIRST CITIZEN: Your belly's answer? What!
The kingly-crowned head, the vigilant eye,
The counsellor heart, the arm our soldier,
Our steed the leg, the tongue our trumpeter.
With other muniments and petty helps
In this our fabric, if that they –

MENENIUS: What then?
'Fore me, this fellow speaks! What then? What then?

FIRST CITIZEN: Should by the cormorant belly be restrain'd,
Who is the sink o' the body, –

MENENIUS: Well, what then?

FIRST CITIZEN: The former agents, if they did complain,
What could the belly answer?

MENENIUS: I will tell you
If you'll bestow a small – of what you have little –
Patience awhile, you'll hear the belly's answer.

FIRST CITIZEN: Ye're long about it.

MENENIUS: Note me this, good friend;
                  Your most grave belly was deliberate,
                  Not rash like his accusers, and thus answer'd:
                  'True is it, my incorporate friends,' quoth he,
                  'That I receive the general food at first,
                  Which you do live upon; and fit it is,
                  Because I am the store-house and the shop
                  Of the whole body: but, if you do remember,
                  I send it through the rivers of your blood,
                  Even to the court, the heart – to the seat o' the brain;
                  And, through the cranks and offices of man,
                  The strongest nerves and small inferior veins
                  From me receive that natural competency
                  Whereby they live: and though that all at once,
                  You, my good friends,' – this says the belly, mark me, –

FIRST CITIZEN: Ay, sir; well, well.

MENENIUS: 'Though all at once cannot
                  See what I do deliver out to each,
                  Yet I can make my audit up, that all
                  From me do back receive the flour of all,
                  And leave me but the bran.' What say you to't?

FIRST CITIZEN: It was an answer: how apply you this?

MENENIUS: The senators of Rome are this good belly,
                  And you the mutinous members; for examine
                  Their counsels and their cares, digest things rightly
                  Touching the weal o' the common, you shall find
                  No public benefit which you receive
                  But it proceeds or comes from them to you
                  And no way from yourselves.

                                    (*Coriolanus* Act 1, Scene 1)

Shakespeare, life and theatre

He'd have loved the telly, Shakespeare. And email. After years of pleasing South Bank punters in a draughty wooden O, he could have worked by broadband out of New Place, Stratford in the morning, strolled to the pub for a light lunch beside the Avon and indulged the grandchildren in the evening.

But the current digital revolution was far off for our man. His digital revolution was the first one – curling fingers around a quill. His medium, though, the stage, was not unlike today's entertainment forum. Most of what he dealt in was romantic comedies, brutal thrillers, big historical bio-epics, lurid chronicles of the downfall of the wicked and even worse tales of the downfall of the worthy. And a little current affairs and poetry thrown in for the higher-minded. A bit like the best of BBC1, 2, ITV and Channel Five, really.

Like most who work in the media, he saw his trade as a microcosm, and its language permeated his daily thinking. For him, drama was life and life was drama; the world a stage, and its inhabitants actors. As a source of appealing metaphors, this idea served him well. Who has not relished the extended business he makes of it in *As You Like it*?

JAQUES: All the world's a stage,
          And all the men and women merely players:
          They have their exits and their entrances;
          And one man in his time plays many parts,
          His acts being seven ages....

(As You Like It Act 2, Scene 7)*

It's an image that re-appears, sometimes, as in the above, for benignly satirical effect and sometimes, as in Macbeth, to express a bleak relativism that takes mortality off its pedestal:

MACBETH: Life's but a walking shadow, a poor player
           That struts and frets his hour upon the stage
           And then is heard no more:

(Macbeth Act 5, Scene 5)*

The realist-nihilist streak in Shakespeare emerges in his probing of extremities of experience. How empty and foolish a spectacle seems 'All of Human Life As We Know It' when Lear reduces it so starkly:

KING LEAR: When we are born, we cry that we are come
            To this great stage of fools:

(King Lear Act 4, Scene 6)*

It's not all bleak pre-existentialist angst, however. There's some potential in the idea of Life as Drama for hope that *All's Well That Ends Well* if the 'Great Director in the Sky' wills it. Oddly enough, Shakespeare did little to exploit this potential in the plays. A shrewd secularist, he never extended the theatrical imagery to postulate a divine scriptwriter hacking out a happy ending in Act 5. However, he did contrast the flawed and transient human drama with some 'Force' beyond – natural or celestial, and possibly spiritual:

    When I consider every thing that grows
    Holds in perfection but a little moment,
    That this huge stage presenteth nought but shows
    Whereon the stars in secret influence comment...

(Sonnet XV)

It's his insider's view of his medium that makes it so practically comparative. How better to show the way lesser mortals draw notice in the wake of more illustrious predecessors than to observe the habits of an audience:

DUKE OF YORK: As in a theatre, the eyes of men,
               After a well-graced actor leaves the stage,
               Are idly bent on him that enters next,
               Thinking his prattle to be tedious;
               Even so, or with much more contempt, men's eyes
               Did scowl on gentle Richard;

(Richard II Act 5, Scene 2)*

As a writer and prime investor in his own theatrical company, Shakespeare would have been only too aware of the way duff actors let the whole company down. This experience is easily translated to the social drama where a political thespian proves unequal to the part:

CORIOLANUS: Like a dull actor now,
             I have forgot my part, and I am out,
             Even to a full disgrace.

(Coriolanus Act 5, Scene 3)*

Shakespeare's craft was in writing for a large open-air theatre and for a mixed popular audience. Sometimes, it is true, he played for small audiences in grand houses and courts where an educated elite attended appreciatively to the cultural menu provided, but most of the time Shakespeare's crust was earned by putting on performances in daylight, for punters wanting entertainment. Until he opened at the Blackfriars in 1610 (Indoors! Heating! Lighting! Sound effects! Seats for all!) his playing space lacked refinement. It certainly lacked such modern refinements as sound amplification, realistic set design and controllable lighting. Not for him the dying of the houselights and the starting of floods and spots to still an audience into listening. The dramatic event itself had to grip attention and stop the chat as the play got started. Hence his opening lines are designed to gain attention by various means. (see section on openings in 'The Close Shakespearience', page 10.)

Shakespeare must have been aware that he was taking drama into new territory unexplored in the English heritage. Extending his human canvas from the biblical and masque traditions with their modest demands upon costume, cast and realism, he was writing scripts embracing ten-year sieges (*Troilus and Cressida*), land and sea wars (*Antony and Cleopatra*) and campaigns involving French and English infantry and cavalry. Without the means to make all this realistically believable on stage in *Henry V*, he had to trust his audience to support the fiction, but he did not take this support lightly. He knew how much he was asking: his audience's imagination was essential to remedy his frankly-admitted deficit:

CHORUS: But pardon, and gentles all,
           The flat unraised spirits that have dared
           On this unworthy scaffold to bring forth
           So great an object: can this cockpit hold
           The vasty fields of France? or may we cram
           Within this wooden O the very casques
           That did affright the air at Agincourt?

In a clever use of apology to flatter and win acceptance, Shakespeare charmingly draws attention to his inadequacies, enlisting the audience, in the prologue to *Henry V*, as an active contributor to the creative effect:

CHORUS: Piece out our imperfections with your thoughts;
           Into a thousand parts divide on man,
           And make imaginary puissance;
           Think when we talk of horses, that you see them
           Printing their proud hoofs i' the receiving earth;
           For 'tis your thoughts that now must deck our kings,
           Carry them here and there; jumping o'er times,
           Turning the accomplishment of many years
           Into an hour-glass:

The same winning appeal is clear, and the same modest confidence in his resources as writer and director is evident, in *Romeo and Juliet*:

PROLOGUE: The fearful passage of their death-marked love
           And the continuance of their parents' rage
           Which, but their children's end, naught could remove
           Is now the two hours traffic of our stage:
           The which, if you with patient ears attend,
           What here shall miss, our toil shall strive to mend.

Underneath the charm, there is a realistic sense of what he can do and what he is willing to do with resources that are limited. Cuts and time-shifts are essentials in reducing great events to the two-hour traffic of the stage. If necessary, a story can be cut, adapted, shaped to the medium and tailored to the audience in a way that a more modern adapter like Andrew Davies has done with *Pride and Prejudice* and *Bleak House*:

PROLOGUE: And hither am I come
          A prologue armed, but not in confidence
          Of author's pen or actor's voice, but suited
          In like conditions as our argument,
          To tell you, fair beholders, that our play
          Leaps o'er the vaunt and firstlings of those broils,
          Beginning in the middle, starting thence away
          To what may be digested in a play.

*(**Troilus and Cressida**)*

What may seem – or may have been – a crafty expedient to get over technical inadequacies is really the foundation of Shakespeare's dramatic achievement. His scriptcraft makes a virtue of necessity, exploiting the relationship with his audience to draw it in to action, to make it sympathise or judge or want to call out 'He's behind you!' Priming an audience is the basis of dramatic irony, and making an audience complicit in the unfolding of a devious plot, or even reluctantly associate with an unworthy character, undermines its security as a judge of what it sees. Brecht was, centuries later, to set himself the task of cracking the complacency of an audience feeling safe as an observer. Shakespeare would have understood this. Going beyond the basic audience cues referred to here, he developed the art of the aside and the soliloquy to combine artifice and realism in an astonishingly effective way.

Shakespeare himself – a personal view of this bloke from the Midlands …

Other writers offer successful takes on Shakespeare as 'Renaissance Man', 'Shakespeare Our Contemporary', or 'Shakespeare, A Writer for All Seasons'. This book shares some of those takes, but it's more about getting close up and personal. Personal and professional, I should say. Michael Bogdanov goes beyond the usual tags in writing of him as 'England's Greatest Living Playwright' and I share his assumption about his continued presence amid the mortal coil. As I see it, he's been so good to me, and for me, throughout my teaching career that I presume a special relationship, albeit not a reciprocal one. I'll finish this section by trying to explain my odd relationship with a regular guy, Mr. William Bloke, from somewhere in the sticks near Coventry.

This 'Lad from the Midlands' did really well for himself, despite not going to university. There wasn't a University of the Central Midlands then. Well there was, but it was called Oxford, and Bill didn't have the necessaries to do the gentleman scholar bit there. Not that missing out on university did him any harm. His education as a jobbing actor set him up for later life as a writer. He wrote more plays and pulled more audiences than his university-educated rivals by taking them on at their own game. What they did, he did. And better. Re-modelled stories out of Greek and Latin? Done. New twists on Ancient and Modern History? Easy. Deft replications of Kings and Queens, Princes and Nobles? Loads of.

Move over, Jonson, Marlowe, Webster – Bill's in town. And writing his way to buying the smartest house back in Stratford. Ghosts, jokes, murders, treachery, passion, farce and satire in ink and on the boards from 1590 to 1613. The only downside is that the writing left him only three years of deserved retirement.

But the 'Theatrical Impresario' is only part of it. Apart from doing the grand stuff – the heart-wrenching, spirit-lifting, brain-tingling themes – and the word-coining, metaphor and pentameter, there's another side to Shakespeare. It's the sanely reassuring voice of the level-headed realist who sums up life's quirks and pains and offers quiet comfort, consolation and common sense. This is just what you need over a pint after a frustrating day: Bill Bloke, leaning on the bar, tutting away and telling you life's a bitch but get on with it – and it's your round.

Play the scenario with me. You've been taken in and let down by some cheapskate who looked honest or sincere?

Bill: 'Swine. **There's no art to find the mind's construction in the face.**'

You've discovered that what looked attractive at first, packed some nasty small print that spoils the deal?

Bill: 'It's a sod. **Things sweet to taste prove in digestion sour.**'

You've done your best to truthfully describe the disastrous situation facing everyone and been given the evil eye and no thanks?

Bill: 'Hard cheese. **The nature of bad news infects the teller.**'

You're an English teacher suffering from target-setting Heads, OFSTED inspectors who wouldn't last a day at your school and Inset providers who get you into groups with a flipchart and coloured markers?

Bill: 'It doesn't have to be this way. **The fault, dear Brutus, is not in our stars / But in ourselves, that we are underlings.**'

Murmuring the right words is what we want from a friend, but there are times when we need a bit more, a bit of stirring of reluctant sinews. That's when he grips your elbow and looks you in the eye:

Bill: 'Don't go there, mate. **'Tis one thing to be tempted, Escalus, / Another thing to fall.**'

And if you're too timid to do what you know is right, he makes it all seem so much more sensible:

Bill: 'Go for it. **Out of this nettle, Danger, we pluck this flower, Safety.**'

He's seen it all before. You're not the first to try the line about getting away from it all, dropping out of the rat race to live on spliffs and vino on the Costa:

Bill: 'No way, Jose. **If all the year were playing holidays, / To sport would be as tedious as to work.**'

He's got the knack of making you see that 'No sweat – no get' is part of Life's rich pattern, and putting in some graft can give you a buzz that outdoes woes:

Bill: 'Get stuck in. **The labour we delight in physics pain.**

He knows that too much brooding means nothing else gets done. He's seen the ineffectual, dithering, navel-gazing intellectual before:

Bill: 'Just do it. **Conscience doth make cowards of us all/ And thus the native hue of resolution / Is sicklied o'er with the pale cast of thought.**

He's observed the ebb and flow of circumstance before and doesn't want you dithering on the foreshore thinking it's too cold or you don't like the wet:

Bill: 'Stop faffing. **There is a tide in the affairs of men which, / Taken at the flood, leads on to fortune; / Omitted, all the voyage of their life / Is bound in shallows and in miseries.**'

Like any wise counsellor or bar-tender, he knows that sometimes telling us what we don't want to hear means repeating the same advice in a different way, changing the analogies;

Bill: *'I know, I know, but **a little fire is quickly trodden out/ Which, being suffered, rivers cannot quench.'***

When we need to be consoled, he's realistic. If you're half sorted, be thankful – don't envy the wholly sorted, the rich and famous:

Bill: *'Forget them. **They are as sick that surfeit with too much as they that/ Starve with nothing.'***

A smart young woman enters the bar – a real looker, and for a moment there's something that takes attention away even from the foaming pint. Thoughts pass rapidly through the mind as she takes off her jacket and arranges her limbs on a bar-stool. There's a cough and a sotto voce mutter:

Bill: **'Is it not strange that desire should so many years outlive performance?'**

If there's one thing that makes Bill Bloke a friend in need, it's his willingness to take us, spots and warts and moans and bleats and all, and not expect too much:

Bill: *'Sup up and stop complaining. **The gods give us some faults to make us men.'***

Cheers, Bill.

7. Shakespeare and examinations

The whole of this book has been dedicated to helping students to enjoy taking ownership of Shakespeare by active explorations and practical activities linked to performance. If that sounds like a recipe for shared pleasure and satisfaction beyond the merely academic, that's good, but teachers may think this recipe may not sit easily with the demands of the examination system. Fortunately, it does, particularly at GCSE from 2010. The spirit of this book and the nature of the activities suggested in it are, healthily and happily, a firm basis for preparation, and a route to success at all grade levels. It is not always possible as an English teacher to have one's cake or eat it, but with Shakespeare, we can have it, eat it (with cream and the topping of your fancy) and still win grades for our students that will satisfy the philistine accountants whose interest in youngsters and education goes no further than league tables.

GCSE

The examination system, despite its trappings of cooped-up writing tasks in the Hall at the end of year 11, has been increasingly adapted over the years to be attuned to the special nature of Shakespeare study. There was a time, and in living memory, when O level Shakespeare tasks seemed designed to test memory, comprehension and mugged-up vocabulary glossing, all in a spirit of catching out the unprepared and sifting the educated wheat from the ignorant chaff. As late as 1982, before GCSE began to make literature and examinations more accessible, I recall, as a young examiner, my dismay at discovering the paper I was to mark allowed 8 marks for remembering what happened before a given excerpt, 8 marks for glossing three phrases, and 4 marks for commenting on character.

> Question on *Julius Caesar*:
>
> (i)   Explain: *your wisdom is consum'd in confidence*;
>   *for thy humour, in very happy time*; and *portents*   8 marks
>
> (ii)   How, immediately after this extract, does Decius go on
>   to interpret Calphurnia's dream?   4 marks
>
> (iii) What do you learn of Caesar's character
>   from his speeches here?
>   8 marks

My dismay gave way to something else when I received from the Principal examiner the instructions on how it was to be marked.

> *Your judgement* (1) *is destroyed* (1) *by over-confidence/self-confidence*
> (1) and nothing else.
> *Just* (1) *to please you* (1) [accept *satisfy your whim or caprice*, 1 mark
> only for *humour you, keep you happy* or *for your peace of mind*.]
>
> *At a very convenient moment or time* (1)
>
> *Strange happenings that are signs of some evil thing that is going to*
> *happen* (2) *omens* (1), *ominous* (1) *Ill-omens* (2)

At the standardising meeting, the Principal Examiner instructed us to add some refinements to the mark-scheme. He had decided, after some reflection, that we should be instructed to allow a mark for those candidates who offered 'satisfy your whim or caprice' for 'for thy humour', and that it would be acceptable to award one out of two marks for those glossing 'portents' as 'omens'.

What was going on here was nothing to do with making Shakespeare accessible and pleasurable, or with setting a teaching and learning agenda based on enquiry, response, practicality or performance. Note that the choice of 'happy' and 'humour' work well to disadvantage those who try to get meaning from context, but are limited to today's usage of those terms. No marks. When one bold new examiner asked if it was fair to penalise candidates who had not used editions that explained the Elizabethan meaning of these words, the Principal Examiner explained that he could not be responsible for teachers' poor scholarship or their choice of inferior editions of the plays.

GCSE changed all that. It had to. It had to cater for the whole range of ability, and it had to provide tasks that did not simply favour those candidates who had received a traditional, grammar/public school form of instruction. Since 1988, various developments within the GCSE system had gradually improved the way that Shakespeare is assessed, placing more emphasis on the texts as Drama, and more emphasis on reader's (audience) response. Prioritising the dramatic qualities meant that Shakespeare study had to be different from prose study: Shakespeare, after all, was not a novelist with an odd penchant for dialogue. In this sense, the examination system was catching up with the earlier twentieth century shift in academic study, where the old Bradleyan emphasis on character and the Spurgeon emphasis on patterns of imagery placed Shakespeare firmly in Literature, as the maker of texts to be read, rather than performed, or seen and heard. This shift has been increasingly evident in GCSE questioning and mark schemes, and is especially evident in the 2010 specifications. The result was a residual lingering of the old attitude to Shakespeare in the National Curriculum's specification of Shakespeare as part of the literary heritage to be read, and to be part of the assessment of reading, in the government-favoured and teacher-despised Key Stage 3 SATs. Even these made a token reference to the understanding of Shakespeare as a dramatist in the occasional question on directing a scene, but the main focus of this assessment tool was on language comprehension, character and plot.

The assessment objectives for 2010 on provide an 'assessment for learning' basis for teachers to build on. There should, therefore, be no conflict between the assessment framework and the ways in which Shakespeare is taught.

Here are five positive aspects of GCSE that make the Shakespearience model right for all, whether students are entered for English or for English Literature. If they are entered for English, Shakespeare is assessed as part of the Reading (literary heritage) strand.

1 GCSE Assessment Objectives

Reading (En2) AOs

Candidates are required to demonstrate their ability to:
AO1 read and understand texts, selecting material appropriate to purpose, collating from different sources and making comparisons and cross-references as appropriate
AO2 develop and sustain interpretations of writers' ideas and perspectives
AO3 explain and evaluate how writers use linguistic, grammatical, structural and presentational features to achieve effects and engage and influence the reader
AO4 understand texts in their social, cultural and historical contexts.

'Social, cultural and historical' was formerly an AO in Literature only. It is to be welcomed as an assessment objective in English Reading, because it allows textual understanding to be more than print decoding and comprehension: it includes the more engaging and personally valuable response based on preference, relevance, similarity to or difference from students' own cultural experience and norms. It invites reading with and for ATTITUDE and VALUES.

Literature AOs

AO1 respond to texts critically and imaginatively; select and evaluate relevant textual detail to illustrate and support interpretations
AO2 explain how language, structure and form contribute to writers' presentation of ideas, themes and settings
AO3 make comparisons and explain links between texts, evaluating writers' different ways of expressing meaning and achieving effects
AO4 relate texts to their social, cultural and historical contexts; explain how texts have been influential and significant to self and other readers in different contexts and at different times.

Literature AO4 is something to celebrate. How often can an Assessment Objective bring joy to an English teacher's heart? The change in AO4 from the previous formula 'relate texts to their social, cultural and historical contexts' is a significant and very helpful one. It helps teachers and students to see the importance of a personal and another perspective on a text, and it helps task-setters to focus questions on this aspect and build in rewards for it in the mark-scheme. The removal of 'understand texts in their literary tradition' from the old AO4 is a realistic recognition that very few students are likely to know anything about the theatrical antecedents of Shakespeare or the development of the epistolary novel in the eighteenth century.

2 GCSE Grade criteria

Grade description

A
Candidates select suitable styles and registers of spoken English for a range of situations and contexts, showing assured use of standard English where appropriate. They confidently vary sentence structures and choose from a broad repertoire of vocabulary to express information, ideas and feelings in an engaging manner. They initiate conversations and demonstrate sensitive listening through contributions that sustain and develop discussion. They recognise and fulfil the demands of different roles, whether in formal settings or creative activities.

Candidates respond personally and persuasively to a variety of texts, developing interpretations and evaluating how details of language, grammar, structure and presentation engage and affect the reader. They identify and discuss writers' perspectives in narrative, argument, explanation or analysis. They choose apt quotations and make telling comparisons and cross-references that illuminate the purpose and meanings of texts, explaining the impact of their social, cultural and historical contexts where appropriate.

Candidates' writing shows confident, assured control of a range of forms and styles appropriate to task and purpose. Texts engage and hold the reader's interest through logical argument, persuasive force or creative delight. Linguistic and structural features are used skilfully to sequence texts and achieve coherence. A wide range of accurate sentence structures ensures clarity; choices of vocabulary, punctuation and spelling are ambitious, imaginative and correct.

C

Candidates adapt their talk to the demands of different situations and contexts. They recognise when standard English is required and use it confidently. They use different sentence structures and select vocabulary so that information, ideas and feelings are communicated clearly and the listener's interest is engaged. They explain and evaluate how they and others use and adapt spoken language for specific purposes. Through careful listening and by developing their own and others' ideas, they make significant contributions to discussion and participate effectively in creative activities.

Candidates understand and demonstrate how meaning and information are conveyed in a range of texts. They make personal and critical responses, referring to specific aspects of language, grammar, structure and presentational devices to justify their views. They successfully compare and cross-reference aspects of texts and explain convincingly how they may vary in purpose and how they achieve different effects. They comment on how social, cultural and historical contexts affect readers' responses to texts.

Candidates' writing shows successful adaptation of form and style to different tasks and for various purposes. They use a range of sentence structures and varied vocabulary to create different effects and engage the reader's interest. Paragraphing is used effectively to make the sequence of events or development of ideas coherent and clear to the reader. Sentence structures are varied; punctuation and spelling are accurate and sometimes bold.

F

Candidates talk confidently in familiar situations, showing some awareness of purpose and of listeners' needs. They convey information, develop ideas and describe feelings clearly, using the main features of standard English as appropriate. They listen with concentration and make relevant responses to others' ideas and opinions. They show some awareness of how they and others use and adapt spoken language for specific purposes. In formal and creative activities, they attempt to meet the demands of different roles.

Candidates describe the main ideas, themes or argument in a range of texts and refer to specific aspects or details when justifying their views. They make simple comparisons and cross-references that show some awareness of how texts achieve their effects through writers' use of linguistic, grammatical, structural and presentational devices. They are aware that some features of texts relate to their specific social, cultural and historical contexts.

Candidates' writing shows some adaptation of form and style for different tasks and purposes. It communicates simply and clearly with the reader. Sentences sequence events or ideas logically; vocabulary is sometimes chosen for variety and interest. Paragraphing is straightforward but effective; the structure of sentences, including some that are complex, is usually correct. Spelling and basic punctuation are mostly accurate.

3 GCSE Teaching and learning priorities

a) AO4 Social, cultural and historical contexts

'Social, cultural and historical' is problematic because, realistically, candidates cannot be expected to make informed comments on sociological and historical aspects of textual contexts. If teachers treat the threesome as a coagulated triple, they will lead candidates to an indiscriminate grasp of the matter. An indiscriminate grasp often results in naïve assertions such as 'in Shakespeare's day, women were inferior' or 'there were social classes and poverty in Dickens' day'. If 'historical' means opening an assignment on Dickens with the statement that he was born in Portsmouth in 1844, it is of little value in terms of interpretation, analysis or response. The understandable urge to write something that appears 'social and historical' often results in candidates exposing an ignorance to which they are, realistically, entitled to in an assessment which is based on Reading or Literature. What matters in the triple is the 'cultural' bit. This is about differences from today and similarities with today, not just in language but also in appeal and relevance. Students should be able to comment on ideas, values and attitudes displayed in the plays, and how they are similar to or different from those of today. This justifies study which explores notions of honour, virtue, weakness, and attitudes to race, class, marriage, gender, justice or politics.

Students need an understanding that all texts embody some implicit cultural priorities and preferences – comment on 'cultural' aspects is more successful when it relates to the possible cultural package of the writer, and how the writer's implied values impact on the reader (and other readers). It helps to distinguish the three components as follows:

i) *Social* relates, unsurprisingly, to the public space providing a context for writing, publishing, reading or performing a text. Students are unlikely to know much about the social contexts of authors or texts other than simple facts assumed to influence an author. They will be on more secure ground if they understand 'social' aspects as 'interpersonal and inter-group' aspects, or even, more broadly, 'relationships'.

ii) *Historical* relates to the factual matter of the time of writing, publishing a text – or the way these may be reflected in a text. Students are unlikely to know much about historical contexts other than simple facts linked to content or language.

iii) *Cultural* relates, more interestingly, to the nexus of inherited or chosen opinions, beliefs, faiths, attitudes and values. Students can do more with this because it allows fruitful comment on these things (implicit or explicit) in the text and in its time, and these things in the reader, and the reader's mind and context. 'Cultural' is the most useful of the three because it allows more open comparison and contrast with values and attitudes. The essence of 'social/cultural/historical' is 'What's changed and what's stayed the same', which raises more interesting matters re. belief and behaviour than form and language.

'Social, cultural and historical' can be most effectively addressed by exploring ways in which Shakespeare's writing was shaped by catering for a contemporary audience and for a contemporary stage. Linking social, cultural and historical and theatricality/stagecraft allows better dealing with dramatic devices and structures. Students may also want to comment on what Elizabethans thought about life, morality and society, but they will do this more effectively if they focus on how things are the same or different today, rather than on any reliance on generalized (and second-hand) comment making sweeping claims about seventeenth century people and society.

b) Theatricality and stagecraft

Drama before Shakespeare amounted to learned re-creations of Latin and Greek plays and stories, or simple moralistic tales in the Everyman tradition, or masques and shows by Mummers and travelling troupes of singing, dancing artistes. Shakespeare was more than these. He took what he wanted from earlier traditions, and added things that others had not dreamed of. And he was not bothered by academic notions about Aristotelian Classical Unities, or the integrity of genres of tragedy, comedy or history. 'Mix, match and lay on whatever keeps the punters coming' seems to have been his working motto.

The blending of genres in the plays – history, comedy, tragedy, romance – and of styles – dialogue, monologue, chorus, song, dance and spectacle – appealed to a wider audience than the scholarly, the cultured and the privileged. Studying examples of script shaped by the needs of his stage, his audience and his actors gives a more practical approach to Shakespeare's craft. Three obvious features are worth emphasising:

Shakespeare's theatre

- open and in daylight
- no sound amplification and no lighting
- no curtains and no set changes

This means that Shakespeare's scripts needed to help audibility in an acoustically poor environment. Changes of setting and passages of time had to be signaled by embedded cues in the dialogue. Events too difficult to stage needed to be described rather than shown.

Shakespeare's audience

- literate, educated and familiar with history and modern politics
- illiterate, uneducated and paying for entertainment
- men and women

The appeal of any single play for this paying audience had to be wide, and the structure of a three-hour performance needed pace and variety.

Shakespeare's actors

- male ensemble but individual favourites
- uncertain employment dependent on successful repertoire
- rival companies and no copyright

Parts needed to be written to make the most of the talents of individuals in the company. Popular characters may need to be re-written into other plays. Actors could not be given scripts in case they got into the hands of rival companies, so had to learn lines by heart. Hence, the rhythms of blank verse helped memory.

c) Audience appeal

Shakespeare's own audience was very mixed. Whilst he did cater for an educated elite in performances at court and grand houses, most of what he wrote was for a public playhouse and a paying public. Appealing to the varied tastes of this wide audience meant putting together plays with something for everybody – comedy, violence, romance, suspense and references to current and past events in English life and history. Those best pleased by verbal abuse, drunkenness and foolery could enjoy Falstaff, Sir Toby Belch, Petruchio – others best pleased by witty puns, parodies and conceits could enjoy the subtler parts of *Much Ado About Nothing*, *Twelfth Night* and *Hamlet*. But each play had something for both tastes.

In his time, Shakespeare offered the equivalent of a modern multi-channel, multi-modal entertainment: *Only Fools and Horses*, *News at Ten*, *Eastenders*, the History Channel, conjuring tricks and a bit of a dance-show thrown in.

4 GCSE Controlled Assessment

For English, Shakespeare is part of the 60% controlled assessment within the school. Although the awarding body will provide a bank of suitable assignments for the school to use, there will be freedom for teachers to choose the texts and the approaches to them. This allows a preparation/study period based on active methods and on selected parts of the chosen play or plays.

For English Literature, Shakespeare is part of the 25% controlled assessment within the school.

Teachers wanting to develop a coherent rationale for teaching Shakespeare have only to adapt their daily classroom practice to the essentials of the AOs and the grade criteria. For example, questioning strategies that continuously reflect the aims and objectives of GCSE Shakespeare can be part of a lesson repertoire.

Examples of question prompts:

- How do *you* respond to this scene/situation/behaviour?
- How may *someone else* respond to…?
- Do you think this situation/behaviour is *different from today* or do we find the same situation/behaviour today?
- What attitudes/values do you think *Shakespeare held* in regard to what he has presented here?
- What hints/suggestions are there in *the language* to make you feel there are these attitudes/values involved in the situation/behaviour?
- How might an audience react to seeing the situation/behaviour on stage?

5 GCSE Awarding body recommendations for suitable approaches

AQA specifications and approaches

For **AQA English** and **AQA English Literature**, the options are very well suited to the Shakespearience approach. Active, collaborative and performative approaches to text and stage/screen performance are necessary for the creative/interactive tasks exemplified in the Sample Assessment Materials.

The **AQA English** specification links Shakespeare (Unit 3 Controlled Assessment) with English Literary Heritage poems and Different Cultures prose, so that the Shakespeare study is a separate one-third task of three discrete studies.

For example, students can choose to work on 'Themes and Ideas' or 'Characterisation and Voice'. If they choose the latter, there is plenty of scope for working on their own characterisation and voice or those of professionals on screen or stage. One suggested task for English is:

> *What aspects of voice, movement and relationship with others bring the character of Shylock to life on stage or screen?*

In **AQA English Literature**, the Controlled Assessment option is worth 25% of the total marks for English Literature so a CA task linking Shakespeare with an ELH prose or poetry text would make the Shakespeare part worth approximately 13% of the total marks for English Literature. This CA task requires students to make links between any Shakespeare play and one English Literary Heritage text of any genre. This means that students can study and be assessed on two Shakespeare plays if this is a preferred option. From a Shakespearience point of view, this is a superb opportunity to compare the way Shakespeare handles a theme in two plays, or uses a dramatic device in two plays. It means that the Shakespeare study can be worth the full 25% of the total marks for English Literature. Careful selection of parts of two plays can result in practical work to explore either the differences (hence variety) of his stagecraft, or the similarities (hence the consistency) of his stagecraft.

For example:

> *Explore the similarities and differences in the ways Shakespeare dramatises father/daughter relationships in **King Lear** and **Romeo and Juliet**.*

Another allows linkage with a prose text, using screen version of both:

> *Explore similarities and differences in the presentation of Shylock in* **The Merchant of Venice** *and Fagin in* **Oliver Twist**. *Explore the ways that screen representations of these characters reflect the original written representation.*

One of the very positive prompts to students' own active Shakespearience as a preparation for Controlled Assessment lies in the repeated guidance on a number of tasks that:

> *You may want to refer to how actors and readers portray these attitudes in performances of both texts, including your own readings.*

Students can draw on any version of the texts, including stage or screen productions, to inform their understanding of the text.

The AQA CA mark schemes are very well suited to reward the Shakespearience route to GCSE study. In English and in Literature the mark band descriptors all feature the four skills of: interpretation; engagement with ideas and attitudes; analysis of language and structure; significance of contexts.

It is especially rewarding to students who have been encouraged to interpret and evaluate Shakespeare on an ownership basis that **Literature Assessment Objective iv** no longer stands as *Understand texts in their social cultural and historical context*, but the vastly more personal, engaging and motivating: *Relate texts to their social, cultural and historical contexts; explain how texts have been influential and significant to self and other readers in different contexts at different times.*

The External examination option requires the study of one play from a choice of five, and encourages appreciation of how the social, historical and cultural context of the text informs its content and lays special emphasis on consideration of how dramatic devices engage an audience, showing a clear understanding that the play was written for performance.

Edexcel specifications and approaches

In the **Edexcel English** specification, Shakespeare appears in the exam whilst in the **Edexcel English Literature** specification Shakespeare appears in Controlled Assessment. In **English Literature** the Shakespeare study compares the chosen Shakespeare play with another version (such as a film or television adaptation). The Shakespeare study in **English Literature** is in the same unit as Contemporary Drama, so there is a clear genre focus, with an emphasis on dramatic craft and performative purposes and effects.

Preparing for the tasks

Students must study one Shakespeare play and one Contemporary Drama text. Guidance about studying these drama texts may include:

* developing understanding of the drama texts on page, stage and/or screen
* paired discussion, reading and speaking the lines
* group discussion of how to edit and present the drama texts for stage or screen performance
* group performances of the drama texts
* class discussion of ways in which the drama texts have been performed on stage or screen
* exploring links and connections between two interpretations of the Shakespeare play (e.g. a reading and a performance).

Responding to the tasks

The response to a task must show that students can:

* respond to the chosen drama texts critically and imaginatively
* evaluate writers' different ways of expressing meaning and achieving effects

- in English Literature make comparisons and explain links between the Shakespeare play and another version of the play, evaluating different ways of expressing meaning and achieving effects
- support ideas by choosing evidence from the drama texts.

OCR specifications and approaches

The **OCR Literature** specification is well suited to the study of Shakespeare in performance because it refers specifically to screen or stage performance in relation to the text. This makes practical classroom work on interpretation, improvisation, adaptation and performance a necessary preparation for exploring the ways in which the text has been professionally produced. Close study of students' own performances of scenes can be matched to professional performances, with students' comment, criticism and analysis based on something more personal and active than print reading.

For example:

OCR Literature

Shakespeare and Film/Audio/Live performance (10%)

Candidates respond to one task on one of the set plays and a film, audio version or live performance of the same play.

Shakespeare and Film

Candidates study one of the following plays and a film, audio or live performance of the same play:

Julius Caesar
Macbeth
Merchant of Venice
Romeo and Juliet

On each play, one task will be set requiring comment, criticism and analysis of aspects of the play and of linked scenes from the film, audio or live performance.

WJEC specifications and approaches

The **WJEC English and Literature** specifications link Shakespeare with poetry, and require a thematic approach, with some scope for study of his methods of portraying themes, ideas and relationships. The focus of the tasks is largely on the themes, ideas and relationships themselves and how they are presented, with more limited opportunities to apply the spirit or the methods of Shakespearience.

WJEC English sample task:

Many plays and poems are concerned with the relationship between men and women. Choose one relationship between a man and a woman in the drama you have studied and compare it with a similar relationship in the poetry you have studied.

More examples of specific tasks:

1. - *How does Shakespeare portray the role of women in* **The Taming of the Shrew** *throughout the play?*
   - *The role of women is also presented in a number of the poems you have studied. Discuss the way the role of the women is portrayed in the poetry you have studied.*
   - *What is your personal response to the literature you have studied? In your answer you must explore the links between the poetry and the Shakespeare play.*
2. - *Look at the way Shakespeare presents Katherine's relationship with Petruchio in* **The Taming of the Shrew** *throughout the play. Consider what Petruchio says about how women should behave and Katherine's reaction to his views.*
   - *Consider the way the role of women is presented in poems in the collection. Write about one poem in particular but make references to others.*

- *What is your personal response to the literature you have studied? In your answer you must explore the links between the poetry and the Shakespeare play.*

A level

Practical Shakespearience is a valid preparation for all kinds of Shakespeare study, making understanding and appreciation a matter of personal engagement with playscript in a performative context – the source and end-product of Shakespeare's art and craft. The grounding in Shakespearience that is promoted by GCSE can help students when they move on to post-16 study of Shakespeare. This is because the approach is firmly rooted in Shakespeare's authorial craft. GCSE and Shakespearience together ensure that students don't make the mistake of dealing with Shakespeare's characters as real people. It's *characterization* that matters more – because this engages the reader with the why and the how of his creation of fictional characters.

The matching of text to performance, both their own and on stage and screen, ensures a closer relationship with the plays than mere reading. Most of the AS/A2 specifications represent largely thematic approaches to the plays, but students who have worked on characterization and voice will be far better equipped to appreciate script than those whose main contact with a play is the story, not the story-teller. Even if the main repertoire of questions at AS level is thematic, it's the classroom experience of playing the lines that will make them – and the themes they portray – come alive.

8. A selective Shakespeare bibliography

I have listed works that have taught me something new, made me see what I thought I knew in a different way and given me delight even if I disagreed. Titles in bold are those key texts that have most materially influenced the way I have thought, felt and written about Shakespeare, and enjoyed plays and performances that I have not seen myself, but wished I had.

Performances

More than any of the books and articles I have read, some stage performances have stayed with me as a personal store of riches. More than any others, these have shaped my understanding and enthusiasm:

1965 RSC David Warner *Hamlet* (Hall)
1973 Bogdanov Leicester *The Tempest, Richard III , Hamlet* (Action Man Trilogy)
1978 RSC Bogdanov *Taming of the Shrew*
1990 Ian McKellen *Othello* (DVD)
1987 Regents Park *Much Ado About Nothing*
1978 RSC *Antony & Cleopatra*

The flavour of these and other productions can be derived from the many reviews which exist in print, either in the collected individual reviews of writers for the national press or in production surveys, as listed below.

Collected press reviews

Brief Chronicles	Agate, Cape 1943
A view of the English Stage	Tynan, Poynter 1975
We'll hear a play	Trewin, Carroll & Nicholson 1949
The rest of the evening's your own	Brahms, WH Allen 1964
The Unfinished Hero	Bryden, Faber 1969

Production surveys

The Shakespeare Revolution	**Styan, CUP 1977**
Shakespeare on the English Stage 1900-1964	**Trewin, Barrie & Rockcliff 1964**
Shakespeare in the Theatre	David, CUP 1978
Changing Styles in Shakespeare	Berry, Allen & Unwin 1981
RSC Playing Shakespeare	Barton, Methuen 1984
English Shakespeares	Holland, CUP 1997

The following list includes books based on Shakespeare's relevance and Shakespeare in performance, the two driving forces behind *The Complete Shakespearience*. I have not included works which approach Shakespeare as literature. There are excellent works which do this, but they are a separate case. If you want a book that is interesting and illuminating on Shakespeare's poetic language, Samuel Clemens book *Shakespeare's Imagery and what it tells us* is hard to beat.

The book which has had the biggest influence on Shakespeare enjoyment and performance over the last hundred years is Jan Kott's *Shakespeare Our Contemporary* which was the text that animated the directorial work of Peter Hall and Peter Brook at the RSC in the 1960s, an animation that was followed up by Michael Bodganov in the eighties and can still be seen in the productions of the noughties. It influenced a whole tradition of writing about Shakespeare as a popular entertainer rather than a heritage monument, a scriptwriter rather than a moral philosopher, a TV sitcom writer rather than a refined delicacy for a bourgeois educated elite. What Kott did was rather like what Luther did to the Catholic Church: he opened up an exclusive and revered institution and made it available to the common man, without the need for an intermediary priesthood. He was followed in this by Hawkes, Eagleton, Holderness, Drakakis and Dollimore and Sinfield – writers whose approach can be broadly described as cultural materialist. If you want a flavour of the resistance to this strand, try McLellan.

The person who, more than any other, enthused teachers with the spirit of Shakespeare for all in classroom performance, was Rex Gibson, whose Shakespeare and Schools courses and newsletters did what no government minister or quango could do.

Alternative Shakespeares: philosophical, psychological, political & popular

Shakespeare Our Contemporary	**Kott, University Press 1965**
Shakespeare & Society	Eagleton, Chatto & Windus 1967
Whatever happened to Shakespeare?	McClellan, Vision 1978
Shakespeare & the Critics' Debate	Powell, Macmillan 1980
Alternative Shakespeares	**Ed. Drakakis, Methuen 1985**
Political Shakespeare	Ed. Dollimore & Sinfield, MUP 1985
William Shakespeare	Eagleton, Blackwell 1986
That Shakespeherian Rag	Hawkes, Methuen 1986
The Shakespeare Myth	Ed. Holderness, MUP 1988
Clamorous Voices	Rutter, Women's Press 1988
Is Shakespeare still our Contemporary?	Ed. Elsom, Routledge 1989
Naughty Shakespeare	Macrone, Ebury 1998
Shakespeare – the Basics	McEvoy, Routledge 2000
Shakespeare is hard but so is life	O'Toole, Granta 2002
Shakespearean Afterlives	O'Connor, Icon 2003
Looking for sex in Shakespeare	Wells, CUP 2004
Why Shakespeare	Belsey, Palgrave Macmillan 2007
Shakespeare on Toast	Crystal, Ion 2008

Speaking Shakespeare

Speaking Shakespeare	Pritner & Claiannni, Santa Monica 2001
Shakespeare's Advice to the players	Hall, Oberon 2003
The actor & the text	**Berry, Virgin Books 2000**

Directing Shakespeare

Free Shakespeare	Russell Brown, Heinemann 1974
Directors' Theatre	Cook, Harrap 1974
On Directing Shakespeare	Berry, Hamilton 1989
Shakespeare on Stage	Ed. Wells & Stanton, CUP 2002 English
Shakespeare: the Director's Cut	**Bogdanov, Capercaillie 2003**

| *Constructing Shakespeare on Screen* | **Ed. Bechervaise, St Clair 2003** |

Actors on their roles

Players of Shakespeare 1	Ed. Brockbank, CUP 1985
Players of Shakespeare 2	Ed. Jackson & Smallwood, CUP 1988
Year of the King	Antony Sher, Limelight editions 2006
Characters: Paintings, drawings and sketches	Antony Sher, Nick Hern Books, 1989

Shakespeare in the classroom

Into Shakespeare	Adams & Gould, Ward Lock 1977
Shakespeare for all in Secondary Schools	Ed. Gilmour, Cassell 1996
Teaching Shakespeare	**Gibson, CUP 1998**
Secondary School Shakespeare	Gibson, CIE 1990
Shakespeare & the young writer	Fred Sidgwick, Routledge 1999
Shakespeare & Classic Works in the Classroom	Carter, David Fulton 2002
The North Face of Shakespeare	Stredder, Wincot 2004
Shakespearience	Thomas, NATE 1998
Routes through English: Shakespeare - Page and Stage	Thomas, Longman, 1999
The RSC Shakespeare Toolkit for Teachers	Methuen Drama, 2010

Audio resources

| *The Essential Shakespeare Live Encore (3 CDs)* | RSC/British Library sound archive |
| *Shakespeare for shepherds* | Tim Baker, Loose records 2007 (Cumbrian dialect verse versions) |

Best live performers

Bringing Shakespeare to an audience needing persuasion that Shakespeare is fun: **Oddsocks**

Shakespeare the man

There are many pseudo-biographies, all of them beginning with the caveat that attempts to write a biography of Shakespeare depend on little documentary evidence and a profusion of conjecture.

If you want to get a social, cultural & historical fix on Shakespeare's world, try:

| *In search of Shakespeare* | Wood BBC 2003 |
| **1599** | **Shapiro Faber 2005** |

If you were going to read only a handful of books from the list, try the ones in bold.
(If you were going to read only one, then you already are…)